12 WHO DON'T AGREE

Valery Panyushkin

12 WHO DON'T AGREE

*Translated from the Russian
by Marian Schwartz*

Europa
editions

Europa Editions
116 East 16th Street
New York, N.Y. 10003
www.europaeditions.com
info@europaeditions.com

Copyright © 2008 by Valery Panyushkin
First Publication 2011 by Europa Editions

Translation by Marian Schwartz
Original Title: *12 nesoglasnych*
Translation copyright © 2011 by Europa Editions

Library of Congress Cataloging in Publication Data is available
ISBN 978-1-60945-010-6

Panyushkin, Valery
12 Who Don't Agree

Book design by Emanuele Ragnisco
www.mekkanografici.com

Prepress by Grafica Punto Print – Rome
The book is supported by Mikhail Prokhorov Foundation
(translation program TRANSCRIPT)

Printed in Canada

CONTENTS

CHAPTER 1
Another Russia - 11

CHAPTER 2
*Marina Litvinovich: Young Woman Leaning
Over a Map* - 33

CHAPTER 3
*Vissarion Aseyev: The Man at the Table
on the Right* - 60

CHAPTER 4
*Anatoly Yermolin:
A Man with a Child's Smile* - 82

CHAPTER 5
*Maria Gaidar:
Young Woman in a Pretty Dress* - 110

CHAPTER 6
Ilya Yashin: Young Man in a Tweed Jacket - 127

CHAPTER 7
Sergei Udaltsov:
Young Man in a Leather Jacket - 145

CHAPTER 8
Maksim Gromov: A Smoker Who Pockets His Butts
Rather Than Throw Them Away - 162

CHAPTER 9
Natalya Morar:
A Beautiful Brunette with Brown Eyes - 182

CHAPTER 10
Viktor Shenderovich: A Man Who Laughs
and Gestures Because He's Sad - 204

CHAPTER 11
Andrei Illarionov: A Man Who Takes
a Detached View of Everyone - 223

CHAPTER 12
Garry Kasparov: The Missing Man - 239

EPILOGUE - 254

ABOUT THE AUTHOR - 261

12 WHO DON'T AGREE

CHAPTER 1
Another Russia

A KILOMETER OF FREEDOM

I spent the night of November 23–24, 2007, serenely. No doubts, no disturbing visions on the edge of sleep, no sleeping pills or sedatives. At the alarm, or rather, at the click that preceded the alarm, I rose, scraped my cheeks with a new Gillette, and instead of a shower since I was at my dacha—I bathed in the snow. Outside, it was not yet growing light. My children were asleep.

While I was pouring myself a cup of coffee the color and strenght of diesel fuel and heaping some Faulkneresque ham and eggs onto a plate, I got a call from the young woman who was standing in for our political desk chief at the paper.

"Valery, are you going to the Dissenters' March today?"

"Sure! How could there be a Dissenters' March without me?"

"And tomorrow, are you going to Petersburg for the Dissenters' March there, too?"

"Absolutely, Anya!"

"And you'll get hauled in by the police again?"

"That I can't promise. Should I?" My effervescent pre-march excitement made me flaunt my politics, which infuriated my boss.

"Why do you always have to make everything complicated?"

It was too late to appear reasonable and modest, so I replied, "That's what you pay me for."

I put on two sweaters, two pairs of warm socks, a down jacket, a wool Afghan pakul brought back from Mazar-i-Sharif the year the Americans went into Afghanistan, and thick-soled boots that were once Tod's but were now shapeless leather bubbles that had escaped the trash bin only by virtue of their amazing durability. I also stuck two pairs of gloves in my pockets.

When you attend rallies often, you get in the habit of dressing warmly.

All the cars were going in the opposite direction, out of town. My lane was empty. I smoked at the wheel and cranked the music up to the max and enjoyed the hell out of the mix of music, tobacco smoke, and speed. As usual on a Saturday morning, downtown Moscow was deserted, if you didn't count the army trucks and paddy wagons parked on the Garden Ring Road, Bulvarny, and the adjacent side streets. "When the oil runs out and our president dies," the band DDT sang on my tape deck for all they were worth. Not only weren't there any cars, there weren't any people, if you didn't count the OMON—the special-purpose police—hiding out for now in their buses behind tinted windows and the soldiers cordoning off block after block, frozen stiff but receiving no order to get warm or jump in place or even wipe the snot from their blue noses.

"They've got you under their thumb," I whistled, driving by in my warm car, with a feeling of distinct superiority over the soldiers, a feeling which, at the march, would be leveled by a single blow of the truncheon.

There were still a couple of hours left until the march. But before it started I still had to go to the Shokoladnitsa Café on Sretenka to meet up with Marina Litvinovich and Denis Bilunov, members of the United Civic Front's political council, to exchange secret telephone numbers purchased the day before and never used and probably never tapped, and to agree on our travel to Petersburg that evening, but mainly, it seemed to me, to prolong for at least an hour this anxious anticipation of the march, which was probably going to disappoint us before it had barely begun when we saw the low turnout, the sluggishness, and the muddle of everyone at cross-purposes.

Besides us there were four others in the café. Two young men worked as correspondents for either Dutch or Danish television; the brawny smiling guy at our table worked as Marina's guard; and the brawny glowering guy in the far corner as Marina's tail. The guard was telling jokes, the tail was looking at a book, pretending he could read, and the correspondents were talking to Denis Bilunov in broken Russian.

"We want to film one day out of your life. You our hero. Whatever happens, we will ask you to stay and make comment."

Denis smiled at the image: five OMON men dragging Denis to a paddy wagon, his arms twisted behind his back, and the Danish correspondents at that very moment asking him to stick around and comment on what was happening.

When the ham sandwiches were gone, we went outside. Instead of paying, the spy assigned to us showed the waitress his ID. Marina got a text saying that all the underground passages across the Garden Ring Road had been closed on the pretext of emergency repairs. We walked down the sunny, deserted side streets. On Kostyansky Lane, or maybe it was Dayevy, the Danish journalists searched among the Mercedes and Lexuses until they found a rusty, Soviet-era Pobeda with a cracked windshield and asked Denis to record his first commentary in front of that car. Evidently they thought that in the film Moscow should look like a Havana descended upon by a glacier, the final touch on all our totalitarian misfortunes.

Broad Sakharov Avenue was blocked off on both sides by a triple police cordon. To get through it, the few thousand people who had come for the march were compelled to pass through five or six metal detectors. A line formed that was no fun to stand in. According to long tradition, the authorities drove a couple of hundred homeless to every opposition rally for the purpose of displaying the drunken riffraff who constituted Putin's opponents. In exchange for participating in the country's political life, the homeless demand vodka but not to be allowed to wash.

While I was standing in this crowd of intelligentsia, students, and bums, I told my friends a tale about how not long ago one oppositionist politician planning to run for president went to see a famous banker to ask for money for his campaign. The meeting took place in a restaurant. The banker was eating oysters. No sooner had the politician walked in than the banker said to him, as he scooped a *fine de claire* out of its shell, "So, I guess you want to run for president? Have you really thought this over? Have you thought about the fact that your wife, Tanya, and your son, Vadik, could be abducted tomorrow and you'd never find them?" The politician was taken aback. He broke out in red spots, muttered something, and took his leave. And no sooner had he gone than the banker said to the intermediaries in the talks between the politician and businessman who were still at the table, "So what? He's asking for twenty million of my money, by the way. Don't I have a right to know whether he's going to piss his pants at the first attack?"

My friends laughed at my tale. The line was moving slowly. In the crowd, trying not to miss a single face, systematically, like farmers plowing their field, FSB—Federal Security Service— agents were going around with video cameras. Without consulting each other, Marina and I turned to one of them.

"Can we say hello?"

"Yes." The agent pointed his camera at us.

"Hel-lo!" we shouted, waving and smiling, like hick kids on a school trip to the Kremlin who happened to come under the lens of central television.

The rally was boring, of course. The leaders of the various

Lilliputian opposition parties were less concerned about attracting a crowd with fiery speeches than about the leaders of each party getting their fair share of time and the party flags in the crowd not intermixing. God forbid anyone might think some liberal SPS (Union of Right Forces) activist wearing a jacket and tie there on the pavement was hugging that activist chick in a leather jacket from Limonov's National Bolsheviks, while the blue and white liberal flag over their heads snuggled up to Limonov's black and white hammer and sickle.

"I can't stand the sight of hammers and sickles," liberal leader Boris Nemtsov complained as he climbed onto the back of the small truck serving as an improvised tribune. "They killed my relatives in the Civil War."

The crowd stood there apathetically. Every so often the orators' speeches were drowned out by a special machine that Nemtsov said was called a Helmholtz resonator. The resonator was set up on the next side street and wailed as if the city were just about to come under bombardment. There were FSB agents sitting inside the resonator, and I had no idea how their eardrums didn't burst from the wail.

The only people who found it interesting were the Tajik guest workers building the new high-rise on Sakharov Avenue. They had dropped their tools and were watching the rally from the scaffolding. The only interesting speech was the one given by young SPS activist Masha Gaidar, who fulminated against the illegality rampant in the country and promised President Putin that one day he was going to be tried in accordance with the law and in full observance of his civil rights.

"Even now," Masha shouted, "I can read you your rights, Mr. President. You have the right to remain silent. You have the right to one telephone call. You have the right to an attorney . . ."

At the end of the rally they read out a resolution from the back of the truck. This was all happening just ahead of parliamentary elections and three months prior to the presidential elections. The resolution said that if the elections were not held freely, if all the parties did not get equal access to television time, if all the presidential candidates weren't registered, if constitutional violations occurred, which had obviously already happened, then the dissidents would come out and protest. The plan was for the rally's leaders to take this resolution to the Central Electoral Commission and for the crowd to disperse to their homes. The authorities had given permission for a rally on Sakharov Avenue. They had not given permission for a march after the rally. But the leaders of the Other Russia coalition, Garry Kasparov and Eduard Limonov, who were standing on the back of the truck, would have been lying if they'd said they really intended to go to the commission without hoping that the crowd would tag along. They didn't have to lie. They were hoping.

Kasparov and Limonov stepped down onto the pavement. Flanked by guards and comrades-in-arms, they headed for the subway. The crowd fell in behind them. For a while we moved down the swath cordoned off by the police, but the columns marching in front felt the heft and power of the crowd behind them.

"Let's move! Move! We're moving!" Aleksandr Ryklin, leader of the Moscow United Civic Front, said.

"They're moving! They're moving! They're moving!" the police radios squawked in fear.

We came out on the Garden Ring Road. We were still marching down the sidewalk, but faster and faster. To control us better, some police official had ordered traffic shut down on the Garden Ring, and that was a mistake. The cars would have kept us from breaking through. Now there was nothing but an empty street behind the police cordon set up along the sidewalk. Faster! Practically running! Arm in arm! "We need another Russia!" someone in the crowd shouted. The crowd chimed in, and from the rumble of voices we realized, without turning around, how many we were. So many! Banners and flags soared over our heads. "We need another Russia!" Faster! Practically running! Arm in arm! "Let's break the cordon!" shouted someone behind me who had realized that the crowd could be controlled only if his orders didn't contradict its troubled, murmuring will. "Let's break the cordon!"

We turned to face the policemen bearing down on us, and this cordoning off of theirs, this crowd-control technique worked out in training, this solid wall of shields, these locked arms—all this snapped like a rotted thread. The crowd splashed out onto the Garden Ring's roadway. The people walking behind us carried us across the road, like a river carrying a splinter. We started down Myasnitskaya Street. It was empty. Only at its far end did the OMON cordon, reinforced by heavy equipment, loom. But we had about eight hundred meters—maybe even an entire kilometer—of freedom before reaching the cordon. And if we did not travel this kilometer under our unfurled banners, our heads held high, then we weren't worth a brass tack.

We were walking and smiling. People who had been terrified in 1999 by the Moscow apartment building bombings and who had chosen order over freedom had themselves asked for a firm hand and considered Putin Russia's necessary Pinochet. They had unleashed the second Chechen war because they didn't have the brains to imagine peace. They had allowed the state to take away our independent television because they didn't like its owner. They had agreed, after terrorists seized the theatre on Dubrovka, that they could not allow their enemies to speak and could not broadcast counterterrorism operations live because we had to understand. They were used to seeing enemies everywhere and were themselves called enemies. We were walking and smiling. I didn't even feel like smoking as we went, the way you don't feel like smoking in the mountains or at the sea. I felt like breathing.

From time to time an OMON unit would start toward us from the depths of Myasnitskaya. An officer would line the soldiers up across the street, but the soldiers did not stop us. They let us through, parted. Only if old women beat soldiers over their helmets with the lightweight plastic sticks from the banners did the men take away the old women's sticks. I didn't realize right away that the chains of OMON men who let the head of our column through were not disobeying an order but closing ranks behind us, cutting off our march at the tail and gradually stripping us of the strength propping us up from behind.

By the time we had gone down Myasnitskaya, our momentum was sapped. The cordon blocking off the street at the end looked solid and decisive enough that it was clear they were going to start beating us now. Ilya Yashin, leader of the Yabloko party's youth wing, who was walking beside me, tried to turn the crowd into a side street and away from OMON truncheons. But not a chance. Ilya even climbed on the roof of a car parked at the curb and started shouting at people to turn around, turn around, but no one listened to him. This attempt to avoid a confrontation only resulted in their showing, on the evening news, on state television, from the whole Dissenters' March, besides homeless drunks, just Ilya Yashin stamping on someone else's car, thus demonstrating graphically what vandals all these opponents of the current regime were.

We had nowhere to go. We walked right up to the OMON chain. The stalwarts in helmets divided our crowd into sectors, as their military science would have them do, and started beating us with truncheons and shoving us into paddy wagons. I saw them arrest Kasparov. His hat flew off. The crowd tried to repulse them twice, but couldn't. Limonov went missing. Ilya Yashin, when I called to ask where he was, replied, "Where could I be? I'm sitting in an OMON van."

As a rule, journalists weren't touched, unless they happened to cross someone's path. But for an OMON private to consider you a journalist, you had to be wearing a special fluorescent vest. I had attended a meeting of the Public Chamber in which the law pertaining to these vests, which would distinguish journalists from the crowd during mass upheavals, and I'd rejected the vest. I'd said that the Third Reich had sewn yellow stars on Jews for their own safety, too, and that ended in gas chambers. Now wearing a journalist's protective vest was a dishonor, and to be honest, I regretted it.

When they bore down on and divided the crowd, I ended up in the same sector as Masha Gaidar. She was wearing a pretty fur coat and stylish boots, delicate and beautiful. I had nothing to do while waiting for arrest other than manifest my chivalry. I took Masha's arm, trying to defend her from shoves and strikes. An OMON colonel, a blue-eyed beast, the kind that goes into the police for the pleasure of causing other people pain, when his detachment's bloody reaping got as far as us, suddenly shouted, "Leave these two alone!"—evidently thinking we were an amorous couple who had ended up on the street by accident. That is how I learned that lovers aren't touched when marches are dispersed.

We were left on the street. We heard muffled blows and shouts from the paddy wagons pulling away from the sidewalk. Masha pounded her fists on the vans' steel sides.

"Stop beating them! Stop beating those people, you pigs!"

A SUSPICIOUS INDIVIDUAL

Masha and I spent the rest of the day riding around town. As soon as the march was routed, we and thirty other activists who had avoided arrest took the subway to the Central Electoral Commission in order to hand over the rally's resolution. Masha presented her deputy candidate certificate and was allowed through the cordon, but then they immediately dragged her to a paddy wagon, drove her away from the commission, and released her on Polyanka Street. Masha called and said she was sitting in a café and asked us to come by for her. Half an hour later, in the café, I tried to calm Masha's outrage over police tyranny with brandy.

"They have no right to detain a candidate for deputy except with the sanction of the general prosecutor!" Masha said.

"No, they don't." I nodded, sipping my cup of milky oolong, which had cooled a little and really did taste of milk. "But they do it."

The café was crowded. The four young women at the next table were yakking about clothes, money, jobs, lovers, children, theater, sometimes even books. They didn't care about us or democracy or the march. A server of indeterminate gender leaned over us and said, "Try the cheesecake."

Then we drove from police station to police station where investigators were questioning Kasparov and our other comrades. Then we drove around to the courts where they were trying the detainees. Theoretically the trials were open, but they wouldn't let us into the courtroom. Standing at the entrance was a police cordon that wasn't letting anyone in and had closed off a small area on the sidewalk in front of the courthouse entrance. Four bailiffs carried an unconscious man out of the Basmanny courthouse and put him down in that area. We shouted for the bailiffs to call an ambulance. The ambulance took a long time to come.

It was nearly midnight when we parted. I let Masha out on Tverskaya Street, which was flooded with light and people rushing about their cheerful Saturday affairs, left the car on a Tverskaya side street near a little restaurant where an Azeri wedding was in full swing, and started for the subway on foot. In the underground passage that leads to the Leningrad train station, a beggar woman was sitting on the ground holding a bag made out of a blanket in which there was presumably a baby. No one was giving her anything. Muscovites are sure that beggars are a mafia controlled by people from the Caucasus who pay off the police. They are just as certain that the participants in the Dissenters' March are extremists financed and directed by the American CIA. And that Vladimir Putin is the father of the nation and has brought about order in the country. You cannot change anyone's mind. The woman was breastfeeding, but I walked on by without putting a ruble in her bag.

The platform was crowded and subdued. Here and there foreign tourists, especially the disciplined Japanese, had heaped their suitcases into huge piles and were waiting for some command. In the intervals between announcements of train departures, the loudspeaker admonished: "Citizen passengers, if you discover suspicious individuals, immediately inform a policeman . . ." What suspicious people looked like the loudspeaker did not specify, thinking it sufficient to know what a policeman looked like.

An armed patrol was on duty at the platform entrance. A sergeant twirled my ticket in his hands and reluctantly allowed me to go to the train. The loudspeaker over my head reminded citizen passengers to be vigilant "in order to prevent terrorist acts," and then a bravura march started playing, practically the Moscow hymn, the text of which rhymes "kupola" (dome) and "kolokola" (bells), "zoloto ikon" (icons' gold) with "letopis vremyon" (chronicle of the ages); this tautological chronicle, in turn, rhymed with the "preiskurantom tsen" (pricelist) decorating the door of the small café at the head of the platform.

I walked toward my car and held out my ticket to the conductor. The young woman took it the way people accept a telegram about the death of a close relative. Her eyes started darting, her hands shaking, and her lips whispered to a policeman standing a little ways off, "It's him."

"It is me," I confirmed. "So?"

"Hello, I need to ask you a few questions." The policeman hurried over, saluted, and introduced himself.

"On what basis?"

"Here, this fax." The policeman held out a poorly printed sheet of paper. "From the FSB." The FSB being the Federal Security Service, today's KGB.

The rolled-up piece of fax paper said, "Check citizen V. V. Panyushkin, who bought a ticket for train number such-and-such car such-and-such seat such-and-such in connection with executing law such-and-such on counteracting extremist activity." No punctuation marks. Whether I bought my ticket in connection with executing the law or should be checked in connection with executing the law was impossible to tell. At the bottom of the page, where there should have been the signature of the official sending this instruction to the train station police, there was just a torn edge.

"And how are you going to verify that?" I asked the policeman.

"Let's step aside. A few questions. It won't take long."

We moved to the side. The policeman asked me where I lived, where I worked, where I was going and for what purpose, and whether I belonged to any extremist organization. I said I lived at such-and-such address, worked for the newspaper *Vedomosti,* was going to St. Petersburg to write about the Dissenters' March, and did not belong to any extremist organization. While I was correcting the spelling mistakes in the police document and confirming that "my words had been taken down accurately," and signed, the policeman said confidentially, "They're probably checking you because of your newspaper. You must work for the wrong kind of newspaper."

I nodded. Indeed, I knew full well why they were checking me. These checks had begun on April 14, 2007, when I'd had the imprudence, during another Dissenters' March in Moscow, to wind up at the police station. The march had started on

Pushkin Square. The march participants weren't holding any signs or banners, just roses. By law, we could not be considered demonstrators; we could only be considered citizens strolling down the city's central street holding flowers. We weren't shouting anything. But Voronezh OMON men (brought in from the provinces intentionally so that during the routing their provincial hatred for well-dressed people from the capital would seethe) blocked our way. As soon as Kasparov tried to explain to them that they could not keep people from simply walking down the street, the soldiers overpowered him and everyone walking with him, me included. They kept us in the bus for a long time, but it's true that that time they didn't beat us. Even when one of our comrades pushed out a window, jumped onto the street, and fled. Then an OMON officer came onto the bus, chided us for the pushed-out window, and said, "We have to go back to Voronezh on this bus. We're going to freeze." Then he complained that OMON men were poorly paid and allowed us to step out for a smoke. At the police station an official, an elderly major, greeted us joyously and did not put us in cells, but offered us the assembly hall. He called Kasparov into his office, where he asked Kasparov's permission to have his photograph taken with him as a souvenir.

We sat in the station for five hours, they drew up papers on our detention, and ever since then my name has been on the confidential list of suspicious persons. Now, every time I buy a plane or train ticket, the information that I'm planning to go somewhere ends up at the special services and they send a policeman to my train car. When they do these checks on the real leaders of Other Russia, they get detained for a long time to keep them from making it to a march or make them miss their train altogether. As for me, I get a reminder that Big Brother is watching, so to speak. I already knew that. In *The Gulag Archipelago* Solzhenitsyn tells you to shout when they're arresting you. So I did. I called everyone I knew and told them

I'd been detained at the train station. Half an hour later, the radio station Ekho Moskvy—Echo of Moscow—trumpeted my five-minute detention, and, perfectly content with this, I decided to go to the dining car for dinner. There was no one else in my compartment. I asked the conductor to lock my door while I was gone. The woman gave me a terrified look. In her mind I was a dangerous criminal whom she had handed over to the authorities and whom the authorities had let go, and now here I was riding in her car, and God only knew what kind of vengeance I would inflict on her. She had probably never heard of the presumption of innocence; on the other hand, she heard constantly about suspicious individuals.

I walked through the cars. There was the smell of coal smoke coming from the boilers. People were standing in the corridors in various states of undress and peering out the dark windows. Outside, along the rail bed, were mainly dumps, which, according to the keen observation of the playwright Grishkovets, people usually admire and about which people usually say with patriotic feeling, "What beauty!"

"Sure is beautiful!" a man in boxers and T-shirt said to me as I was walking past, nodding out the window.

It was midnight. Emptiness reigned outside. The train was traveling through a dark stretch of forest. The forest's edge was heaped with the rubbish passengers had thrown out the windows as they were moving. All you could see were the dark shadows of pines, the white snow-covered earth, and the blots of plastic bags spoiling the snow's whiteness. There was the smell of onions cooking.

The dining cars on our domestic trains are of a certain quality, and so are the dinners in them. As an appetizer they serve a slice of bread with red caviar crowned by a pretty and thoroughly frozen butter rose, or else tongue with horseradish that looks like a felt innersole. For the first course they serve a little pot of solyanka or borscht. For the second course they serve either a breaded pork cutlet or a breaded sturgeon fillet with a complicated garnish. The point of the garnish is so that passengers can tell the meat from the fish, because there's no way to distinguish them by taste. But that's not what matters. It's believed that any dish gives pleasure if you wash it down with vodka. They always serve Sinopskaya vodka on the train, but if you order, say, Russky Standart, then the solicitous bartender pours Sinopskaya out of a Russky Standart bottle. The menu has always listed Indian tea, even after the Indian government refused to buy a submarine from Russia that was unable in tests to hit anything with a single missile and the Russian Epidemiological Service stated in response that Indian tea was infested with khapra beetles. That's all right. We drink it with beetles, too.

Right up until closing, which is to say, until we get to Bologovo, there is a video of the "Russia Onward!" patriotic concert playing on the television attached high on the wall. On the screen, cultural figures sing the manly song, "How Entrancing the Evenings Are in Russia," known in artistic circles as "Kakupa"—a mash-up of the Russian title—or else the maidenly "Down the Nighttime Roads." The cultural figures look appropriate, wearing high heels, underwear, and virtually nothing over it. The video pirates have lovingly cut the uplifting speech wedged into the concert by the newly fledged father of our nation. In short, it's cheerful in the car, there are no empty seats, and it's all right to sit down at a table with complete strangers, introduce yourself, and tell whoppers about yourself—you're an engineer for an elevator company, you're going to Petersburg to design a supersonic elevator in the Gazprom Tower being built, and you spent your last vacation traveling through Shaolin monasteries, or maybe through Caracas's filthiest bars.

I'd already polished off the tongue, the solyanka, and a hundred grams of vodka and was ready to face my second hundred with whatever breaded item I got when a bulky, gray-haired man of about fifty walked up to my table.

"May I?" The man nodded at the seat across from me.

"Please," I mumbled with a full mouth, accompanying my mumble with a gesture of invitation.

"Seryozha." My new friend stuck out his hand.

"Valera." I shook it.

We ordered vodka. Leaning his elbows heavily on the table and propping his heavy head on his heavy fists, Seryozha looked at me with a heavy gaze and asked questions. How old was I, where did I work, was I married, did I have children, did my younger daughter go to school. I answered without thinking, and after the first round of questions Seryozha raised his glass: "Let's drink to our meeting."

I tossed back the shot, noticing only that my companion didn't sip more than half of his. And he was already continuing his questions. Why was I going to Petersburg, how had I gotten involved with "dissenters," wasn't my newspaper owned by Americans, and wasn't Garry Kasparov an American spy.

"Well," my companion said, pouring me a full glass and himself a few drops, "let's drink to Russia, Valera."

"Let's." I held out my glass across the table to clink.

"Will you drink?" My companion looked at me with what's called a leaden gaze, the way President Putin sometimes looks at Western journalists, for that is exactly how the KGB had taught him to look at enemies.

I drank up. My companion put his unfinished glass on the table, sighed heavily, and said, "You see, we're going to take you in now, Valera. I am FSB Colonel Shcheglov."

I smiled. Just as in chance acquaintances with young women a drunken pig will introduce himself as a film director or oil magnate, so too in chance acquaintances with men a drunken pig will introduce himself as an FSB officer. It lends importance. And I smiled.

But Shcheglov continued. "Do you think we're going to take you in over the Dissenters' March? No, Valera! You're wrong! You're the Bitsevsky maniac. You killed four little girls. Children, Valera! They were children, and you killed them!"

A chill ran down my spine. For the last few months, stories about a Bitsevsky maniac had indeed been running in the tabloids. It was easy to assume that in Shcheglov's (or whatever his name was) drunken mind all the prevailing myths that had held sway in Russians' minds had gotten mixed up: patriotism, the FSB standing guard for the Homeland, American spies, the Bitsevsky maniac . . . Sock the drunken pig between the ears, finish my vodka, slip the server a hundred rubles not to call the guard, and go to bed. But a treacherous chill ran down my spine, and the blood rushed to my head, and my temples started pounding—from my awareness of the surefire lowdown trick that had given birth in my companion's drunken brain to this pseudo-FSB, pseudo–special op to arrest me.

I and everyone who participates in the Dissenters' Marches—we've prepared for repression, we've often talked about it, but we imagined we'd be arrested for unsanctioned rallies, antigovernment articles, and public opposition. Why didn't I think of this? The Bitsevsky maniac! Young Limonov supporters go to prison not because they've posted antigovernment flyers or organized Dissenters' Marches. They go to prison for selling drugs, like good little children, even though the drugs were planted on them by operatives during the arrest. Even their parents believe their own children's involvement in the drug trade. Mikhail Khodorkovsky is in prison for money laundering, not for going into politics. Manana Aslamazian came under investigation for contraband, not for running a free journalism school.

Idiot! You were hoping to be repressed for your little freedom-loving articles? Like hell! What are you going to do if you're repressed because of well-edited FSB videos of you assaulting minors? What will it be like when neither your friends, nor your own children, nor even your own mother believe that the proof of your guilt, quoted in the tabloids and on television on *True Confession,* is bullshit from first word to last?

The idea of putting me down as the Bitsevsky maniac was so low I actually believed for a second that there really was a special operation under way and the man sitting across from me really was an FSB colonel. I grabbed him by the collar and pulled him toward me across the table. His breath stank. Shcheglov's mouth reeked of decay, cigarette butts, and garlic.

"Look me in the eye!" I shouted. "In the eye! Who are you?"

"Aha! Scared?" Shcheglov dissolved in a drunken smile.

"In the eye! Who are you?" I remembered the phrase one of the Beslan mothers had shouted at an FSB man who didn't want to introduce himself. "Who are your father and mother?"

I must have been shouting pretty loudly. All the restaurant customers turned toward me, and the server, a buxom blonde who could barely squeeze between the rows of tables, came up to us and said conciliatorily, "Boys, don't you go fighting."

I unclenched my fists and Shcheglov, no longer held up by me, fell face down on the table, overturning his unfinished glass and sticking his ear in the mayonnaise-y salad recently served him. As if on command, the guards accompanying the train entered the dining car, picked Shcheglov up, and carried him off. I paid calmly and finished my beetle tea. And I was all set to stroll through the cars to my compartment when the train stopped at a major station, and it was Tver.

The train car doors opened. The restaurant customers and a few midnighters from other cars went out on the platform to smoke. So did I. The train was supposed to stop there at least ten minutes. I lit up and headed down the platform toward my car. Standing near the car next to the conductor was a well-dressed and perfectly sober young man. Lighting a cigarette, he said, "That was a dreadful scene in the restaurant. But you handled yourself well."

"Meaning?" I asked, not remembering this young man among the restaurant's customers.

"It's terrible when people have too much to drink and introduce themselves as FSB officers. Understand? I too have some connection to that bureau, so I'm embarrassed."

"What, were you in collusion?" I looked at the young man and immediately thought that maybe they really had been in collusion. I threw my cigarette butt under the train and went to my car, asking the conductor to open my compartment.

In the dark compartment, a fully clothed man was sleeping on the lower berth. He had a build worthy of service in the so-called *spetsnaz*—the special ops units. I realized that I was being overtaken by a persecution mania, possibly heightened by vodka. Nonetheless, I took my jacket off the hook, grabbed my backpack, and got the hell off the train. The train pulled away. I was left on the platform. The conductor hurried to close the door so I wouldn't change my mind and jump on as it was moving. Her worst suspicions had been confirmed. In her eyes I was a criminal, since I had hopped off in Tver while having a ticket for St. Petersburg.

BETWEEN MOSCOW AND THE CAPITAL

"Where are you?" I texted Marina Litvinovich from my secret number. "They closed in on me on the train. I had to hop off in Tver. Can you come get me?"

The last time Marina and I had seen each other was that evening near the Basmanny courthouse, where they were trying Kasparov. I knew that Marina, fearing arrest, was not taking the train to tomorrow's Petersburg march but was driving a car rented in her bodyguard's name. Right then Marina should have been on the road somewhere near Tver.

The platform was deserted. Every other hour, Moscow trains like the *Red Arrow* stopped at Tver, one after the other. I could have boarded any of them, but I didn't feel like taking the train. Recent events had made me feel claustrophobic in trains. I strolled along the platform for five minutes and was starting to freeze, when I felt a text in my pocket from Marina: "Let's meet at Gregor's. Just don't bring them with you."

I had told Marina about Gregor's, in my opinion the best café on the Moscow-Petersburg highway. The café was in the forest outside Tver, run by a young Armenian named Gregor and his Russian wife, Olesya. The café looked like an unfinished wooden booth. It was heated with a wood stove and had no plumbing or even running water. But Gregor made fantastic *shashlyk*. Although a Christian, he got his meat from a halal slaughterhouse owned by Chechens and insisted that if you were going to slaughter cattle properly, you had to live according to Sharia law. Every day Olesya and Gregor's children walked hand in hand to school along the highway about five kilometers, to the next village. On the way to school, the passing trucks splattered the older boy with mud; on the way back, the younger. But the boys weren't afraid of the trucks; they were only afraid of feral dogs.

I left the station and woke up the taxi driver sleeping in his car parked in front of the station. When he heard I wanted to go out of town, the driver for some reason took down the yellow, checkered roof light that meant the car was a taxi. I don't know why provincial taxi drivers always do that. Marina Litvinovich didn't have to worry about me bringing a tail. Even without looking at the square in front of the station, which was completely deserted at that hour, I told the driver to take a couple of loops through town to be sure. The city was hung with posters: "Putin's Plan Is Russia's Victory." The province's dramatic theater was also adorned with a portrait of the president and again some slogan about his nonexistent plan. I told the driver a tale about a recent congress of Putin supporters held in that theater. At the congress, I told him, a deputy from the Tver legislative assembly spoke and got so carried away with his loyal outpourings that at the end he said, "I suggest that since the founding congress of our movement in support of Vladimir Vladimirovich Putin is being held in Tver, the movement's headquarters should be set up in Tver, too, halfway between Moscow and the capital!" The driver laughed. The driver said the deputy was a known thief in the town, that under the Communists he had worked on the Young Communists' city committee, under Gorbachev he'd been a vehement democrat, in the 1990s he had joined Chernomyrdin's party, Our Home Is Russia, and now it was no wonder . . .

"The land does have that kind of louse, after all," the driver summed up philosophically.

We had no tail. We drove out on the highway, which even at night was full of trucks carrying all manner of goods in exchange for our oil from Europe to Moscow via Finland and back. And the kilometers started flashing by on either side. And the chemical agent under the wheels started throwing dust in our eyes. I drifted off briefly, lulled by our Fatherland's monotony.

"Hey, wake up." The driver nudged me. "Is this your Gregor?"

We really were parked in the concrete lot next to Gregor's, and Gregor himself was working his magic at the grill under the awning and waving to us in welcome. In the half year since I'd been here, Gregor, who had built the café and house according to the principle "no day without a nailed board," had managed to construct an unpretentious but sturdy mansard roof over the house and had equipped the café with windows where there had been just plastic. A doghouse had appeared at the café entrance, too, and settled in the doghouse was a huge Caucasian shepherd pup, indecently good-natured for a guard dog.

Gregor and I greeted each other with a handshake. Or rather, I shook his wrist, because his hands were coated with spices and meat juices.

"Go on in, all your people are already there," Gregor said, turning a strip of lamb suet as thin as a featherweight kerchief and wrapping lamb's heart and kidneys in the fat. "*Khan shashlyk* for you?"

"Yes, Gregor."

"Go on in, only there's no light. And Chubais broke."

Gregor called his gasoline generator Chubais; without it, the café was pitched into darkness for electricity was only sporadic outside Moscow. I went inside the café, which was well heated. At the door I ran into Olesya. She seemed to be pregnant again. She was carrying two platters of greens. She greeted me cheerfully.

Inside, all the tables were occupied by Dissenters' March activists. There were about ten of them, plus drivers and bodyguards. They were eating cheese and talking in low voices. Laid out on the central table was a map of St. Petersburg, and a few people, including my Marina, were leaning over it. The café's small wooden room was lit only by candles. In this living light, people's shadows rose to the ceiling and flickered on the uneven walls. The whole picture looked like it had been painted by Georges de Latour. And the people leaning over the table looked like conspirators. Which is what they were. I knew almost everyone here. And was friends with several.

The only one missing was Garry Kasparov throughout. The night before, the Basmanny Court had sentenced him to five days' arrest for the morning march down Myasnitskaya—the first prison term in the world chess champion's life.

CHAPTER 2
Marina Litvinovich:
Young Woman Leaning Over a Map

INFORMATION THREATS

The tall wooden door closed slowly, the lock clicked, and Marina was left outside. A blonde with close-cropped hair and a distraught face. Her lips tended to be offended; her eyes, angry. Press Minister Mikhail Lesin, a man who knew how to put on airs even in the steam room, TV Channel One chief Konstantin Ernst, a media beauty who had filled out, and TV Channel Two chief Oleg Dobrodeyev, an administrator, his glasses being the facial feature you remembered above all, had entered the office of Aleksandr Voloshin, the president's chief of staff. It was Friday, October 25, 2002. It had been two days since terrorists under the command of Movsar Barayev had seized hostages in the theatre on Dubrovka. Dank Moscow. The streets around the theater were blocked off, reporters and relatives of the hostages were besieging the police cordon, President Putin was silent and not appearing in public . . . And the traditional Friday meeting devoted to media policy with the chief of staff was happening without Marina Litvinovich.

Marina was standing by the closed door and still could not understand why she was no longer an expert whose opinion was heeded. That never again, neither directly nor indirectly through Voloshin, would she have any influence on presidential decision-making. She was holding a folder with her weekly report, "Information Threats and Recommendations for Their Elimination." In her bag slept her laptop, which was permanently connected to the Internet. Her papers of employment in the president's administration were now with Viktor Petrovich Ivanov, the Kremlin's main personnel officer, for review, and she did not think, "That's it, we're here, dry your oars." She was not thinking that a meeting with Voloshin was some great bureaucratic happiness. She was thinking about the terrified hostages in the theater: without sleep or water, wearing the doglike expression of a person with Stockholm syndrome. She was thinking about the terrified relatives behind the police cordon, desperate, but not letting themselves cry out, as if a cry might detonate the bombs set out in the theater. She was thinking about President Putin, who should have been with those people, if only on television.

A long time ago in school Marina had written a paper, "Mistakes of the Paris Commune"; she had always wondered why people lose and why they win. A long time ago in school, when her teacher, taking advantage of the words' consonance, called a little boy whose last name was Bognyuk "Govnyuk"— "Turd"—instead, Marina jumped up and started shouting about human dignity. Her hands were trembling and her knees were buckling out of fear at reprimanding her teacher, but she had a heightened sense of justice, which expressed itself by the fact that her chest hurt and her cheeks burned unbearably, and her fear only made her shout more loudly than she needed to.

Her mother had died when Marina was seven. Other than cozy childhood memories of a person that you can't tell are yours or what you've fantasized from photographs and stories, she knew her mother had been a deputy to the district council. Marina did not know whether her deceased mother had had any serious connection to power. She had only a vague sense that one could have a connection to power, one could influence decision-making. One could—unlike today, when Aleksandr Voloshin's door had slammed in Marina's face.

Her family did not like politics. When Marina was planning

to enter the political science department at Moscow State University, her father and grandfather, both aviation engineers, had tried to talk her out of it because they did not consider political science a profession. But her father was an environmental activist (although he would have been surprised to be called that) and was constantly assembling the neighbors for volunteer Saturdays: planting trees, hoeing flowerbeds, and sweeping the streets for a few blocks around their building, because by the late 1980s street cleaners had completely disappeared from Moscow's streets. These volunteer Saturdays, these intellectuals with their puny saplings and rusty shovels in their maladroit hands, gave Marina the sense that you could influence life around you, fix things.

In her upper-level classes, since the Pioneers and Young Communists told us to live long, Marina attended the Communard circle or the Leaders School—something like a scout troop. Students from the pedagogical institute tutored the children in history, maritime law, rhetoric, and logic, went on hikes, and organized holidays in villages . . . strange holidays. The villagers, who fed their livestock bread because bread was cheap and milk was expensive, who drank water out of puddles because it was a long walk to the well, and who pictured a holiday as a Saturday dance party with a mandatory brawl at the end, watched in amazement as the youngsters from the city set up tents outside the village fence and invited them to take part in fun games. Some did: serious fellows (who at fourteen bought mopeds so that at eighteen they could start drinking seriously and crash them) lazily climbed the slick pole for the ribbon, lazily jumped over the campfire, and waited for the party to take its usual course, that is, to end in a brawl. But the "young leaders" did get the impression that you could organize a holiday.

In the city the "young leaders" visited children's homes and old-age homes. The old people were desperately sad. It was easy to help them just by talking to them, but as soon as they turned away they immediately forgot anyone had been talking to them. The orphans were cocky and servile at the same time. They wore rags and drank tea from mayonnaise jars for lack of cups. They also played a game where you had to press on your comrade's windpipe with a deft movement of the fingers, so that the other person experienced an instant of oblivion resembling narcotic intoxication. But the "young leaders" still had the sense that they could somehow help both the orphans and the old people.

Marina was planning to go to journalism school. In order to have the publications that the admissions committee required, she went to the tent camp situated between the Rossiya Hotel and Red Square. The Meskhetian Turks living there were demanding some sort of historical justice, but their demands were routinely ignored. Marina went from tent to tent asking how the children were doing in this tent camp. What were they eating, were they going to school, were they sick? It turned out, of course, that the children were not going to school, they had scurvy, bronchitis, and lice, and they were eating canned food meant for adults. Marina sent her article about the children to the editors at *Moskovsky Komsomolets*. The editors rejected the article, and Marina decided she did not have the makings of a journalist. She enrolled in the political philosophy department instead.

Just before she did, the political science department was routed. After the victory of democracy in 1991, a decision was made to shut down the School of Scientific Communism. All the teachers who had been teaching from the old political science books lost their jobs instantly, regardless of whether they were diehard supporters of the Soviet regime or had only been considered Communists because in the Soviet Union you could not work as a political scientist without quoting Lenin and Marx. There was no one to do the teaching. God knows who was now teaching, having snatched their political knowledge from samizdat literature and conversations with dissidents over the kitchen table. After studying for half a year, Marina transferred from political science to philosophy and studied hermeneutics, the science of interpretation. She had no idea how hermeneutics might be applied in real life.

By the time she graduated, Marina wasn't interested in anything, including hermeneutics, and was reading only *Inostranets* (*The Foreigner*). This newspaper, whose fundamental stance boiled down to the idea that nothing could be done in Russia and you had to leave Russia, was very popular at that time. It was a hundred times easier to find out from this newspaper what life was like in London or New York than what it was like in Moscow. The *Inostranets* editors regarded life in Russia as forced exile, temporary and thoroughly unpleasant. In Russia one could only survive and endure, but not really live: not build plans for the future, not hope for anything, and look on everything happening to you and your country as flippantly as possible. The ads in *Inostranets* were flippant, too. Marina needed a job, and (from an ad in *Inostranets*) she went after a position at one of the newly opened FM radio stations that broadcast easy-listening music.

The radio station rented space in a frayed Stalin-era building. At the entrance sat a guard, retired military apparently, who was closely examining *Playboy*, which had only started to come out in Russian then. This magazine was edited by the well-known music critic Artemy Troitsky, who felt guilty just editing a magazine about naked girls. He tried to convince himself that the magazine was meant for the mature man, so it should have serious content. The best writers worked for the magazine. But the words in the magazine only irritated the guard. He was looking at the pictures, not guarding anything. When Marina walked past, the guard didn't even look up.

The director of the radio station was practically loading the

CDs in the player himself, but he thought he was a big shot in show business and spoke pompously.

"Can you read the news?" The director spoke through clenched teeth and in the same tone of voice as the producer did to Howard Stern in the recent movie about the radio star.

Marina shrugged.

"Read something." The director plucked a page from a messy folder on his desk. "What about this?"

Marina went into the studio, moved the microphone closer, and started reading. The news was about a plane that had gone down in the mountains, about how rescuers had been looking for the bodies of the dead for more than two days without success.

"You don't suit us," the director said before Marina was barely out of the studio. "Your voice is too sad."

"What kind of voice should I use to read news about an airplane crash?"

"Well, I don't know. More upbeat. This is an entertainment radio station."

Marina got a real job through a tip from a friend. The friend said that there was apparently a strange office called the Fund for Effective Politics, and the office needed someone to read the newspapers every day and write up a summary. This suited Marina.

The job really did consist of reading all the national newspapers every morning. Marina suddenly discovered, first of all, that there was a Chechen war under way in the country, and second, that there were elections in the country and the current president, Yeltsin, was losing the campaign disastrously to the Communist leader Gennady Zyuganov.

If you read the newspapers not the way normal people do, skimming the headlines and reading only the articles that interest you, if you read the newspaper straight through from cover to cover, your picture of the world changes. Articles by different authors on different topics line up in legions of information and go on the attack. In various newspapers and under various headings Marina found seemingly totally unconnected articles. An article about the horrible state that the largest factory in the town of N was in, for instance. An article about how businessman K had met with young people. An article about how state official M had taken shady money for consulting for some unknown person. Putting these texts together, and bearing in mind that the newspapers that ran all these articles belonged to businessman K, Marina realized that businessman K wanted to privatize the factory in N, official M was preventing him, and so businessman K had started a smear campaign whose ultimate goal was acquiring the factory.

In her surveys of the press, Marina attempted not just to give a brief summary of what the newspapers were writing about but also to group the articles by campaign. Marina began to think that there was nothing going on in the world but PR campaigns. This is the impression a young political analyst always gets, just as an upper-level med student gets the impression that he is suffering from every illness at the same time.

In spring 1996, Marina suddenly discovered that all the newspapers, regardless of who owned them, had begun to write about how much productive work President Boris Yeltsin was doing and what follies the Communists' presidential candidate, Gennady Zyuganov, was committing. Marina guessed that all the owners of newspapers and television channels had agreed to support Yeltsin in the presidential election. She guessed that the Fund for Effective Politics, where she worked, was also in on the conspiracy. She hated being part of the conspiracy, refused to accept her salary, and in the elections voted for Zyuganov in both the first and second rounds.

But Marina was not fired. She found it interesting, by reading the newspapers every day and following the information campaigns, to understand how the world operated, even if the world turned out to operate with extreme cynicism. She found it flattering to be initiated into the secret, even if the secret stank. In addition she saw that, being in on the secret, she could influence the secret course of events, and everyone on the FEP staff was consumed by the excitement of this influence. They spent their days and nights at work, applying political levers to reality, while all the rest of the nation could do nothing but be reconciled to it.

One day Marina was supposed to take her latest report to FEP head Gleb Pavlovsky. She collected the materials in a folder, went up to her boss's door, and knocked softly. No answer. She knocked louder, then cautiously opened the door and peeked inside. Pavlovsky was sleeping peacefully on his sofa, covered with a dark blue blanket, the way Bolsheviks in Soviet films about the revolution had the habit of sleeping in their offices under their greatcoats.

This Pavlovsky, whom people close to politics in Moscow now call "great and terrible," was known to Soviet-era dissidents as someone who had betrayed a comrade, literally telling the KGB where and which forbidden books his friend Vyacheslav Irgunov had, for which Irgunov was put into a psych hospital for two years. After that, human-rights activist Gefter would not shake Pavlovsky's hand. The gentler human-rights activist Alekseyeva said that the betrayal probably occurred during questioning and the application of special methods, that you could admire a person's staunchness, but you could not blame him for weakness. In short, the true heroes of anti-Soviet resistance treated Pavlovsky on a continuum from contempt to condescension, but Marina did not know any Soviet dissidents. In her eyes, Pavlovsky was a true hero.

And here her hero was asleep, under a blanket, which made it seem to Marina that here, in this office, the country's fate was being decided so urgently that one couldn't even go home to sleep. She acquired an e-mail address with the username "*silavoli*" (strength of will) and started spending her nights at work, too.

The elections ended, Yeltsin won, and 90 percent of FEP employees were fired, which is what Pavlovsky always did with anyone he thought he didn't need. But he kept Marina. The analytical press survey she had come up with had gradually turned into a weekly report, "Information Threats and Ways to Resolve Them," and was being sold successfully to the president's administration. On Fridays Pavlovsky started taking Marina with him to meetings with Chief of Staff Voloshin.

Based on the calendar of upcoming events, Marina surmised, for example, that the next week each and every journalist was going to be interested in the president's health because he hadn't appeared in public for several months and now had taken to a hospital bed altogether. As a way to resolve the problem, she suggested that the president record a radio address to the nation, since the president looked so awful he could not tape a television address. The suggestion was received ecstatically.

Another time Marina said that the next week, when another agreement, about bringing nuclear waste to Russia for processing, was going to be signed, journalists would come running like dogs to tear at the topic of nuclear waste. She suggested that the president might also speak out against organizing dangerous production in the country, in order to improve his ratings. But the chief of staff objected. Pavlovsky's eyes narrowed in fright on the other side of his narrow, rimless glasses, and the moment Marina started to argue her case, Pavlovsky took her by the arm and ordered her to be quiet with a single glance. After the meeting he explained that the factories processing the spent uranium belonged to a prominent Kremlin official, and no one was about to shut them down, even if they hurt the president's ratings. The president didn't even know that waste from foreign nuclear plants was being processed in Russia.

Gradually Marina became her own person in the Kremlin.

Confident that the young woman had learned how to tack between the country's political interests and officials' personal ones, Pavlovsky stopped going with her to the Friday meetings at Voloshin's. Besides these Friday meetings, Marina was also busy creating the first two Internet magazines, she did a Web site for Boris Nemtsov when he was deputy prime minister, she tried to prevent the re-election of Moscow mayor Luzhkov, for which she was beaten up by unknown men in her lobby for the first time, and she helped Ukrainian President Leonid Kuchma get re-elected. She was making pretty good money and bought an apartment in downtown Moscow. She spent day and night on the job but gave birth: her water broke right in her office, and while she was in labor she was reading her *silavoli* e-mail.

For Marina, the Ukrainian elections were pure income. It was a tour among savages who had no idea what sophisticated methods a political fight could deploy. Ukrainian television was run by complete political incompetents, or else people who played the fool to safeguard their independence from Moscow's political experts. In Ukraine, her "Information Threats" report didn't work. The television directors couldn't, or pretended they couldn't, draw independent conclusions from it. That was when Marina came up with a list of topics for them, a direct guide to action: which topic should be covered in the news and how, who to get commentary from, and who not to under any circumstances.

These kinds of lists were put to use in Russia as well. At the turn of the century, when the little-known Vladimir Putin became first acting president and then president, there was a need to clarify for the nation who this man was, what he was doing, and why he was doing it. The entire team at FEP sat around thinking up how, for example, after the successful rout of Shamil Basayev's gang from Dagestan in winter 1999, Putin should, in the headquarters tent on the border between Dagestan and Chechnya, raise a plastic victory glass of vodka with the soldiers, but, without drinking all the vodka, put the glass down and suggest that they not drain their glasses until Chechnya was completely free of terrorists. This was meant to tell the nation that the new president, unlike the old one, was not a drunk, and unlike the old one took stopping the war in Chechnya seriously, even if that meant starting a new war in Chechnya.

A definite case of wagging the dog.

Marina truly felt her strength when on August 12, 2000, the *Kursk*, a nuclear submarine, sank in the Barents Sea. People said the sailors in the sunken submarine were alive and were supposedly knocking on the side with a heavy object and putting out SOS signals. Their wives and mothers on shore, in the village of Vidyayevo, were waiting for and demanding the submarine's rescue. But no one was rescuing it. The military leadership refused the services of the Norwegians, who offered their divers. And President Putin sat it out in Sochi. He was on vacation. And politically it was right for the president to have no contact whatsoever with the story of the Vidyayevo ship, not to be associated in any way whatsoever in the voters' herd mentality with misfortunes and disasters. Let them blame the Northern Fleet leadership for everything.

But Marina thought otherwise. At the Friday meeting with the president's chief of staff, Marina stated that the head of the country could not lie around on the beach while his officers and sailors were perishing deep in northern waters, that he at least needed to fly to Vidyayevo to see the mothers and wives, to support them morally, if he couldn't get the submarine off the bottom, to console them somehow, to let them know that the country was with them. Oleg Dobrodeyev, head of the Rossiya television channel, supported Marina then. The president's chief of staff left the office, called Putin in Sochi, and when he returned said that the president was flying to Vidyayevo.

To this day, Marina thinks that going to Vidyayevo was the

right thing. The president retained his human face, showed compassion, and behaved decently, ultimately. But I fear Putin thinks otherwise. A crowd of enraged and desperate women was waiting for him at the Vidyayevo House of Culture. They were shouting at a man who already considered himself an infallible ruler. He got flustered and promised to pay the widows compensation equal to ten years' officer pay but didn't know how much an officer made. He offered condolences, but the women demanded the mourning be postponed because mourning meant the end of rescue operations. Then he lost his temper and in the most foolish way started blaming the reporters for the disaster that had occurred. On the street, a drunken man walked up to him and held out his hand, saying, "I've been wanting to meet an honest man for a long time"— and you couldn't tell whether he meant it or was being ironic. After that Putin never again met with disaster victims, except for one single time when the victims had been carefully selected and coached.

Policy changed. God knows who in the Kremlin decided that when disasters occurred the president should maintain silence. And then a disaster did occur. The hostages had been held in the theatre on Dubrovka for forty-eight hours. The president was silent. Television was silent, except for NTV—Independent Television—which Putin did not yet control. And Marina Litvinovich was not allowed into the meeting with the chief of staff with her "Information Threats" report.

Marina stood in front of the closed door and then got the hell out of the president's administration. The next night *spetsnaz* units stormed the theater using an unidentified poisonous gas, and 130 hostages died, primarily from choking on their own vomit after they lost consciousness.

And the "information threats" were eliminated by the fact that NTV, the last VHF television channel to allow itself to speak freely, replaced its directors. At the time, President Putin reproached the channel's chief, Boris Yordan, for "making ratings on blood." The president was implying that there were so many victims because NTV had broadcast the assault live. The Kremlin's information policy had completely given way to naked propaganda, and no one needed Marina Litvinovich anymore.

LIST OF DEFEATS

By December she had left FEP. Pavlovsky did not try to hold her back, either realizing that the girl had outgrown his organization or else sensing how the Kremlin's attitude toward Marina had changed. But Marina wasn't afraid of being out of work for a second. An election year had come, and the young woman—whom, it was rumored, Viktor Ivanov, the Kremlin's main personnel official, had refused to hire, so as to keep the administration from giving too much power to his deputy chief, Vladislav Surkov, who had invited her—was bound to head up someone's campaign headquarters.

Indeed, before she could get a couple of days' sleep, the telephone rang and Boris Nemtsov, one of the leaders of the Union of Right Forces (SPS), a liberal party, offered Marina a job. Nominally, SPS campaign headquarters were headed up by Albert Kokh, but his functions were to allocate the budget and preside. In fact, Marina organized the entire operation. Marina did not ask for a lot of money for this job, two thousand dollars a month—plus a spot on the party slate. If SPS surpassed the five percent threshold in the elections, Marina would become a parliamentary deputy.

A few days later, hanging over the desk in Marina's new office at SPS headquarters near the Ploshchad Ilicha subway station, was a huge piece of Whatman paper on which a calendar was drawn all the way to election day, and on each day the rallies, actions, meetings, and filming of campaign clips were mapped out. When Anatoly Chubais, the party's main inspiration and one of its significant sponsors at that time, saw the calendar, he was extremely pleased with the new employee, inasmuch as he himself liked to plan his time so that he would have "a call to someone at 14:43, and a meeting with someone else at 14:47."

In spite of the campaign staff's penchant for drunkenness and romances with young female reporters, the work was going full steam when Marina got a call from Vadim Malkin, her best FEP friend, who had also left Pavlovsky, not for the liberal SPS party, but rather for Yabloko, a social democratic party. The SPS and Yabloko electorates overlapped in a lot of ways, and the intelligentsia voted for both parties.

"Dinner?" Vadim suggested.

"Let's," Marina agreed.

They had dinner at a Yolki-Palki, a fast food place that pretends to be a Russian restaurant. Vadim was amused by the inviting slogan stretching all across the façade: "unlimited access to the wagon." At Yolki-Palki, the "wagon" was what they called the salad bar, and the cold dishes were indeed set out on a real wagon, which, for the sake of tacky patriotism, preened in the middle of the dining room. But Vadim interpreted the phrase in the political sense. The young people laughed that "unlimited access to the wagon" could be written into the contract of any state official, apart from the salary, and the word *wagon* could be understood either as the state budget or as oil company revenues.

"The wagon" could also be understood as "the story." Deputy Chief of Staff Vladislav Surkov, accordingly, had "unlimited access to the wagon" in the sense that he could order the directors of the central television channels to distort any story he liked. Marina smiled. She liked this penchant of Vadim's for intellectual games.

"Marina, why are you trying to bloody us?" Vadim suddenly asked.

The laughter stopped. Marina looked at her friend and wondered how SPS could be running a smear campaign against its Yabloko competitor, while she, who basically headed up the staff, knew nothing about it.

"When?" Marina asked.

"Yesterday," Vadim replied. "Your guys went to a Communist rally with Yabloko banners."

There was no reason to doubt what Vadim said. If he said that SPS had sent its people to make it look as though the Communists and Yabloko were together and thereby push the intelligentsia, anti-Soviet by force of habit, away from Yabloko, then that meant he'd found out that the provocateurs were indeed from SPS.

Over the next few days Marina learned that besides the official SPS headquarters run by her and Albert Kokh, there was also an unofficial headquarters run by Leonid Gozman. The official headquarters filmed positive videos about army reform, increasing the birthrate, and fighting corruption, and did everything it could to fight for the unification of all democratic forces, which is what the majority of SPS and Yabloko voters wanted. The unofficial headquarters spread nasty rumors about Yabloko's leaders, arranged provocations like the one with Yabloko banners at the Communist rally, and even harassed Yabloko activists using their personal connections in the prosecutor's office.

After gathering all of these facts, Marina went to see Chubais. She also had a sociological survey that implied that if Yabloko and SPS ran each other down, the voters would be disenchanted with both parties and neither party would garner more than five percent in the elections or get into parliament.

"We can't bloody Yabloko," Marina told Chubais. "We won't get in."

"I don't care," Chubais replied. "As long as Grisha doesn't."

Grisha was what he called Yabloko's leader, Grigory Yavlinsky.

Marina undertook her final attempt to avert a suicidal war with Yabloko in the middle of the summer. She went to Zhukovka with Boris Nemtsov, the only peace-loving member of the SPS political council, to see Mikhail Khodorkovsky. The oil magnate had given money to both Yabloko and SPS, and according to Marina's calculations he could not possibly have liked the fact that the two democratic parties were using his money to destroy each other.

Khodorkovsky met them in his reception building. For a long time he listened, drawing squares, algorithms, and diagrams on a sheet of paper. That was how Khodorkovsky thought. When he was thinking he drew diagrams of his thoughts on paper. Based on the results of the discussion, Khodorkovsky suggested that the two parties he sponsored sign something like a nonaggression pact. But Marina could see that the little squares on his sheet of paper were not shaping up into anything quite so elegant, just like the little boy Kai in the tale of the Snow Queen, who never could piece together the word *eternity*.

In fact, Khodorkovsky did not know how to force SPS and Yabloko not to destroy each other. And Marina, who was always interested in why people lose, thought then that what makes people lose is hatred. You're prepared to lose, you're prepared to die even, as long as you know your sworn enemy will die from it, too. Hatred is stronger than the arguments of reason. It is even stronger than money.

About a week later (evidently Khodorkovsky had called Chubais and tried to admonish him), the Union of Right Forces' political council met suddenly to discuss the progress of the campaign. And what they said! One after another the members of the political council said that it was Marina Litvinovich's fault that flyers hadn't been printed, although they had been and

Marina was prepared to show them. But no one was listening to her. They said it was Marina Litvinovich's fault that videos hadn't been filmed, although they had been, and Marina was prepared to show them. They said . . . in short, they said that Marina Litvinovich had to be thrown out on her ass, and only Boris Nemtsov backed her up, but he was in the minority.

Marina was driven out. She was paid her money but crossed off the election slate. They drove her out after reaching an agreement with her that she would not speak ill of the party and the party would not speak ill of her, but they immediately told reporters "in confidence" that it was Litvinovich who had brought down the campaign. Inasmuch as the legend of Marina's incompetence had to be supported, the actions Marina had planned were canceled and the videos shot by Marina weren't used. The new campaign staff managed to shoot only one video, in which the party leaders—Chubais, Nemtsov, and Khakamada—were flying in a private plane and pontificating about liberalism while leaning back in leather seats. And although Chubais had never in his life had a private plane, and he, as head of United Energy Systems, flew in an old Gorbachev-era IL, this video provoked indignation at the liberals' conceit even among the well-off. And SPS lost any chance of getting into parliament.

And Marina lost her job and her reputation as someone who always succeeds.

Actually, she did not have long to wait for an offer this time either. Before she could get a couple of days' sleep, she had a call from Yukos. Khodorkovsky was inviting her to explain to the country how and why the two oil companies, Yukos and Sibneft, were merging.

In fact, this PR campaign and these trips by Khodorkovsky to various regions to lecture about the social benefit of Yukos and Sibneft merging only appeared to be image support for a major oil deal. In fact, it was politics. It was a campaign trip for a presidential candidate, even if Khodorkovsky didn't plan on becoming president but planned on training the nation to want someone like him, Khodorkovsky, for president. In any case, if a person worth nearly twenty billion goes into politics, it is hard to think he is setting himself a more modest goal than power. Marina didn't. She saw that Khodorkovsky found it much more interesting to find a common language with students at a provincial university, for example, or to understand what some governor was thinking, than to explain to the governor and students how much the capitalization of the merged companies would increase and how many new jobs would be created as a result.

He was a poor speaker. In his first speeches he tried to draw little squares and appeal to diagrams. They flew on a chartered plane from city to city, and every evening Marina gave Khodorkovsky lessons in rhetoric.

"Mikhail Borisovich, you have to map out your high points."

"How's that?" Khodorkovsky listened like a schoolboy.

"Your emotional splashes . . . . That's all people remember."

"For instance?"

"For instance, don't talk to them about state tyranny and corruption. They don't understand what that is. Tell them that if you want to take away an oil company you need a state prosecutor, but if you want to take away a little store, all it takes is a local investigator from the prosecutor's office."

She must have had second sight.

In Nizhny Novgorod, the surveillance that his security service had long been trying to tell Khodorkovsky about became open. A car of FSB agents joined the billionaire's motorcade, and in special service language, that meant "Run!" But Khodorkovsky had no intention of running. Someone very important in the Kremlin had promised that he would not be arrested. He knew there would be an attack on him and his company, but he expected an honest, political, legal attack and fully believed he could fight it because he had the best political strategists and the best lawyers on his team. The motorcade was on its way to the airport and there was a heavy snowfall. Marina shot a glance at the FSB Volga following them and wondered whether Khodorkovsky's chances of winning were all that great. To Marina, they seemed significant.

At the airport they were told it was nonflying weather. They waited a few hours for the weather to clear, stretched out on couches in the VIP lounge, and then went back to the hotel. They went to dinner and unexpectedly drank too much.

One of Khodorkovsky's aides was trying to make Marina understand. "It was always good weather! No matter where MBKh" that was what they called Mikhail Borisovich Khodorkovsky—"flew, there was always good weather."

Because of these drunken conversations Marina missed the telephone conversation Khodorkovsky had that evening. She did not see MBKh talking with an unknown well-wisher who warned the billionaire that he would be arrested the next day. But the expression on Khodorkovsky's face did not change, and even the next morning, when he canceled the whole team's flight to Irkutsk and told everyone to go back to Moscow, he wore a slight smile: not once did this smile leave his lips throughout the investigation and trial. At the time Marina thought that often it doesn't matter whether someone wins or loses. Often what matters is *how* you lose.

And she started losing. Time after time. Knowing in advance that she would lose, but the main thing was *how*. She ran the campaign of the writer Viktor Shenderovich, who was running for the Duma. Shenderovich did not get in. She headed up Irina Khakamada's campaign headquarters in the presidential election. And not only did Khakamada not become president or get into the second round, she did not even accrue any significant percentage, and almost none of her former friends and colleagues even came to the banquet held in honor of the campaign's conclusion.

All she could do was lose. The political world where she had been a fish in water had shrunk. Democratic parties were not getting into parliament, television channels were obeying the Kremlin without a murmur, and so were most newspapers. The judges had learned to be obedient, Khodorkovsky was sentenced to eight years in prison, and finally, after terrorists seized the school in Beslan and children died, Putin eliminated gubernatorial elections. Marina's next project doomed to failure consisted of her helping world chess champion Garry Kasparov, who was attempting for the umpteenth time to unite the democrats. There was a Civic Congress, a congress of human-rights activists, at which Kasparov spoke. During a break at the congress, Marina was approached by a tall, athletically built man with the facial features of someone from the Caucasus. And with kind, absolutely childlike eyes. This was Vissarion Aseyev, the deputy from the Beslan District Legislative Assembly.

"Marina," Vissarion spoke with a slightly French r. "I've wanted to meet you for a long time and am inviting you to pay us a visit. Please come."

It sounded like he was offering his hand and heart, although Vissarion's gentle and manly ways held no hint of flirtation. So Marina agreed to come.

"HELP US"

Marina took a grass green S7 Boeing 737 from Moscow to Vladikavkaz. The three lucky sevens on the airliner's fuselage were a touching attempt to dispel the feeling now characteristic of all passengers on this flight that they were flying to the saddest place on earth. Because the Vladikavkaz airport serves Beslan. Because on September 1, 2004, terrorists took control of the school there. Because they held children there for three days locked up in the gymnasium without food, water, or medicine. Because the mothers there were shouting, "Give us water at least for the children!" And because three days later an assault was launched instead of talks, and federal troops fired a tank gun and heat-seeking flamethrowers at the school, which was filled with children, and the bombs dangling over the children's heads in the gymnasium exploded, and those children who escaped the explosion and fire and ran out of the school through windows opened by the blast were shot in the back by the terrorists.

Now the new Beslan cemetery, 335 flower-strewn graves, if you looked out the little window of your plane coming in for landing, looked like a flower bed, a cheerful, colorful flower bed on the steppe at the mountains' foothills. The plane landed, Marina disembarked, and an airport employee checked to make sure she had taken her own suitcase off the baggage belt.

Two men met her: Vissarion Aseyev and a tall, sorrowful man named Sasha. Vissarion had invited Sasha so he wouldn't have to hire a taxi—Sasha had a car. Also, Sasha's fifteen-year-old daughter had died in the Beslan school.

They were going to Vladikavkaz because Beslan doesn't have a decent hotel, and everyone who goes to Beslan stays in Vladikavkaz. The road ran past the cemetery. They got out and Marina put a few flowers on a few graves—the bouquet she had brought was not enough for even a tenth of the tombstones. Sasha walked up to his daughter's grave and stroked the stone for a long time.

At the turn from the airport toward Vladikavkaz, on the very outskirts of Beslan, there was a nice new playground surrounded by a high fence. A sign hung on the fence announcing that the playground had been given to the children by Sberbank. But there wasn't a single child on the slides, merry-go-rounds, and jungle gyms. Not because the town was in mourning but simply because the playground was too far from any Beslan home for the mothers to take their children there.

They drove past a large brick house planted with small firs. Vissarion told her that the house belonged to someone by the name of Tamerlan, although Tamerlan was rarely home, and if you knocked at the gate you'd be met by Tamerlan's brother, who, as a rule, was washing his car under the grapevine-entwined pergola. This Tamerlan had vowed to find everyone to blame for the children dying, people said, find them and kill them with his own hands. But he considered revenge a sacred obligation and the right of the people of Beslan, and he thought that Muscovites had no right poking their noses into Caucasian affairs. Therefore, a year later, when Marina began aiding Beslan mothers legally and politically, people said it was Tamerlan who sent his men to beat her up.

They drove past vodka factories. There were vodka factories at every step, and Vissarion joked that vodka was the national Ossetian drink and the basis of North Ossetia's economy.

They drove past signs announcing that the Ossetian people through their combined efforts were shooting a film based on an ancient mountain epic. Vissarion explained that the film's screenplay had already been published and that in the last episode of the screenplay the legendary ancient heroes, having vanquished the monsters, having descended into the kingdom of the dead and returned, "are sitting and feasting with parliamentary deputies and members of the government of North Ossetia." That was what was written. But when the hero Soslan descended into the kingdom of the dead, according to this screenplay, dead children ran up to him and said they were the souls of children who would perish millennia later during the terrorist act in Beslan PS1.

They stopped at a gas station. Women were working there as gas station attendants. The men drove up, emerged lazily from their vehicles, told the attendants lazily, through clenched teeth, "fill 'er up," lit up right there, half a meter from the flowing gasoline, and discussed important, mainly family affairs:

about some Zurik who was a deputy's aide, and some Sosik who worked for the police and had won a freestyle wrestling championship . . .

They arrived at the hotel. Marina went up to her room to leave her things. Vissarion and Sasha waited for her in the lobby. Outside, in the nearby mosque, the muezzin was crying out fervently. Marina didn't know the language in which the muezzin was shouting, but he was crying out: "Arise! Prayer is better than sleep!" The Terek flowed noisily.

Having dropped off her things in the room and discovered she had only cold water running from the tap, Marina joined Vissarion and Sasha and they headed off to have dinner at the Alandon restaurant. It was warm. Marina felt like sitting on the banks of the Terek and watching the balloons that some unknown person had launched down the mountain river for some unknown purpose dance in the shallows. But Sasha couldn't sit on the banks of the Terek. Ossetian tradition held that someone in mourning could not sit in a restaurant and feast in front of everyone, even if the person had simply dropped in for a piece of beet-greens pie. They were sitting in a separate, rather stuffy room. They ordered three pies, huge, each the size of a Neapolitan pizza, although they could have barely eaten even one. Vissarion explained that this too was an Ossetian tradition. When a misfortune occurred, there had to be two pies on the table. When there was joy, there had to be three. This day there was joy: Marina had come.

Marina was drop-dead tired. She had gotten up too early and eaten too big a piece of meat pie and drunk a shot of vodka, afraid of insulting the hospitable Vissarion by turning it down. Before drinking, Vissarion mumbled something about the Great God who watches down on us from heaven and knows everything about us in advance . . . Marina thought Vissarion was praying.

They drove to Beslan, to the school, which stood there in

ruins. In the middle of the destroyed gymnasium lay a perfectly fresh mountain of flowers and a great many bottles of the water the children taken hostage had needed so badly. The smell of fire had never aired out, even though several months had passed since the terrorist act. Marina wandered through the school. Vissarion showed her the classroom where the militants had shot the hostages. He showed her the auditorium with the cache in the floor where the militants had kept their weapons. He showed her exactly where the bombs had been hung in the gymnasium. He showed her where the woman terrorist killed by the blast had been standing. A black bloodstain had eaten into the concrete floor.

But Sasha had gone off somewhere. Marina found him as she came out of the school and headed for the car. He was squatting in a vacant spot. His body was shuddering either from dry sobs or hiccups. Marina didn't know how this spot was connected with Sasha's dead daughter, but she put her hand on Sasha's shoulder as he stroked the ground under his feet, rose, and went to start up the car.

She met with people. When someone in a home dies, Ossetians place the deceased's favorite things and photograph on the person's bed. You have to go up to the bed, lean over, and lay your hands briefly on the blanket; this is how they express their condolences. In the first house Sasha and Vissarion took her to, they led Marina to a bed where there were photographs of a woman and four children, a lace blouse, two dolls, a soccer ball, and a wind-up toy train. Alongside this bed the father of the four dead children was silent and then led Marina, Vissarion, and Sasha to the kitchen, poured them some vodka, and talked about the Great God, who was good and just. And he looked at Marina. Marina tried to add to the toast about the Great God words of condolence about the dead children, but Vissarion stopped her.

"Wait. We have twenty-eight mandatory toasts. The first is

to the Great God. The second is to St. George. The one for the deceased is the fourth."

That day they never did get as far as the fourth toast with anyone. They drove from house to house. One man told them that during the assault he had found his son among the dead children in the school, carried the boy's body out to the street and laid him on the grass, and then his cell phone had gone off in his pocket: it was his wife calling to tell him their son was alive and well.

"Imagine what was going on in my mind!" the man said. "How could I mistake someone else's boy for my own son?"

Another person recounted how on the second day after the assault he had sat with his wounded son in the hospital, and all of a sudden the ward door had opened and in walked President Putin, who had flown to Beslan when the terrorists had already been rendered harmless.

"You know what I said to him? I said, 'Get out of here! I needed you four days ago when my son was sitting there in the school under a bomb and no one but Aushev was negotiating for him. That's when I needed you. Now I don't. Get out.' And he did."

In the late afternoon Marina met with the women. The mothers of the dead children. At some house of culture, in a completely empty room. For the first time there was neither food nor vodka on the table. The women were all talking at once, and Marina couldn't understand what they were saying. All she could make out was that in Ossetia, if a woman walks down the street in a black mourning scarf, even the old men stand up out of respect for her grief. Marina tried to talk to these women about legal support, but they only wept.

Later that evening Sasha and Vissarion took Marina to one more house, to see someone named Totraz. There the table was laid, and on the table were three pies, meat, vegetables, greens, cheese, and vodka. Marina tried to refuse because she had been drinking and eating all day. But Vissarion explained that it would be awkward to refuse. They had been waiting for Marina all day and had prepared the dinner especially for her.

Totraz was silent all evening. He only took a photograph of a girl of about fourteen off the shelf and said that this was his daughter. And that the girl's name was Agunda. Vissarion spoke. He made the toasts. To the Great God, who watches us, who is merciful and just. . . . To St. George, who is a warrior-angel and protects us and whose legions of angels . . .

In the intervals between toasts Sasha talked about how after the assault he collected the tubes from the heat-seeking flamethrowers from the entrances of the houses around the school. Based on the inventory numbers it was easy to determine that federal soldiers had fired these flamethrowers at the school, that the fire and blasts that had killed the children had probably been the fault of the federal troops, and that none of the members of the Moscow commission who came had wanted to listen to him or look at the tubes he'd collected.

By midnight Marina was drunk. She stood up, thanked Totraz for his hospitality, and said she was going to her hotel and that there was no need to accompany her.

"Fine." Totraz smiled. "I'll call my nephew right away. He'll come in his car and take you back."

"No need." Marina shook her head decisively, nearly losing her balance. "I'll go myself. I'll take a taxi."

"Is this your first time in the Caucasus?" Totraz smiled again. "Little girl, blondes here do not catch taxis alone at night."

"Then where can I smoke here?" Marina asked, again not taking into consideration that this was the Caucasus and women here did not smoke, at least not so that men knew about it.

Totraz smiled again and said to Sasha, "Take her into the kitchen."

They smoked in the kitchen. It was a tiny kitchen, five

meters square, in a crummy Khrushchev-era apartment. Sasha was telling some story. Marina didn't understand. A certain amount of time passed and a certain number of cigarettes had been smoked when Marina discovered suddenly that she was standing, squeezed in the corner between the table and refrigerator, and that Sasha, a huge man compared to her, had his arm around her shoulders. "Fool," Marina thought. "What a fool!" It was silly to shout, "Take your hands off me!" to someone you'd spent the whole day crying with. It was silly to call for help from Vissarion or Totraz and make yourself out to be a touch-me-not after you'd been sitting and talking at the table with men, after you'd drunk vodka with them and smoked with them in the kitchen. "Fool!" Marina thought. She shut her eyes and did not resist when Sasha now very decisively caught her in an embrace.

Sasha cupped Marina's head in his huge hands and brought her face right up to his. She was expecting a kiss. But no kiss followed. She felt Sasha's breath on her lips, but the man wasn't touching her lips. She opened her eyes. Sasha stared point-blank into her eyes and whispered, "Help us."

"What?" Marina murmured.

"Help us."

CHAPTER 3
Vissarion Aseyev:
The Man at the Table on the Right

The sounds that woke Visa Aseyev were like a squib or a firecracker going off. The clock read nine and change. Time to get up, of course. It was September 1, 2004. Visa thought that if someone was launching squibs on September 1, then it must be people at the school commencement ceremony with fireworks. Beslan is a small town. Nothing happens there but weddings and funerals. The opening day of school is a major event attended by families and it is no sin to mark it with fireworks—assuming, of course, you have extra money to spend on them. Visa lowered his feet to the floor and sat up on the bed. The pops continued, but all of a sudden they formed a neat sequence that squibs going off couldn't: only submachine gun fire could. Visa leapt up. The distant but distinct sound of submachine gun rounds flew through his open window. There's no confusing that sound with anything else. Visa had served in the army. True, he had served in the diving forces. He, a mountain man who didn't even know how to swim, had been taught not to run across the mountains but to walk on the bottom of the Akhtuba River wearing eighty kilos of equipment, while his own boyish weight was sixty. He got tangled up in his hoses, fell to the silty bottom, lay there helpless, watching the silt suck him under, and called for help through his intercom, and his officer replied through the intercom from the surface of the water, through the watery layer, "Suck it up, Aseyev. I'm not sending you any rescuers. Get up yourself." That's what he was taught in the army. But there was also shooting practice. And anyone who has ever heard a Kalashnikov round doesn't confuse that decisive sound with anything else.

Now Visa was preparing for war. In the Caucasus, when a man hears submachine gun fire out his window, it should not occur to him to hide or call the police. He should understand that it's probably the police who have been attacked, as had recently happened in Nazran, where the police who were attacked by militants included relatives, neighbors, and friends, and federal troops wouldn't help because in the Caucasus they were afraid to stick their noses out of their military bases. You had to pick up your gun and go fight before the enemy came to your house, as had happened in Botlikh.

Visa dressed military fashion. The way men in the Caucasus have always dressed for war—track pants, T-shirt, and sneakers. For self-defense he took along only his identification as a deputy of the district legislative assembly. This identification won't protect you from bullets, but if you encounter policemen you don't know, who have come from Vladikavkaz, for example, as reinforcements, and if they ask you why you're walking around town with a weapon, you can show them the identification, proving that you're a deputy, not a militant. By law, the deputy identification doesn't give you the right to carry a smooth-bore Saiga carbine with a clip. But the Caucasus are another matter. A gun and power are one and the same.

After all, Visa didn't just happen to become a deputy. In the Soviet era his father was first an instructor for the Communist Party's district committee and then head of the propaganda office. In the modern era his father had first been deputy district chief and then, after losing the election to Taimuraz Mamsurov, had worked as an advisor in the republic's parliament, maintaining good relations with Mamsurov. His father was well known to people because it's not every person in

Beslan who works as a deputy district chief and parliamentary advisor. When Visa registered for the elections and went from house to house to show voters his campaign platform, people asked, "Which Aseyev are you campaigning for, young man? Volodya?"

"No, Vissarion," Vissarion replied.

"Who is this Vissarion? And who is he to Volodya?"

"It's me," Vissarion replied. "I'm his son."

And people realized that before them stood a young man from a good family. That they at least had to invite him into their home, offer him something, and listen to what he had to say. And he said that they needed to introduce differential payments for water. Because in a five-story building the water flows just fine on the first floor, badly on the third, and only at night on the fifth. He said that the person on the fifth floor shouldn't pay as much for water as the person on the first. And people saw that it was fair.

Later people also recalled that this was the very son of Volodya Aseyev who had studied at the North Caucasus Metallurgical Institute, the graduates of which land in North Ossetian power structures as often as Ivy League graduates in America end up in the Capitol or the White House. People also recalled that this was the very son of Volodya Aseyev who, when the 1992 war began in Prigorodny District, was in commerce and gave cigarettes from his stall to the soldiers at their positions. Someone else recalled that in 1998, when there was a financial crisis and his stall went bust, this young man did not get his father to support him but went to work as a laborer and then a production engineer at the Salyut Zlatoglavaya vodka factory. And how at the plant there he made fun of the security chief. She had started shouting at the workers, who, in anticipation of the search that was mandatory after every shift, had scattered and weren't lined up properly. And this young man had said, "Why are you shouting? A step to the right, a step to the left, a hop in place—that's an attempt to fly away?" She complained about him to the bosses. But the workers stood up for him. The director considered this a strike and Visa the strike's organizer, and he fired him. People also said that Visa was fired not because he had quarreled with the head of security and had enjoyed the respect of his workers but because he had posted flyers for Slavik Bzykov, who was running for deputy and to whom the factory's owner was opposed. This too was unfair, and people remembered that he was a young man from a good family who had been treated unfairly, and that's why they were prepared to vote for him.

This was a time when only a member of the United Russia Party could become a deputy, or if he was a member of another party, then only with the higher-ups' approval. But people voted for him. He was a young man from a good family. He had many respected relatives. They held positions in all of the precinct electoral commissions in the district. When the higher-ups called the head of a precinct electoral commission and demanded that he throw in ballots for Vissarion Aseyev's rival, the head of the electoral commission said, "I can't. I have Vissarion Aseyev's uncle here on the commission, he'll see I'm throwing in ballots against his nephew, and he'll disgrace me in front of all Beslan. How can I walk down the streets after that?" The higher-ups realized that the electoral commission chief really did fear disgrace more than he did the higher-ups. Therefore there was no falsification and Visa won. And therefore his deputy identification, although it did not give him a legal right to carry a carbine with a clip, did attest that if he had a Saiga carbine lying on the passenger seat of his car, then that was fair.

Visa left the house calmly. Slowly, as if he were simply going to work, because he mustn't frighten his wife. But the moment he was through the door he broke into a run because he could not dawdle when people were firing Kalashnikovs in the city.

He ran to the garage. Every Caucasus native has a weapon stashed somewhere in his house or garage. In the Caucasus, militants—or federal soldiers pretending to be militants in order to commit robbery—attack isolated Russian school-teachers, because in an Avar, Ingush, or Ossetian home they would be met by a man with a weapon, whereas in the home of a Russian teacher they are met by the teacher.

Visa kept his weapon, a Saiga repeating carbine, the Kalashnikov's younger brother, in the garage. It took Visa a fairly long time. First he had to get the carbine out from behind the boards, where it was hidden away from the children. Then he had to break open the boxes of cartridges, load two clips, and shove more cartridges in his pockets. Then he had to rev up his dilapidated old Zhiguli-9, a black one with sunken seats, but at least with heavily tinted windows, Caucasus style. All this time the shots continued, and Vissarion thought that somewhere in town a battle was under way without him.

Finally he got going. He was driving toward the Beslan internal affairs directorate, thinking it had been attacked, as in Nazran. He drove past the Internet club he ran, drove about another two hundred meters, and at the door of the district administration building saw someone he knew.

"Hey, listen, where are they shooting?" Vissarion shouted, stopping and lowering the passenger window.

"They're shooting at the school," the man answered, shaking his head and gesturing helplessly, as if to say he could not conceive of there being shooting at a school.

In fact, neither could Vissarion. When two horsemen in the mountains fire at each other over an ancient feud, it's savagery, of course, a savagery Vissarion didn't like, as he believed Ossetians were modern people and Europeans. But it happens. When serious men fire at each other over oil or over control of the vodka market, that's savagery, of course, but it happens. But for men to be shooting at children—that should not be.

And for children to be standing between men shooting at one another—that should not be either.

Vissarion reached the side street leading to Beslan PS1. There was a butcher shop on that street. The sign nailed up on the corner now took on a terrible meaning. The sign said "Fresh Meat." Vissarion abandoned his car. There was a police cordon there and cars were not being let through. Carrying his carbine, Visa ran past the policemen and toward one of the five-story apartment buildings that surrounded the school. He would have liked to peek around the corner, but a police colonel pressed up against the wall there said, "Young man, don't poke your nose out, they're strafing."

Visa ran around the building from the other side, where the path was shielded by bushes and trees. Now all that separated him from the school was a vacant lot, garages, and a transformer booth. Still, he couldn't get a good look at what was going on in the school. Several policemen were squatting behind the transformer booth, their backs leaning against the wall.

"Do we have anyone on the roof?" Vissarion shouted at the policemen.

"No, no one. Why the roof?" one of the policemen replied.

"Ugh!" Visa gestured with his hand. "You have to control the high-points, don't you know that? Two of you follow me!"

He ran for the entry. Two policemen ran after him because he had said very decisively that they needed to control the high-points and because he was the first person to come along who had the slightest idea of what to do when terrorists seize a school. They ran up the stairs, and by the fourth floor Visa could feel himself gasping. He had asthma, which he got at the vodka factory, provoked by his allergy to flour dust. Somehow he dragged himself up to the fifth floor, where he sat down on the floor. If he hadn't, he would have fainted. A door to one of the apartments opened and a woman came out. She brought Vissarion a glass of water. He felt better, but he remembered he had left his spare clip in the car, and he sent one of the policemen to the car for the clip. He asked the second policeman, "Do you have enough cartridges?"

"Ten per clip." The nice young sergeant smiled.

"You mean you came here unarmed, soldier?" Vissarion summed up and he started to climb up to examine the equipment floor.

Meanwhile, the second unarmed soldier brought him the cartridges, which were only enough to frighten the terrorists, who had brought a truckload of ammunition.

No one had taught Vissarion the tactics of street fighting. In the army he had been taught that if you're from the Caucasus and you end up in a barracks where you're the only caucasian, then the first night the old-timers will wake you up and start beating you to break your will. And you have to fight. You're a snot-nosed kid, there are three of them, but you have to fight desperately unless you want to clean the toilet for a whole year with your own toothbrush, shave with a terry cloth towel, and push a matchbox across the floor with your nose to entertain the old-timers. They will knock you off your feet with heavy blows, but you have to get up again and again and fight, until the huge Mordvinian Vanka gets up from the last cot and says in a good-natured bass, "All right already! See, he won't surrender!" And leaning over you, after you've finally allowed yourself to lie on the floor with a busted-up face, he slaps you on the shoulder. "Get up, kid. They won't anymore. You did good, held your own." And that is when real soldier friendship will begin.

He was taught that in the army. But as far occupying the high-points, he didn't remember where he got that.

In the army he was taught that if you defended your right not to be subjected to ridicule from old-timers, that didn't mean they wouldn't wake you after lights out. A senior sergeant comes up to you, wakes you gently, and whispers, "We're going to go teach the young folks. Get up, sit around with us in the depot, drink a little tea, or else, you know, you'll undermine our authority."

So you get up and go to the depot, and you drink tea, because you're strong enough to defend your own dignity if you're prepared to die, but you're not strong enough to defend the dignity of all the platoon's young soldiers if they want to live. You drink tea in the depot and you hear the rookies who've been awakened in the middle of the night carrying out humiliating commands: "Lie down! Stand up! Lie down! Stand up!" The point of the commands being that they're humiliating.

Only toward the end of your service, when you've become squad commander, do you decide to arrange things fairly. You tell your old-timers not to harass the young people at night. And you tell the young soldiers to come to you if they're hazed. And peace and life by the books reigns in your barracks. And you sleep peacefully. You don't know that every night the old-timers wake up the rookies with a whisper: "Up and out, soldier. Quiet as a mouse, soldier. If the old man hears, it's checkmate for you, soldier. Get it?"

They get up and out in their underpants on the parade ground, where they obediently carry out the humiliating commands: "Lie down! Stand up!" There are puddles on the parade ground. But you sleep peacefully and think you've brought order and observance of the rules. They only tell you how it really was in the bus on the way home.

This is what Vissarion learned in the army. But what you do when an enemy carrying a weapon comes to your town, the army didn't teach him that.

In the army Vissarion learned that if you're a good soldier and don't get beaten by old-timers, the deputy political officer will call you in and order you to rat on your comrades: how they brew tea after lights out, how they go AWOL. If you refuse, then on the last day of service your entire squadron lines up on the parade ground and along with the demobilization order they read an order about your demotion to private. And smiling, the deputy political officer tells you that if you don't rip your sergeant stripes off right now, you won't go home. And the bus, there it is, right outside the gates. So you rip off the stripes and ride home in your dress uniform with scrubbed buttons but with threads sticking up on your shoulders. At home your father gets upset and says, "Didn't you write saying you're a sergeant?" And your evaluation says "undisciplined." Your father says, "I thought you'd come home a sergeant with a good evaluation. I wanted to get you a job at the KGB. Ugh! Suit yourself, soldier."

Vissarion learned this after the army. But Vissarion did not know how to protect children from terrorists. He just guessed that you should control the high-points.

"Hey!" a policeman shouted after he glanced at the roof while Visa was finishing up his survey of the equipment floor. "This is someone's lookout."

"What do you mean, lookout?" Visa was taken aback.

"There's a blanket on the roof and a water bottle."

Quick thoughts flashed through Visa's mind. It might mean that the night before an observer, one of the terrorists, a sniper maybe, had come up here on the roof and kept watch on the school. If the seizure hadn't gone according to plan, if someone had resisted the terrorists, he would have fired. Where was he now? Did he go down when the school was seized? Might he have walked past Vissarion running with his carbine? Had he blended into the crowd? Was he walking in the crowd, looking, listening, and reporting to the terrorists in the school what was happening outside the cordon? Or had he seized one of the apartments? Was he looking out the window and might he at any moment fire at the policemen hiding behind the transformer booth? He would see the *spetsnaz* troops, when the *spetsnaz* came . . . .

"Hey, come down," Vissarion shouted to the policemen. "You have to go around to all the apartments on this entry. Make sure everything's all right. Move people away from the windows. But carefully. There might be someone in the apartments."

"I understand." The policeman nodded.

The policemen went off to check the apartments, and Vissarion climbed out on the roof alone. The roof was totally flat and guarded only by metal railings with just the occasional bar. There was nowhere to hide. Vissarion lay down on the tar, crept over to the edge, and for the first time saw the school like an open book. Children were standing in the windows. Vissarion couldn't make out their faces, but he thought they were children because a grown person could hardly stand at full height in a window opening, and they were. Behind their backs there were people moving back and forth, carrying bundles of some kind. Vissarion thought those were the terrorists, that they were mining the school, using the children as shields, and no sniper would ever fire at terrorists while children were standing in the windows.

"Vipers," Vissarion whispered under his breath. "They prepared."

Right then he heard a rustle behind him. Vissarion rolled over on his back, hoisted his carbine, undid the safety, and aimed at a man in camo looking out of a dormer window. Slowly. Too slowly. The other man ought to have had time to fire.

But he didn't. Instead he put a finger to his lips and said, "Easy, sir, we're on the same side. Vladikavkaz OMON."

Visa lowered his weapon. The OMON sniper and his gunner escort hopped out of the dormer window as agilely as kittens.

"Fuck it. Not one lousy brick." The sniper surveyed the totally unprotected roof.

"The gunner can take off his vest and hang it on the railing," Vissarion advised.

He didn't know where he'd come up with the idea that if

you hung a bulletproof vest on a railing you would have a passable weapon emplacement. Maybe one of his friends had told him about it during the endless discussions that men from the Caucasus have about war. The sniper nodded. The gunner removed his vest. Hiding behind it, the sniper began to examine the school through his sight and whispered, "Children in the windows."

Vissarion went with the policemen to check the apartments. He saw women who had been told to move away from the windows and who were sitting in their bathrooms because there weren't any other bulletproof rooms in the apartments. When Vissarion returned to the roof and stuck his head out of the dormer window, the sniper told him, "They took a shot at me." And as if in confirmation of what he said, a bullet struck the roof about two centimeters from the sniper's boot.

"Let me lie here for you," Vissarion said. "I'll shoot and distract them, and you look to see where the sniper is working from and take him out."

Without waiting for an answer, Vissarion crawled to the emplacement behind the vest to take the sniper's place. The sniper rolled to the side, took cover through the window, and put his eye to his sight.

Vissarion lay there, fired occasionally, held the bandanna the sniper had left over the vest, and counted the bullets that buzzed by, the way bullets buzz only when they are very close. Vissarion didn't remember who told him that if a bullet whistles, that means it's a ways away, but if it buzzes, then it's very close. Again, it must have been during the endless Caucasian conversations about war.

"That's it!" the sniper said. "I've pinpointed him. Go."

In order to roll toward the window, Vissarion rose slightly. He moved a couple of inches to the side. First he thought a fly had struck him on the forehead. Then he thought it was a bullet, not a fly. A bullet had hit him in the head.

SIGNS OF SUCCESS

Meanwhile, the news flew around the world about terrorists seizing a school in the North Ossetian town of Beslan and either two hundred or three hundred children being held hostage. The mothers of the children taken hostage stood by the police cordon shouting that there couldn't be three hundred hostages in the school, there had to be more than a thousand. But no one listened to them. Then they drew a sign saying that there were more than a thousand hostages. They were afraid the federal authorities wouldn't worry about three hundred people and would order an assault of the school. They thought the authorities might agree to negotiate for the sake of a thousand people. The mothers stood there with the signs, but the directors of Russia's national television channels didn't show those signs on the grounds that you shouldn't put unverified information on the air, they said.

Shortly thereafter an antiterrorist headquarters was set up in Beslan. One of the headquarters' directors, an FSB man, a general apparently, strutted up and down the street near headquarters talking on his cell phone. A phone with diamonds on it, worth twenty thousand euros.

Later the terrorists handed over a video with their demands. They demanded that the presidents of Chechnya, Ossetia, and Ingushetia come to Beslan. But headquarters told reporters that the cassette was empty, and the television directors immediately broadcast that information on the air, despite the fact that this news was at least as unverified as the sign that the hostages' mothers were holding up: "They have more than a thousand in there."

Then former Ingushetian president Ruslan Aushev arrived, although the terrorists had not called for him and they expressed no readiness to exchange the children for him. But he came and went into the school. No one knows what he said to the terrorists, but the terrorists let twenty-eight children go with him, mostly babies. No more hostages were negotiated out during the talks. There were no more talks.

Meanwhile in the school the terrorists were shooting the men, afraid that if there were men among the hostages, they could organize an uprising. They took the men into one of the second-floor classrooms, made them kneel, shot them in the back of the head, and threw their bodies out the window. One of the doomed men, seeing that his executioner was reloading his Kalashnikov, jumped out the window himself, not waiting for the bullet, onto the pile of bodies. He hurt his leg falling, but he managed to run away. Spetsnaz troops took him to the hospital for first aid and to question him closely on what was happening in the school. He ended up in the same ward as Visa Aseyev, in the next bed.

Visa was wounded. The bullet had grazed him above the eye. The sniper and gunner had dragged him off the roof, bandaged him up, and sent him off to the hospital in an ambulance. When he came to, he lay there for a while, listening to the secret stories of the escaped hostage, and then he got up and went home. He thought he shouldn't take up room in the hospital when that room might be needed for the children. He didn't believe there wouldn't be an assault. That evening they discharged all ambulatory patients from the hospital. No one believed there wouldn't be an assault. Visa walked, swaying, toward his house, looked with his right eye at the unusually crowded Beslan streets overflowing with soldiers and reporters, and he didn't know for sure whether he had a left eye under his bandage or not. The doctors said he did.

Visa spent September 2 at home. On the morning of the third he went to the hospital to have his bandage changed, and no sooner had he returned home than he heard the blasts. He wanted to run back to the school, but he thought a one-eyed man would just get underfoot there. Fifteen minutes later his mother arrived. She brought two boys, neighbors, with her; they had been rescued from the school. The children were dirty-faced, bloody, terrified, and stripped to their underpants. But not hurt. The blood on their bodies was someone else's. His mother bathed the boys for a long time, and then the neighbor came for them, having searched for her children near the school in the confusion of the assault and evacuation until someone told her her children were at the Aseyevs'. This neighbor said that the ambulances that had come from all over Ossetia were taking too long to drive through town from the school to the hospital because the drivers didn't know the city. Then Vissarion realized how he could help. He got up and went outside.

Almost immediately he encountered a lost ambulance with a Kabardinian license plate. He got in. He showed the driver the way to the school, and then showed him the way from the school to the hospital. Their vehicle was filled with injured children. On the second trip the ambulance was again full of injured children, and one was dead. On the third trip there were no injured children in the vehicle—just the dead. When he and the driver drove up to the school for the fourth time, the Kabardinian said to Visa, "Go on, pal, I can manage myself now."

"You remember the way?" Vissarion made sure.

"I'll never forget it, I swear!"

The driver was weeping. Tears hung off the ends of his mustache. So Visa went home. It was late in the afternoon. Near the entrance Visa met his neighbor, who was standing there stock-still, looking at the sky.

"Did you find your little boy?" Visa asked, knowing that the neighbor had a son who went to PS1.

"Yes," the neighbor replied. "In the morgue."

It's the custom in Ossetia that if someone in a building dies, the neighbors arrange the funeral. Therefore, the next day Visa went with the neighbor to the morgue to collect the body. His neighbor went inside and Visa waited outside. Forty-five minutes later the neighbor rushed outside. His face was red and his eyes weren't focusing but spinning independently. He was shouting.

"What do you mean! Who are you! Twenty rubles!" he cried. "Who are your father and mother? What do you mean! Twenty rubles!"

"What do you mean?" Visa shook his neighbor by the shoulders. "What twenty rubles?"

It took him a little while to get some sense out of his neighbor. It turned out that they were putting the children's bodies into coffins in the morgue and giving them out with the coffins. But you had to pay for the coffin. And the neighbor didn't have the twenty rubles in his pocket to pay for the coffin. And until the coffin was paid for they refused to give the father his son's body, with or without the coffin.

Visa paid the twenty rubles. He helped his neighbor carry the boy home. He helped him drag the small, light coffin up the stairs. He heard the boy's mother let up a wail. And he went outside.

He walked to the district administration building. He strode quickly, gritting his teeth and squeezing his fists until they hurt. He could have started a revolution right there. He could have dismantled the administration brick by brick. He could have . . . he could have . . .

A policeman carrying a submachine gun was standing at the door. Visa could have shown him his deputy identification to go through, but instead he just pushed the policeman aside. The only reason he didn't shoot was that he was local and knew Visa by sight.

People were sitting at a table in the administration head's office shuffling papers. Visa shouted at them.

"You've completely lost your minds! Completely lost your minds. Now you're even taking money from the dead?"

For the next few days money was abolished in Beslan. Altogether. Not because the district head ordered it but simply because people realized that anyone walking down the street was either going to or coming from a funeral. The coffin makers let their wares go for free, the builders lined graves with bricks (the custom in Ossetia) for free, the gas stations gassed up any vehicle for free because every vehicle was a hearse, in the cafés they fed people for free because in those days there were no meals in Beslan that weren't funeral repasts.

On the sixth, they buried more than a hundred people at a mass ceremony. The same on the seventh. It was raining so hard that Visa in his leather coat was soaked through to the bone. The coffins kept coming. The earth they sprinkled in the graves was washed away by the water so they couldn't cover the graves. And at a distance, nowhere near the graves, definitely not at the cemetery, there was a platform onto which the officials climbed and held a funeral rally for the reporters standing in front of the platform. No one at the cemetery heard what Moscow mayor Yury Luzhkov or North Ossetian president Aleksandr Dzasokhov said there. And when their funeral rally was over, none of the officials went to a single grave, or bowed over a single headstone, or laid a single flower.

Before closing the coffin, Vissarion's neighbor kissed his dead little boy and said to him, "We were lucky. You're completely whole. Just one little hole. People over there are burying cellophane packages."

Many that day buried body fragments.

WHERE YOUR ENEMIES ARE

Communism didn't last long in Beslan. The funerals went on for both ten days and a month. People collected their children's bodies after a sickening identification procedure that took days. Some children held on for a few days in the hospital and died later, and they had to be buried. But the impulse to give everything away for free held on for about ten days. The coffin makers, gas station owners, and café proprietors had to live too. A couple of weeks after the terrorist act, Vissarion got a call from Lena Kasymova, the curriculum head at Beslan PS1. Twenty years before, Vissarion and Lena had attended that same school where she was now curriculum head and that he had tried to defend with a weapon in his hands. Lena said they needed to meet.

Kasymova's neighbors had a BBC journalist staying with them, Lyosha Shvedov, one of the men who had witnessed the Beslan terrorist act from the first day, were poisoned forever by what they had seen, lived afterward thinking only about what they had seen, and a few years later died of a heart attack. At the time, this Lyosha said that aid had to be organized for the families of those who'd perished. Lists had to be compiled to determine which of the victims were the worst off, and they specifically had to be helped, if only with money. And he said that no one could do that better than the schoolteachers who'd survived because no one knew the schoolchildren and their parents better than the teachers. Lena asked Vissarion to help organize a Teachers Committee to aid the victims.

And he did. He turned the Internet club he ran over to the committee. He found the person who owned the beslan.ru domain. The man was a banker. A couple of years later he would head up the Regional Development Bank in Beslan and be murdered. But now Vissarion reached an agreement with this man, who gave them the domain for free to set up a Web site where the lists of victims compiled by the committee could be posted and where reports could be published about how much charitable money had been given to whom. An account was opened at Sberbank in the name of Lena Kasymova's husband because he had a car and Sberbank was on the outskirts of Beslan; without a car it was hard to go there every day to take money out of the account and distribute it to people. The first hundred dollars was brought to the committee by CBS correspondent Jonathan Sanders. They exchanged that money for rubles, added a little of their own so it would come to four thousand, and took a thousand rubles apiece to the four neediest families. In one of those families, a child and his father, who had been taking him to school, had died, but there were still other children. The teachers bringing the money were met at the door by the mother of the family. When they gave her the money, she started crying. She had just been on her way to a dealer to sell her wedding ring.

Vissarion's job was to keep after the district leadership, which did not want to give out official lists of the victims so that they could be checked against the committee's and wanted all the aid rendered Beslan to go through the municipal budget. Every evening at his Internet club Vissarion consoled some teacher who was crying and saying she couldn't go around to hand out money anymore because when she visited the victims she wept all day, and you can't live when you weep every day from morning to night. Vissarion drew up a schedule so that the teachers handed out the money no more than every other day, giving their tear ducts a rest. It was very important for the teachers to get receipts from every victim when they gave them money. Vissarion did not believe that anyone might think that the teachers could be dishonest about distributing the money or steal anything. But just in case they decided to take receipts. And rightly so. Less than a year later, the prosecutor's office began to investigate the committee's financial activities. Had it not been for the receipts, Vissarion as well as the teachers would have been thrown into prison.

Basically, Vissarion took on all the organizational work. It was winter when Vissarion finally got around to gathering up the documents and heading off to the Registration Office in Vladikavkaz to register the committee as a public organization. He took a jitney. There were women standing with signs where the road out of Beslan joined the Caucasus federal highway and where the other way led to the airport and the new cemetery. These were the Mothers of Beslan, women who had lost children in the terrorist act. Their signs demanded the resignation of North Ossetian President Aleksandr Dzasokhov and an international investigation into the circumstances of the terrorist act and assault.

All these months, relations between the Mothers of Beslan and the Teachers Committee had been strained. The Mothers of Beslan were on the official commission involved in the investigation and in distributing budgetary assistance. They accused the committee, possibly after prompting from officials, of obstinacy and a reluctance to work together, and they accused the teachers of negligence that had made it easier for the terrorists to plan their seizure of the school. Nearly six months passed before the Mothers of Beslan realized that they were not being given access on the official commission to investigation materials and that the budgetary assistance was being distributed without consultation with them. They guessed that the investigation was purposely being conducted so that neither President Dzasokhov, nor the special services, nor the Moscow authorities could possibly be found culpable for their children's deaths. That was when they went out on the federal highway with their signs. They were demanding Dzasokhov's resignation. But Vissarion rode past.

When Vissarion returned from Vladikavkaz that evening, the women were still standing there. They were soaked through and freezing, but they intended to stand there until their demands were met. Then Vissarion called his friend, a businessman, and asked him to bring the women a tent. Then he called several store and café owners he knew and asked them to bring the women hot tea and food. And he himself joined the women on the Caucasus highway because they were his constituents and he was their deputy. The tent stayed up for three days. Other people joined the protesting women as well. There ended up being a lot of people. The first day, sturdy fellows arrived, sent by the district head, Taimuraz Mamsurov, who would soon become the Ossetian president replacing Dzasokhov. They shouted that the tent had to be taken down and the picketing halted, but they didn't dare take down the tent or drive out the women, who were dressed in mourning.

On the second day Ossetian deputy Arsen Fadzayev came, the only person who had political weight in Ossetia but was not part of Dzasokhov and Mamsurov's team. Fadzayev tried to talk the women into folding up their tent and stopping their picketing. When they heard this, Mamsurov's men started trying to talk them into continuing their picketing, because Mamsurov had no time for anything that came from Arsen Fadzayev, even if it were the pastures of heaven.

On the third day Deputy General Prosecutor Vladimir Kolesnikov arrived. After getting out of the car, Kolesnikov walked up to the protestors and started reprimanding them as if they were children. He said, "What? You've gone into politics? Who are you to go into politics?"

Visa listened and thought that standing here was a representative of federal power saying that only the select few in this country could engage in politics and the people had to be silent, even if their children were being killed.

Kolesnikov said, "It's indecent for a woman to stand on the road with a sign. Or are you the kind of women who stand on roads?"

As Visa listened, fury began to boil in his heart. In the Caucasus you must never, not even by the slightest suggestion, insult a woman dressed in mourning.

But Kolesnikov said, "And the men? Are you men? Why are you standing here with posters? There are your enemies!" The deputy general prosecutor pointed in the direction of Ingushetia. "If you are men, then go and sort things out with your enemies, don't stand here with signs."

Visa could not believe his ears. At the time, many people in Ossetia were saying that the Ingush were to blame for the terrorist act, on the grounds that there was an ancient enmity between the Ossetians and the Ingush, and also because many of the terrorists were Ingush. These nationalistic conversations had gone on at the funerals, at the funeral repasts, at the condolences, and simply in the cafés. Journalists often asked whether there was any great danger that the terrorist act might spark an Ossetian-Ingush war. But for a federal representative to unambiguously call on the Ossetians to go to Ingushetia and start a slaughter!

Visa shouted, "Quiet! What are you doing!"

When he saw Visa's eyes in the crowd of protestors, the deputy general prosecutor got back in his car and drove away.

That same evening, Beslan prosecutor Alan Batagov invited Vissarion Aseyev to his office. He said that the protest on the federal highway was illegal; the protest organizers would be held responsible; and Visa should take responsibility for organizing the protest, otherwise the prosecutor's office would accuse Visa's friend who had given them the tent of organizing the protest.

So Visa took responsibility. And not just because he didn't want to leave his friend holding the bag. Now he truly was opposed to the state. Because the state was in favor of war.

At the time he didn't know that in addition to this administrative case they would also bring criminal charges against him. He didn't know that they would never let him run for deputy again. He didn't know that on the Web site Vissarion Aseyev had set up for them, the Teachers Committee would post a notice saying they did not share the political views of Vissarion Aseyev and did not consider Vissarion Aseyev to be a member of the Teachers Committee. He didn't know he would be beaten up at the door of his own building.

But he felt that whatever happened to him, it would be better than war.

S old!" The auctioneer rapped his gavel and the audience filed out of the hall.

Anatoly was standing in the doorway watching the people walk past and thinking that they had a uniform, too: by that time crimson blazers had gone out of style and Versace had come in. All these people at the auction were dressed either in black Versace jackets or Versace leather jackets and polo shirts. "Just like us," Anatoly thought. "A dress uniform and a field one."

"Tol!" The head of auction security gave him a shout. "Let's go."

He led him to a room with soft leather couches and a television and handed him an envelope. In it was a nice new hundred-dollar bill. Good money for 1994 Moscow. An amount equal to Anatoly's monthly salary when he'd served as commander of the Vympel *spetsnaz* group with the rank of major.

"For crying out loud," Anatoly thought. "Stand in a doorway for four hours and there you go, a hundred dollars."

He still couldn't get used to the fact that there was money like that and people like that wearing Versace jackets moving millions around. He'd grown up in a military family and spent his childhood in military towns: Kushchevskaya in the Krasnodar Region, Michurinsk in Tambov Province, Werneuchen outside Berlin. To him, East Germany had seemed the pinnacle of beauty, culture, and prosperity. He'd rejoiced each time he'd left Werneuchen for his vacation in the Soviet Union because that was his Homeland, and he'd rejoiced each time he'd returned to Werneuchen after vacation because the streets were swept there and the bakeries smelled of cakes and marzipan.

He was sorry when his father was transferred to the village of Siversky in Leningrad Province. Fourteen-year-old Tolya Yermolin had a dream. He wanted to go to Moscow's Higher Border Forces Institute and become a military translator. He'd read in the newspaper *Krasnaya Zvezda* that their department trained "officers with the highest specialized military education as translator-advisors." He tried on "officer with the highest specialized military education as a translator-advisor" for size and realized that a boy about to enter Railroad School No. 43 in Siversky outside Gatchina didn't have a snowball's chance in hell.

But he did it. Despite the fact that he was distracted from his school studies nearly every day by the need to fight with the local riffraff. Despite the tremendous competition. Despite his grades. He got in and on practically the first day was ordered to the kitchen, where his work consisted of scooping the dishwater out of the stone basin where they'd just washed the dishes for the whole institute. The basin was the size of a small tub. Tolya stood up to his knees in the dishwater holding a rusty bucket. Over the barbed wire that topped the fence he saw a glow. That was Moscow. Tolya looked at the glow and thought, "Four years! What have I gotten myself into? Four years!"

Their department was considered élite in the institute. Because of this, the drilling of the cadets in their department was particularly strict. Yermolin didn't get his first leave until the end of his second year, and on his very first leave he met the girl he later married, had two children with, spent twenty-five years with, and still lived with today. The only breath of air, literally, in this barracks life were his foreign-language classes, for the classes were led by young women who smelled of Dior's Poison or by impressive, intelligent colonels who smelled of the then fashionable cologne Aramis Devin. One of these colonels, seeing that cadet Yermolin was nodding off in class after night duty, said to him, "Are they driving you hard?"

"Yes, comrade colonel."

"Hang in there. It's all right. External pressure develops a person's ability to resist. His core, you know. As long as the intention is not to break that core . . ."

The institute's head had no intention of breaking that core. His intention was to rear good officers. They loved him. And if he called a cadet in, that was a good sign. One day, in his last year, Yermolin was called in by the institute's head. Sitting in that office, his heavy hands folded calmly in his lap, was a man in civilian dress with an intentionally thoughtful face.

"Do you know who I am?" this civilian asked.

"Yes sir." Tolya nodded.

Of course he knew who he was. What soldier, no less cadet, did not then know Colonel Karpukhin, the legendary commander of the Alpha *spetsnaz* detachment?

Karpukhin continued: "Afghanistan. The war. You might die. Your decision?"

Damn! He was inviting the boy to serve in Alpha!

"I agree," Yermolin replied without a moment's thought.

"Go." Karpukhin smiled, and with this their conversation was over.

For several months Yermolin quietly rejoiced that he was going to be serving in the country's most heroic army unit. And the girl who had become his wife quietly rejoiced that she would not be following her husband to some Providence Bay but would be staying in Moscow.

A few months later the head of the institute called Yermolin back in and said, "Tol, four people have been chosen for Alpha. Three are regular, the fourth is reserve." The cadet's heart sank and the head continued. "You're the reserve, Tol. Don't get upset. You won't get into Alpha, but you can choose where you want to serve and we'll try to make it happen."

Cadet Yermolin nearly wept. But he smiled and replied with a lieutenant's saying: "Comrade general, you won't get less than a platoon or be sent farther than Kushka. Vladivostok maybe? Great. The ocean. Trepangs. Caviar . . ."

"Think it over. Consult with your wife."

"She might ask to go to the Baltics. Or the Crimea."

This was a test. The institute head had to know whether the cadet wanted to serve in Alpha and hang his ass out for Afghan bullets in order to stay in Moscow and get an apartment in Moscow or whether he wanted to be a hero. Whether he would wriggle around trying to get a job at headquarters or respond with the lieutenant's cheerful saying. His reply was well taken. A few days later, when Yermolin went to the institute head to say he was prepared to serve anywhere but would prefer the Baltics, the general interrupted him.

"Cutting to the chase, Yermolin, there is another detachment. I can't tell you what it's called. It's just like Alpha, except the work is abroad. Tomorrow you'll go to kilometer 25 on the Gorkovsky highway. And don't even think of wearing your uniform."

That was how Lieutenant Yermolin ended up in the Vympel special ops group. These were real ninjas. They could handle every type of weapon, but they could also assemble a bomb from a tin can, moss, and saltpeter. They skydived and swam underwater, but they could also hide on level ground in an open field. They could handle any military vehicle, but they could also handle people. They knew how to drink and chat with someone in such a way that he didn't even notice he was revealing the military secrets entrusted to him. They were the intellectual *spetsnaz*. Their mission was formulated as follows: to deploy underground partisan activity in the enemy's rear. They fought in Nicaragua, Angola, Mozambique, and Afghanistan. Even now, only Yermolin's training exercises have been declassified. In his free time from Afghanistan he and his special ops group determined whether military sites were well secured and whether a good saboteur could find them and take them out. For example, he found and symbolically took out a rail-mobile missile system—a BZhRK—equipped with Satan missiles, each of which held eighteen nuclear warheads aimed at eighteen cities in the United States of America and capable of reducing those cities to dust.

It was the late 1980s. The politicians in Moscow kept harping on perestroika and glasnost. But the saboteurs and rocketeers were playing hide-and-seek without any glasnost. A rocket general told Yermolin, "There's this thingamajig, and if it fires, America won't be able to wage war. It travels over the rails. I'll even tell you the region where it's moving. But you won't find it, captain. Never!"

A couple of days later Yermolin's special ops group, seven men, were sitting in a dacha in the middle of the district the rocket general had indicated. They were drinking tea and thinking. If this thingamajig was moving over the rails, what did it look like? A train car. What kind of train car? A freight car. It couldn't look like a passenger car because a passenger car has windows. So what kind of freight car did it look like? A refrigerator car, because an ordinary freight car had slits, and the tank was round and bulky. What made this refrigerator car different from all the rest? It had missiles inside. It was very heavy. It had to have more bogies, and when it moved it had to make a particular sound. Who might know that this thingamajig was traveling along the railroad? Rocketeers, but they wouldn't say anything. Railroad men, dispatchers, repairmen . . . They compiled a list of people possibly initiated into the secret and went to talk to those people about a very heavy refrigerator car that had a lot of wheels.

But not directly, no. Not head on. By the end of the second week of searching, having spoken fruitlessly with a couple dozen people, Yermolin finally met an officer in the railroad forces who seemed to have excessively important stars on his shoulders to be serving at such a remote station. They were sitting on the platform, smoking, and Yermolin was telling him how he had supposedly missed his train (having first checked that there actually was such a train and one could in fact miss it at this station). They talked about how the country was falling apart and what a mess they were in. It was a popular topic at the time. Yermolin cited examples and babbled on about some factory where he supposedly worked as an engineer. Or look, Yermolin said, just take the rolling stock on the railroad. It's falling apart as it goes. Recently they'd stopped his train on some siding and a freight train had gone by that made so much noise you'd think it was about to fall through the earth, the sound was unreal, why didn't they grease the wheels?

For one instant an expression of superiority flashed across the railroad officer's face. He knew what kind of train it was that the silly, unlucky Moscow engineer thought was falling apart as it went, and on ungreased wheels. The rest of the pumping was a matter of technique. He just had to find out when this officer was on duty to know when the BZhRK would pass through his zone of responsibility.

There were several branch lines in this zone, but they all met at a hub station. A freight car filled with missiles would have to pass through that station and it was fairly obvious at what time.

There were forty rail lines at this junction. To see them all, Yermolin based himself on a rail bridge over the track. He held a bouquet of flowers. A besotted fool meeting his wife, who was coming home from vacation. Her train was late (Yermolin checked to make sure several trains coming from the south at once were late). He stood on the bridge with his bouquet of flowers, looking off into the distance. He looked like a total idiot. She'd doubtless had all kinds of holiday affairs there, and he was waiting on the bridge with a bouquet of flowers. Hidden in the bouquet was a theoretical bomb with which he was theoretically going to destroy the Rail-Mobile Missile System.

He waited less than an hour. About an hour later Yermolin heard a roar. Not the noise of a train but a roar, as if a fairy-tale ogre were creeping down the rails. There weren't just more wheels than refrigerator cars usually had, there was nothing but wheels. They didn't make the usual clickety-clack; the car's weight was pressing them into the tracks.

Yermolin felt a sense of pride. A boyish joy and pride that his Homeland possessed a thingamajig of such incredible might, capable of wiping America off the face of the earth. A minute later he tossed his theoretical bomb, which was theoretically supposed to blow up in twenty minutes, on the refrigerator car's roof. Now all he had to do was return to base and watch the rocket general who had boasted of his missile complex's invulnerability turn red, then white, and sweat and listen to this general shout, "It can't be!"

Then it was August 1991. The putsch in Moscow. After the putsch, articles appeared in the newspapers for the first time about the Vympel group. It was decided to declassify them or at least give the newspapers a chance to write about the super-warrior-ninjas who had fought in Angola and assaulted Amin's palace in Afghanistan. Meanwhile, the super-soldiers were turning into super-terrorist-statists. Approximately half a year passed between President Yeltsin's victory in Moscow and the breakup of the Soviet Union. That entire time Yermolin and his group were running through the Caucasus Mountains catching partisan separatists, the leaders of the Armenian Popular Front or the Azerbaijani Popular Front. It was a manhunt. Yermolin's small group headed off on a free-form hunt with orders to "kill so-and-so." Their methods were just like the partisans'.

Later, when the Soviet Union fell apart and the hunt for Azerbaijani separatists lost its meaning, Yermolin started hunting for Ingush separatists or escorting Acting Prime Minister Yegor Gaidar on his Caucasus trips. Only on television did Gaidar's visit to Vladikavkaz, Nazran, or Nalchik seem to proceed "in a friendly, businesslike atmosphere." In fact, Gaidar was taken through the Caucasus like particularly precious cargo; hiding around every bend in the road were troublemakers who considered it a matter of honor and valor to abscond with this precious cargo.

It was the creeping Caucasus war. No break for sleep and common sense; on the other hand a break for winter, when the leaves drop in the mountains, snow falls, and a man is too easily spotted by a sniper. Yermolin ran through the mountains and thought that at least his family was living quietly outside Moscow in peaceful Balashikha, and that was worth running through the mountains.

Once (in winter 1992, when the fighting had quieted down again in the Caucasus), the military command remembered that Russia was not only a country bogged down in partisan strife but also a nuclear power. It was decided to verify how reliably the workshop that produced nuclear arms in the closed city of Arzamas 16 was guarded. Yermolin's group received an order to penetrate the closed city, seize the shop, and theoretically destroy it.

A couple of days later seven men in tracksuits with backpacks and hunting skis got off at the train station in Nizhny Novgorod, the closest big city to Arzamas 16, a place where you could go unnoticed. Their backpacks were crammed with weapons and explosives. From the train station, as law-abiding citizens, they headed straight for their hotel, made themselves comfortable in the lobby, and started to settle in, that is, enter their passport numbers—fake, naturally—in the hotel register. Yermolin was leaning over the little table and writing his numbers in the register when suddenly he heard a voice over him.

"Hello, excuse me, I'm Pyotr Smirnov, the ITAR-TASS correspondent for Nizhny Novgorod Province. Do you have some kind of group here, if I may ask?"

Failure, Yermolin thought, not without feeling a touch of pride for his country. They protect these nuclear sites damn well if all you have to do is get off the train at Nizhny and they already have you scoped out. He looked up. The man standing over him looked like a typical special services agent very typically pretending to be a reporter: checked jacket, dumb smile, plum-shaped nose . . . Yermolin was in the habit of not giving in, so he started weaving a tale about how they were a tourist company working out a ski route through places connected with St. Serafim of Sarov.

"Yes, yes! Serafim of Sarov!" The reporter waved his hands. "You must! You must! I've been working on that for a long time. True, Arzamas 16 is there and no one will let you through, but you can go from the Diveyevo convent . . ."

This man turned out not to be special services but an actual reporter, as well as a local historian. Yermolin even felt ashamed that instead of working, this Smirnov was sitting with him in the archives and laying out in front of him prerevolutionary maps that depicted in the most detailed fashion all the surrounding area of Sarov and the town itself, which in the mid-twentieth century had been renamed Arzamas 16 and disappeared from maps.

The local historian's help was invaluable. Using the prerevolutionary maps, Yermolin's group completed several ski sorties, studied the location, and found an undefended gap in the closed nuclear city.

At a meeting with his command, Yermolin said, "We'll go under the river's ice. There's a small stream there. In the winter no one guards it, so we'll put on diving equipment and go under the ice."

It pained him that the workshop where the country's nuclear shield was forged could be so easily reached by seven special ops men and one local historian. The training operation was considered complete, but the general said, "Major, could you take the perimeter head on?"

"The guarded perimeter of a secret city head on?" Yermolin smiled.

"Well yes, we won the game and hurt the muzhiks' pride"—the general was referring to Arzamas 16 security. "We at least have to give them a chance to catch you, major. Can you, head on?"

"Yes," Yermolin was sad to say. He thought he really could simply get through all barriers. "I just need a three-meter pole and six meters of rope."

At the time set by the command, Yermolin's group completed a twenty-four-kilometer sprint on skis and skirted four pickets in the forest. Some of the soldiers were smoking, some were talking, a couple of times the soldiers, alerted, ran right over Yermolin's head after he buried himself in the snow. Using the pole and rope, Yermolin's group avoided all the traps. The sensors had been desensitized so the alarm wouldn't go off every time a bird flew by, and the defensive perimeter had been built haphazardly, or else building materials had been stolen during its repair.

At three in the morning, Yermolin's group was standing at the gates of the secret shop where nuclear warheads were made and no one had detained them. For all its nuclear might, Russia had not simply lost to seven saboteurs, it had lost big time. One of the special ops kicked one of the secret sensors to finally catch the guard's attention. The alarm went off and soldiers with dogs rushed toward the gates from all sides. Yermolin took the first dog to reach him by the collar and patted him on the head.

To the boy soldier who was the first to aim a submachine gun at Yermolin, the major said. "You hit the jackpot, soldier. You're going on leave. You caught a saboteur."

It was insulting and nauseating. Even though Vympel won the training exercise. Even though, at the debriefing, one quartermaster turned red and tried to blame it on the shortage of barbed wire for the enclosures. Yermolin felt himself burning out like a light bulb. He'd started burning out long before. Back in the Caucasus, when he'd had to hunt down people in the mountains whom he had long considered fellow countrymen, when his battle comrades had died and no one knew for what. But that time he'd restrained himself and had not submitted a resignation letter.

He did not restrain himself later. In October 1993, after the assault on the White House, when the political confrontation between the president and parliament turned into a military confrontation, there was shooting on the streets of Moscow. President Yeltsin called the head of Vympel, General Gerasimov, to the Kremlin, to order the assault. The president's eyes bulged so when he said the word *assault* that Gerasimov realized he expected blood from him, he expected Vympel to make mincemeat of all the White House's defenders, whom Yeltsin considered mutineers.

"Comrade president, we don't have the troops," the general said, trying to dodge the cruel mission.

But the president wasn't listening. He waved his arms in the air and shouted, "Aviation, artillery, encirclement."

Gerasimov thought that if Vympel didn't storm the White House they would call in paratroopers, who would certainly make mincemeat of all the Supreme Council deputies.

Vympel was put on alert while Major Yermolin was sitting alone at home with his son in Balashikha. His wife had gone somewhere. Yermolin called his mother-in-law, but she couldn't get to him in Balashikha through Moscow, which was jammed with military equipment and paralyzed by a curfew. He had to take his son to the base with him.

The boy was sitting on a box of cartridges when Vympel, in

full battle dress, formed up, and General Gerasimov went out to his soldiers.

"Whose is this?" He nodded at the boy. "Yours, major? You brought help? Go home and wait for your mother-in-law, and when she comes you'll be in command of the reserve."

Yermolin was bitter. He had always thought that the reason you needed to run through the mountains and fight in Afghanistan and Angola was so that here, in peaceful Moscow, your family . . . But there were tanks in the streets! He took the boy's hand and headed for the door.

But General Gerasimov continued, "Muzhiks, there is an order to storm the White House. I can only carry out this order with volunteers. Volunteers, two steps forward."

None of the officers budged.

"Muzhiks, besides us and Alpha, no one can take the White House without blood."

About two-thirds of the officers took two steps forward.

Yermolin did not take part in the assault itself, but he heard enough stories from his comrades to consider the operation the height of *spetsnaz* virtuosity, and the president's reaction the height of official ingratitude. They burst into the White House lobby, and Deputy Valery Shuikov shouted to his supporters who were scattering in panic, "Don't be afraid, it's Vympel, there won't be any blood!"

Shuikov knew many Vympel officers personally; they had guarded him on his trips to Ingushetia.

They took floor after floor. One of the officers flung open the door to some deputy's office and saw a gun barrel aimed directly at his face. The deputy whose office it was was either aiming the gun at the special op or raising the gun to his temple and just could not bring himself to fire.

"Muzhik," the officer said to the deputy. "Do you have children? Give me your gun to list in inventory and go to your children."

Colonel Protsenko, the legendary Colonel Protsenko, who had also stormed Amin's palace, walked up to the door of Vice President Aleksandr Rutskoy and told the soldiers guarding it, "I am Colonel Protsenko. I need to speak with the vice president."

And they let him pass without a word.

General Rutskoy knew Colonel Protsenko from Afghanistan. When Protsenko walked in, the general was sitting at his desk, his head lowered glumly.

"Hello, colonel."

"Good day, comrade general. I have orders to arrest you. You understand."

"Yes." Rutskoy nodded. "Come on, let's have a smoke. What do you have?"

"Prima." Protsenko smiled as he took the crushed pack of cheap, unfiltered cigarettes out of his pocket.

"Sonofabitch!" The vice president snorted. "The best *spetsnaz* in the world smokes Prima. Enjoy."

The vice president held out a pack of Marlboro Reds. They smoked in silence like two old battle comrades. Colonel Protsenko led the arrested Rutskoy to the buses, where they had gathered the other arrested deputies from the mutinous parliament.

These buses drove to the Krasnopresnenskaya subway station. The doors opened. The people got off the busses, stood against the blank subway wall, and prepared to be executed. Some prayed. Some wept. Some looked apathetically at the *spetsnaz* officers standing next to them.

"Why are you standing there!" one of the officers shouted. "Get on the subway! Go home! Home!"

The next day the president's aide who had attempted to command the assault and had been told to fuck off, military style, reported to Yeltsin that Vympel had refused to carry out the order of the commander in chief, that only volunteers had participated in the assault, that they hadn't fired, and that they had released those arrested. By presidential decree the Vympel group was transferred to the Interior Ministry, renamed Vega, and assigned to disperse demonstrations. The intellectual *spetsnaz*, the best special ops in the world, were now supposed to learn how to build a "turtle" of plastic shields against unarmed demonstrators and wave truncheons against an unarmed crowd.

Of Vympel's ninety officers, eighty resigned. Including Yermolin. And that was why he was now working at auctions as a guard.

LESSONS OF THE REPUBLIC

That evening he returned home with his hundred-dollar bill in his pocket and his wife told him, kissing his cheek as usual, "You had a call from Menatep."

"Where? Menatep the bank? I don't know anyone at Menatep."

His wife shrugged. They sat down to supper, which was sausages and macaroni.

A few days later, after working as a guard again at the door of another auction, Anatoly returned home and his wife said, "You had a call from Khodorkovsky."

"Who? The oligarch Khodorkovsky? I don't know him."

"Tol"—his wife made a face of minimal reproach as good officers' wives allow themselves only when it is a matter of their husband's careers—"call Khodorkovsky back. I thought you were looking for a job."

She did not even say out loud that she had married an officer, not an auction bouncer. But Anatoly understood and called the number his wife had written down on a scrap of old newspaper. Khodorkovsky's receptionist was very glad to hear from him. The meeting was scheduled for the next day.

At the time, the Menatep office was located in the very center of Moscow, on Kolpachny Lane. It was a handsome private residence behind a high fence with video cameras along the perimeter. Passing through the gates, Anatoly wondered whether the building could be taken by a group of seven, say. Looking around, he decided it could.

Mikhail Khodorkovsky himself, Menatep's owner, was the same age as Anatoly and considered it his duty to give him a stern look. In response, Anatoly smiled his child's smile, which you would never expect to find on the face of a military officer.

"You were recommended to me as someone who knows how to educate little boys," Khodorkovsky said.

And this was true. A few years before, between two raids in the mountainous districts of Ingushetia, Anatoly had also been an inspector in Frankfurt-am-Main, where Pershing missiles were being destroyed under a treaty between Russia and America. He observed the Pershings being destroyed, and his NATO colleagues observed him observing. In the evenings spies from all over the world gathered at a bar for a stein of beer and a ham hock and observed each other in informal surroundings. One day a British officer, Richard Moore, who was serving there at the airbase, dropped a comment: "Those kids are driving me crazy."

"What kids?" Yermolin asked.

"Oh, I'm chief scoutmaster at the base." The kids may have been driving him crazy, but Moore smiled gently. "I used to meet with them once a week, but now all their fathers are on military missions, so we meet every day."

Operation Desert Storm was under way. The children of NATO pilots hadn't seen their fathers and were afraid for them. Every evening their leader, Moore, assembled his scouts to distract them from their military worries with orienteering or lighting a fire with a single match.

Yermolin expressed interest, and the next day Moore brought

him some scouting textbooks. The minute he opened them, Anatoly realized he would be doing this for the rest of his life—educating boys using this pedagogy of adventures, which was so similar to the Vympel group's survival training. At home in his military town he organized a scout troop, Kavalergard. He went on hikes with the boys, tied sea knots . . . And the officers' wives were happy their little goofballs weren't hanging around at loose ends. The officers helped him, too. General Shebarshin, the intelligence chief, even canceled an entire military mission to the Caucasus so that Major Yermolin could be back in time from assignment to run a summer scout camp outside Moscow.

He really did know how to educate boys. Only he did not understand why a shark of capitalism, the owner of Menatep, Mikhail Khodorkovsky, cared.

"You see," Khodorkovsky said, "I can never pay a cashier as much money as the gangsters do for him to open a door and simulate an attack."

"So?" Yermolin still didn't understand where the banker was going with this.

"So I want company employees to look on this company as their own. I want to educate them."

"That's it?" Yermolin looked at Khodorkovsky, searching his face for the signs of lying that were well known to a professional interrogator.

"That's it." There were no signs of lying on Khodorkovsky's face.

"Then I agree."

"Then come to work here," Khodorkovsky summed up. "Tomorrow."

Khodorkovsky apparently had in mind educating not current company employees but the whole country, for the future. In any case, Yermolin would not be involved with team-building programs for bank clerks or their children but would be deputy director of a boarding school financed by Khodorkovsky for orphans and the children of soldiers serving on the border or in hot spots. The director was General Mamonov, who dealt with administrative problems and relations with the head of Odintsovsky District, where the school was located. Yermolin dealt with educational work.

But first they had to assemble the children, and this was a problem. Director Mamonov went to the Russian frontier post in Tajikistan and brought children out in APCs, under fire. Deputy Director Yermolin took on the Caucasus. An unending war was under way there, and there were plenty of orphans at every frontier post.

One day Yermolin arrived at one of these posts not far from Gyumri. The border command told Yermolin that there was a boy, the son of a dead Russian officer, living in Gyumri, in a half-destroyed orphanage.

The orphanage was indeed half-destroyed. Because half of Gyumri itself had been destroyed by an earthquake. And no one was rebuilding the town. The orphanage director was an intelligent, not yet old man. Yermolin was struck by how this man managed, given the destruction and the smoldering war all around, to maintain the orphanage in relative order; to feed, clothe, and teach the children something other than bearing weapons; to make a wall newspaper with the children; to memorize poems with the children.

The orphanage director was thrilled that Russia had finally remembered the son of its dead officer and began to prepare the boy for the road. On the eve of departure he invited Yermolin to his home for supper. They had a simple meal— cheese, greens, flat bread, brandy—and the director told him that he had formerly been a professor of philology in Erevan. Later, when perestroika began, he joined the Armenian Popular Front and was one of its leaders. At the time, many intellectuals in the Caucasus became leaders of separatist movements, if only because they knew how to speak. He even had to go off into the mountains. For a few years he traded teaching for leading a partisan detachment. Soviet special services, Azerbaijani special services, and Armenian special services hunted for him. When Armenia seceded from the Soviet Union and the time came to divvy up the pie, his former comrades started hunting for him. That was when he left, he left political and public life completely. And now he was living in the mountains educating little children.

"Listen," Yermolin said. "You know, I was a *spetsnaz* commander for many years. I was under orders to arrest you. My group hunted for you through the mountains for four months. We might have killed each other in battle."

"There, you see?" The director smiled. "It's a good thing you didn't kill me. Who would you be sitting with now and drinking brandy?"

They raised their glasses and drank to each other's health.

One way or another, Mamonov and Yermolin managed to assemble children for the boarding school from all over the country. Many came from orphanages, but not necessarily. Little Tanya, for example, was brought by her father, who had been given an assignment in Chechnya, where he would become a general and a Hero of Russia. Little Kolya was brought by his father, a warrant officer serving as a helicopter pilot in Providence Bay. This same warrant officer was told by a taxi driver at the airport that it would cost him five hundred dollars to drive to Koralovo, outside Moscow, where the school was located. The warrant officer believed the taxi driver and gave him all he had saved over the several years during which he, his wife, and his son had seen nothing but sea and snow and for half the year did not see the sun. Yermolin took Kolya through the school, showed him the room where he would be living, his own shower, the gym, the auditorium, the armor displayed in the lobby, and the salt room where they would do therapeutic inhalations, and asked, "Well, what do you think, Kol?"

"It's okay," Kolya, who had never seen anything but barracks in his life, replied.

Kolya's father was afraid the boy would refuse to stay. But he stayed.

Not all the children were from orphanages, but the orphanage parasite syndrome engulfed everyone almost immediately. The children's good clothes were in tatters in a week; their boots, in a month. Nothing they did could make the children pick up the trash in their rooms or stop dropping their laptops, which each of them had been given, on the floor. Then Yermolin asked the educational game designers to develop a game for the children that would teach them independence and responsibility. These pedagogues suggested using play money.

For useful things like school cleanup or gardening each child now could earn a reward in play money. For property damage each would pay in play money. At semester's end there was an auction in which they could use their play money to buy something that was not for play at all: a portable CD player, a camera, a toy for the little sister you would see during vacation, perfume for your mother . . . In a few days the children had completely scoped out the way economic life works. The rooms were clean, the clothing stopped ripping, and the only problem was how to divide up the work if everyone wanted to work and there weren't enough jobs. The children asked whether they would get compensation if they wore a pair of boots for a year instead of six months, as planned. The children demanded that Yermolin let the cleaners go because they were taking jobs away from schoolchildren.

The teachers explained to the children that in order to achieve social justice in the school they needed a government, and for a government to work they needed a parliament and laws. The school turned into a republic run by the children themselves. Just in case, Yermolin retained the right to declare an emergency, but in all his years as director he never once did.

The final institution of power whose mechanism had to be explained to the pupils, who had already mastered the government and parliament, was the court. Yermolin doubtless did not want an occasion to arise that would require him to explain to the children why they needed a court or how trials were conducted, but it did. That same Tanya whose father had gone to serve in Chechnya committed a crime.

She was the daughter of a regimental commander and was used to bossing everyone around. But here at the school the children didn't obey her much. Moreover, Tanya was disliked for this authoritarian bent and for her arrogance. One day Tanya took a pair of scissors and cut the hair off all the Barbie dolls, including her own. The girls came back from classes, discovered the damage, and started to cry, and Tanya cried too. Suspicion fell (Tanya made sure it would) on an orphanage boy who was on duty that day and could have gone into the bedrooms. The investigation went on for nearly a month. The boy would not admit his guilt.

One evening, when the girls started talking again about their disfigured Barbies, the instructor said, "All right, girls, it's time to forget this story. God sees everything. He knows who did this so we don't have to."

At that moment Tanya burst into tears and said she had shorn the dolls and had framed the orphanage boy.

Yermolin could have simply expelled Tanya or punished her somehow, but the teachers council decided to add a third branch to the legislative and executive branches of school power—a judiciary. The orphanage boy who had nearly suffered from Tanya's guilt was appointed prosecutor. Kolya, the son of the helicopter pilot from Providence Bay, agreed to be Tanya's attorney. All the rest of the students were the jurors.

"What are you going to charge Tanya with?" Yermolin asked the orphanage boy on the eve of the trial.

"But she hurt everyone!" the boy replied. "Who made her boss here?"

"No, wait," Yermolin said. "What law did she break?"

After thinking hard, on the third or fourth try the prosecutor finally charged Tanya under two articles: damaging state property and slandering a citizen of the republic.

It was easier for Yermolin with attorney Kolya. Kolya said immediately, "You'd never have found out she cut off the dolls' hair if she hadn't confessed."

The defense had the defendant's sincere confession, written out in her own hand. Yermolin had a good laugh. It was obvious that the girl who wrote the statement had spent her whole life in a barracks: "I, Tatyana Imyarek, the worst slut on earth, admit my guilt, that I cut . . ." and so on.

At the trial, attorney Kolya gave a fiery fifteen-minute speech and at the end exclaimed, "A fault confessed is half-redressed!"

The jurors stood up one by one and told Yermolin, who was acting as judge, "Tatyana is guilty. Don't expel Tanya."

There were a lot more than twelve jurors. But they arrived at a unanimous decision. They had complete consensus.

Gradually these school republics spread throughout the country. One day Khodorkovsky, who had just bought the Yukos oil company, came to see how the school he was financing was getting on. It was raining. Khodorkovsky entered the lobby, saw the surgical cleanliness all around, and took off his shoes so as not to muddy the floors the children had mopped. He walked in his stocking feet through the schoolrooms and said to Yermolin, "Anatoly Aleksandrovich, what are you doing tomorrow?"

"Whatever you say. I'm a military man."

"There is a proposal to fly to Nefteyugansk."

In Nefteyugansk, as in other towns where Yukos had operations, the educational situation was the same as throughout the country. They had schools but no system of education.

Yermolin taught the children to elect their own parliaments, the members of parliament were invited to summer camps, and later, for activists, they organized something like a scout jamboree. All of this was called the New Civilization project. Serious problems did not arise for New Civilization until August 1998, in connection with the country's economic crisis. At that time Khodorkovsky was forced to stop financing all his philanthropic programs, except for the school in Koralovo. That's when Yermolin informed the teachers involved in New Civilization all over the country that they would no longer be paid. But the people kept working for free. The school republics held on for an entire year on pure enthusiasm. At the end of the year Yermolin went to see Khodorkovsky.

"Mikhail Borisovich, we have saved New Civilization, but the crown of the program is the summer camp. We have to keep it going. I'm prepared to squeeze down to the minimum, but still . . ."

"How much does it come to?"

"Twenty thousand dollars."

Khodorkovsky took a piece of paper and on it wrote his own name and the names of his three partners. Opposite each name he wrote $5,000. He went into his safe and pulled out five thousand in cash and later, in exactly the same way, the other Yukos directors went into their personal safes. A year later the company pulled out of the crisis and New Civilization's financing was restored in full.

MEMBER OF PARLIAMENT

In 2003 Khodorkovsky was imprisoned. By this time Yermolin was one of the directors of Open Russia, a philanthropic fund headed up by Khodorkovsky personally, and New Civilization was just one of the educational projects the fund financed.

Yermolin was also a deputy to the State Duma from United Russia, the pro-Kremlin party. Yukos had recommended Yermolin as a deputy, and Anatoly looked calmly on the fact that major companies were installing their own lobbyists in parliament. Yukos gave Yermolin no orders and let him act at his own discretion, except that Yukos's discretion and Yermolin's for the most part coincided.

Before running for office, Yermolin went to the Kremlin for a talk, for it was the Kremlin, not the election precincts, that decided whether or not someone would become a deputy. The Kremlin liked the former *spetsnaz* officer, and he did not find conversing with Kremlin officials unpleasant. For the most part they were the type of FSB officers Yermolin knew from his service in the Caucasus. Yermolin thought that President Putin was setting up his power heirarchy in the country in exactly the same way as Khodorkovsky had set up management in his oil company. He had set it up, put things in order, and started to delegate authority to his subordinates, including the right to make mistakes. Yermolin thought Putin was doing the same thing with the country.

He wasn't even very worried when Khodorkovsky was arrested. The best attorneys were working for Khodorkovsky. The charge was flimsy even at first glance. There was every reason to think that the billionaire would beat the charges in court and life would continue on as before.

After Beslan, though, Yermolin suddenly realized he was wrong. After terrorists seized the school in the North Ossetian town and three hundred hostages were killed, Yermolin saw that the regime had no intention of bringing about order and had no plan or strategy. It pitied no one and was simply steamrolling all its opponents as flat as a pancake.

There in Beslan, thirteen of Yermolin's military comrades from Vympel died, unprecedented losses for the *spetsnaz*. The Vympel officers who returned from Beslan told Yermolin that

there had been no plan to free the hostages, no assault prepared, no unity of command, no intelligence gathering, no common sense, not even simple pity for the children taken hostage.
There had been nothing but cowardice and confusion, they
said.

The only sensible decision headquarters made was to pull
Vympel and Alpha fighters back to a distance of a fifteen-
minute drive from the school. The professionals realized that
the terrorists who had settled inside the school probably had
informers on the outside who were reporting what was happening on the perimeter, beyond the cordon. So that the terrorists wouldn't think an assault was beginning or detonate the
bombs hanging over the children's heads, Vympel and Alpha
were pulled back farther, leaving only a few *spetsnaz* observers
near the school.

The assault began spontaneously. Either the terrorists deto-
nated one of their bombs or else federal soldiers fired on the
school with a flamethrower or from a tank. But the assault did
begin spontaneously, and the *spetsnaz* observers had no choice
but to run into the school and save children. The terrorists
were using the children for cover and shooting. The Vympel
officers did not fire back because on the run no ninja can hit a
man hiding behind a child without injuring the child. They ran
toward the bullets in the hope that their bulletproof vests
would save them. They ran to get close enough to the terrorists to use a knife. Some did. Some officers managed to put
their knife to use before dying. For this operation everyone at
headquarters, including the high command, should have had
their hands severed. Instead, President Putin canceled gubernatorial elections in the country, as if the governors were to
blame for the fact that children died and *spetsnaz* officers ran
down school hallways toward certain death.

Deputy Yermolin laid out his thoughts on the assault on the
radio at Ekho Moskvy. Tears of despair and fury choked him,

but he tried to speak calmly, as an expert. After the broadcast, Yermolin had a call from an aide to Deputy Chief of Staff Vladislav Surkov. In Surkov's name he praised the calm tone of the commentary and suggested that he deliver another commentary on Channel One.

"I'll send you a fax with the text you need to read," the man said.

A little while later Yermolin received the fax. It said, first, that in the face of the terrorist threat citizens should be vigilant, and Yermolin absolutely agreed. Second, it said that one cannot negotiate with terrorists, and the antiterrorist headquarters in Beslan did the right thing in not negotiating because negotiations only make terrorists more brazen.

"So?" Surkov's aide called back. "Did you get the fax?"

"Yes," Yermolin said calmly. "Only I'm not going to say you shouldn't negotiate."

"Why?"

"Because you should always negotiate, no matter what the circumstances, to the bitter end. I'm telling you this as an antiterrorism specialist."

Surkov's aide harrumphed and hung up.

An hour later two television men arrived, a cameraman and a soundman. They didn't even have a reporter with them to ask questions. The cameraman set up his camera, the soundman his microphone, and Yermolin himself said for the camera everything he felt necessary to say about the operation to free the hostages in Beslan.

When his words, reedited twenty times over, were aired, Surkov's aide called again.

"Anatoly Aleksandrovich, you didn't say what we asked you to say after all."

"No, I didn't."

"Well, you'll see."

Fear can have an amazing effect. People crushed by tragedy

think that now, in the face of these children's deaths, they should sacrifice something important. And the regime takes advantage of that. As a rule, after terrorist acts, the regime demands that people sacrifice freedoms in no way connected with the reason behind the terrorist act. President Putin openly demanded then that gubernatorial elections be canceled throughout the country. Secretly, Deputy Chief of Staff Vladislav Surkov demanded that parliamentary deputies obey him absolutely and from then on vote strictly as Surkov ordered.

Among the ruling party's deputies there are quite a few competent and intelligent people. As a rule, they have major companies behind them. Before Beslan, if the Kremlin submitted an idiotic law to the Duma, the idiots would vote for it, but no one made the competent people do so. They did not vote against the Kremlin law, of course, but they had the right to abstain.

That is what happened, for example, with the laws about the eastern oil pipeline and the victory banner. On Surkov's order, the deputies voted for the pipeline to follow the shore of Lake Baikal and for the victory banner not to look like it did on the Reichstag. President Putin criticized these laws publicly, on television. He said that Baikal was our national treasure, the victory banner our sacred symbol, and he, the president, would not let laws be passed that inflicted harm on a national treasure and a sacred symbol. This was a PR move to elevate the president in the people's eyes and discredit the parliament, which is to say, any power other than the president's. The president came out smelling like a rose. The deputies looked like morons. Only those deputies who had abstained from voting for the laws on the eastern pipeline and the victory banner managed to save any face.

But that was before. Now, after Beslan, you couldn't abstain. Anatoly Yermolin and the other United Russia deputies were invited (or summoned) to Surkov's office. Surkov demanded that henceforth none of the deputies express any personal opinion.

He shouted at the legislators, "How are you going to press your buttons? Who do you think you are? Who's asking you?"

And when the deputies tried to object that it wouldn't do to vote for laws that knowingly discredited the party, Surkov replied, "The decisions are taken without you. Anyone who doesn't understand, look at the Yukos case."

This conversation took place soon after Khodorkovsky had been sentenced to eight years' imprisonment. Not in court, but on the television channels controlled by the Kremlin, the billionaire was accused not only of tax evasion but also of financing terrorists. The lobbyists of the major companies realized that now, after Beslan, anyone could be charged with abetting terrorism. And in the public consciousness anyone was worthy of death merely if it was said about him on television that he was connected with Chechnya. This was a serious threat. So the deputies obeyed, becoming mere dummies pressing buttons as they were told.

Everyone except Yermolin. Maybe because Yukos was no more and because Khodorkovsky was in prison. Maybe because his comrades had perished in Beslan. The conversation with Surkov was secret, naturally, but Yermolin sent an official letter about the conversation to Zorkin, the head of the Constitutional Court, asking what the hell business was it of the president's deputy chief of staff to line up State Duma deputies like corporals, and what the hell business was it of his to order them how to vote. After writing the letter to Zorkin, Yermolin told reporters that he had written the letter.

He learned that Surkov was furious. He realized he was going to be driven out of the faction and would no longer be a deputy. He realized that open insubordination to Surkov would spell the death of any career he had other than that of chief scoutmaster. But he also realized that sending the ruling party and deputy chief of staff to hell was no more dangerous than serving eight years in a Russian prison, like Khodorkovsky. No more dangerous than running toward the bullets, as his comrades had, in the hope of getting close enough to a shooting terrorist to use a knife.

CHAPTER 5

Maria Gaidar: Young Woman in a Pretty Dress

DELIGHT

Masha Gaidar was trembling with excitement. Trembling in a good way, as in childhood when she used to go for matches. When she was a little girl and her name was Masha Smirnova. When she still lived in Moscow and her mother and stepfather had not yet taken her away to Bolivia. There were a few extra cupboards in her room on Tishinka, cupboards filled with soap, matches, and toilet paper. Life, if you didn't count school and her serious water-skiing lessons, was a perpetual hunt for all kinds of things like that, things people stockpile if they think war is going to break out any day. Salt, matches, sugar, groats, tea, macaroni, and toilet paper. For some reason people think they will definitely need toilet paper during a war.

Masha was all of nine, but her parents were not afraid to let her go outside alone if she was going to buy something that would be useful in the event of war. She liked to buy matches. The end of the line would stretch out the store. People stood along the sidewalk in silence. Their clothing was gray and worn, like that of soldiers in a march-weary army. And the little girl would stand there with them. After an hour and a half a gloomy salesclerk would hand her ten boxes of matches wrapped in gray paper, and Masha would walk home, shying away from the rats so prevalent in Moscow then, and place these ten boxes in the cupboard with what must have been the same feeling a soldier has on the eve of war when he adds a box of cartridges to his arsenal. Sometimes at night she would get out of bed, open the cupboard, take one box out of her arsenal, and light matches, the way a soldier makes sure his ammunition is good: the only possible way—by shooting.

At the time, in the late 1980s, Masha thought that acquiring and stockpiling essential goods in the apartment was a fascinating game. She had fun imagining that war and famine really had begun, and how they would get canned meat from the cupboards and survive the winter. Later, when her parents decided to flee hungry Moscow for Bolivia, where her stepfather had been offered a contract, Masha imagined the exciting adventures involving Indians that awaited her in Bolivia. Now, fifteen years later, she thought it was a fascinating game to drive with her brother, a friend, and a mountain-climbing instructor to the Bolshoi Kamenny Bridge, which crossed the Moscow River, to jump from the bridge. She trembled with excitement the same way.

Their spy had been standing near them on the bridge since morning, and Masha's friend Ilya now called out to him: "Well? How goes it? Nobody there? Excellent! Get out of there!"

It was now apparent that more than anything in the world Masha feared not heights, not jumping from a bridge, not hitting the water from a height of twenty meters, and not even dying. What she feared was failing, not completing the jump. She feared that an OMON bus would be waiting for them on the bridge, that OMON men would block off the street, force her brother's car over to the shoulder, drag all of them and their climbing gear out, put them face down on the asphalt, twist their arms behind their backs, handcuff them, and smile at Masha's clumsiness and their own cleverness.

From the day Ilya came up with the idea of jumping off the bridge, they had applied maximum effort to keeping their intentions secret. From the very first telephone call. When gubernatorial elections were canceled, when the Kremlin's obedient deputies made amendments in the election law and people started being elected only from party slates, when the bar for parties was set at 7 percent, an incredible hurdle for the opposition, Ilya phoned and said, "I think I know what to do."

They met on Staraya Square, walked down Varvarka, came out on the embankment down Vasilievsky Slope, and when Bolshoi Kamenny Bridge appeared before them in all its glory, Ilya said, "See that bridge? We're going to jump off it!"

"Wow!" Masha said, because it really was a brilliant idea.

Then, for another whole month, they attended the mountain-climbing club at Moscow State University and trained. They secured safety ropes and clambered to the peak over steps that were narrow and icy, since it was already October. Masha was afraid, even with a safety rope; she still had to step down almost into emptiness. Even scarier, though, was not taking that step, since she had just seen Ilya do it.

All that month they did not talk on the phone about bridges, ropes, banners, elections, firecrackers, or paint. They told the minimum number of their very closest friends about the upcoming jump and only at the last moment. They still needed someone to drive them to the bridge, someone who would stand guard on the bridge and make sure there wasn't an ambush awaiting them, and also someone to assemble and bring the reporters, because without reporters jumping off the bridge made no sense whatsoever.

In fact there wasn't anyone on the bridge. In the middle, at the worst possible spot, Masha's brother, Pyotr, stopped the car, his passengers got out, and he immediately drove off to park and come back. The mountain-climbing instructor quickly started securing safety ropes to the bridge railings, and Masha and Ilya started putting on their climbing gear and orange hard hats. The helmets made no sense if the point was jumping into the water. But the helmets served to convey to any policeman who happened to turn up on the bridge that they were industrial climbers, they were working on bridge repair, and their boss would be bringing the permission for high-rise jobs any minute. Not without a certain satisfaction Masha noted that there wasn't a single policeman around. On the other hand, a crowd of reporters was walking down the embankment from the Balchug Hotel led by the person assigned to public relations.

They clipped the carbines to their belts. Ilya picked up the thin but durable cord he was supposed to yank to unfurl the banner tucked inside Masha's shirt. They separated on the bridge the width of the banner, climbed over the railing, and Masha looked down.

It was high. Damn, it was high. Far below, logs were floating in the gray water of the Moskva River, and Masha thought it would be pretty bad to fall on a log instead of into the water. Meanwhile, Ilya stepped off the parapet, swayed on his rope, and started lowering himself quickly but smoothly toward the water. The cord connecting them stretched taut, the banner started coming out of Masha's shirt, and if Masha didn't want to tear the banner she too had to step off the parapet. So she did, and she started descending too. At that moment she felt a sense of relief and the joy of victory because now no one could keep her, Masha Gaidar, leader of the Yes youth movement, and her friend Ilya Yashin, leader of the youth wing of the Yabloko party, from hanging right near the Kremlin between Kamenny Bridge and the water and stretching out their banner: "Bastards, give the people back the elections!"

After dropping the full length of his rope, hanging ten meters above the water, Ilya tugged on the cord. He pulled slowly for fear of ripping the banner. The words crept out of Masha's shirt one by one. "Bastards" (because you are bastards for taking away the people's natural right to elections), "give back" (because we aren't demanding anything new or unprecedented, we're demanding what we had and had taken away, what belongs to us by rights), "the people" (not just us, young intellectuals from good families, but the people), "the elections" (because the people need elections, freedom, the right to decide their own fate).

A minute later the yellow banner was unfurled. Masha was pleased to note the photographers' flashes twinkling below on the embankment. Ilya lit a firecracker and shouted with all his might, "Russia without Putin!," "Down with Chekist power!" At this Masha remembered she was supposed to light a firecracker, too, but in all the turmoil she had forgotten to take it from the back seat of her brother's car.

On the other hand, on the embankment below, Masha's friends lit firecrackers, and even one of the reporters lit a firecracker, too, because there were plenty of Masha's friends among the reporters. So she calmed down. She was hanging under the bridge by a rope, the wind was swinging her and Ilya, using the banner as a sail. Masha just waited for the police to come and for the policemen to start hauling them up comically.

But for twenty minutes or so nothing happened. The police were in no hurry. Masha was freezing so she got some chocolate out of her pocket in hopes of warming herself. Then she got out her phone and called her papa, Yegor Gaidar, a former prime minister of Russia, during the Yeltsin era, the man who had averted the famine that little Masha had hoped to guard against by buying canned goods and matches. A man who sacrificed his own political career in order to stop a famine and civil war, for people always hate a minister who frees prices, even if that is the only way out.

She phoned and said, "Papa, I'm calling to tell you I'm fine. I'm hanging from a bridge, but please don't worry. I'll call you back when everything's okay."

"Oh, my heartache," her papa said from the phone, accustomed to answering all of Masha's calls that way.

But he was busy with something and promised to call back when he was free.

Ilya Yashin hadn't even planned to call his father. His father made the call himself.

"Son, I've made the arrangements. Tomorrow morning at nine they'll bring the crushed stone to you at the garage. You just have to decide about the money."

"Papa," Ilya replied hoarsely because he'd lost his voice shouting "Russia without Putin!" "I can't decide about the money right now. I'm at a demonstration."

"Ilyush, this is important. I have the men here now, and I have to tell them right now—"

"Papa! Listen! I'm hanging from a bridge!" And he hung up.

Meanwhile, Masha's words hit Masha's papa. He called back and shouted into the phone.

"What are you doing hanging from a bridge? You mean what Ekho Moskvy is reporting, that's you hanging from the bridge, my heartache? And when will this 'everything is okay' of yours be?"

"Papochka, don't worry."

Ilya Yashin's father also realized that his son was hanging from a bridge. He called back and shouted into the phone.

"What are you doing there? You're hanging from a bridge?"

And Masha's brother, Pyotr, standing on the bridge, shouted, "No! You can't cut that rope! No! They'll fall and get smashed to pieces!"

Masha looked up. A policeman was leaning over the bridge railing. He looked drunk. He was fiddling with the climbing knot and shouting, "What protest actions! No protest actions on my watch!"

Masha's brother, Pyotr, grabbed the policeman by the arms so he wouldn't untie the knot.

FEAR

In that moment Masha was genuinely afraid. There are two kinds of fear. You can be afraid of heights or speed. You can be afraid your airplane is going to fall out of the sky. Or that your train is going to be derailed. Or that the bridge under you is going to collapse. Or that the earth is going to gape open. You can be afraid of fires, floods, earthquakes, plague, loneliness, old age, and death. But you can also be afraid of people, and that's different. The fear instilled by people resembles the symptom of some shameful disease. It feels like a cold plaster being applied to your spine. You're not even afraid of the pain or of death but of how that pain and death will be inflicted.

When Masha was in to Bolivia with her mother and stepfather—while in Moscow Masha's papa became prime minister—Masha's brother, who had stayed to live with their father, was once supposed to fly to Bolivia. And Masha, a little girl who was used to going to the Russian embassy to visit the little embassy boy Seryozha and play soccer, saw how just before her twelve-year-old brother's visit all the Russian diplomats suddenly started living with that sticky fear down their back. They drove the cleaners to mop the floor and dust the shelves three times over. They ran around with documents that had been lying there for years like deadweight. They prepared for the arrival of Petya Gaidar as if Acting Prime Minister Yegor Gaidar himself were coming. And not just on a visit, but to inspect. When Masha's papa in Moscow retired and Masha came once again to the embassy to play soccer with Seryozha, they would not let her in. Standing under the doorkeeper's incinerating gaze, she experienced the sticky fear inflicted by people.

At home in Bolivia every night, Masha listened to the conversations of her mother, stepfather, and their friends about Russia and thought that these people were inflicting that sticky fear on themselves in order to justify their emigration. From their conversations you'd think that in Moscow, if you so much as went outside you'd be shot. That there was no electricity in the city so it always seemed to be night. That the children had no milk and the old people no medicine. To some degree this was true, but Masha's beloved grandmother was still in Russia, and Masha didn't understand why, if things were so terrible there, her mother didn't take her grandmother out of that hell instead of only sending her money and gifts.

In October 1993, when the standoff between the president and parliament turned into a brief street war, Masha in Bolivia saw her papa on television, and he was calling on people to take to the streets and defend democracy, which was to say, the president. Later Masha saw the television anchorman Aleksandr Lyubimov, who with feigned unconcern in his voice, on the contrary, admonished people not to go anywhere or defend anything and let the legislators and executive branch choke on the gruel they'd cooked up. Masha sympathized with her papa. Not because he was her papa but because even though he was awkward, stout, and bald he spoke without fear, whereas the handsome, imposing anchorman spoke with fear.

Later, in 1996, when she returned to Russia, the first thing Masha did was go to see her grandmother in the hospital. Her grandmother was very ill, and she couldn't wait hours for the doctor, who would give her or tell the nurse to give her a shot for the pain. Her grandmother was very ill, and Masha ran through the empty hospital corridors in search of a doctor. She peeked into the wards, where, on ragged beds made up with dirty sheets, lay women in pain. The medicine had run out in the drips for some, but the nurse had not come by to pull the needle out of the vein. The women were wearing flowered flannel robes they had brought from home. On the stands at the foot of the beds lay the food and medicine they had brought from home. Essentially, it made no sense for them to leave home and go to the hospital in order to take the medicine they had brought with them. They were lying there only out of fear. The doctors weren't helping them, but the women hoped that if they were about to die, if their heart stopped or they needed an emergency operation, the doctors would stop their lazy, sleepy tea drinking in the lounge for a while, set aside their overt flirting with the nurses for a while, and save them from death, and then they'd be back in God's hands.

They were sick, these women, but they were afraid to bother the doctor over something as trivial as pain. They were afraid the doctor would get angry at them and at the critical moment would fail to save them from death.

In some wards, men were sitting on stools next to a few of the women. Husbands. Frightened and indecisive. With soup in a thermos. When the doctor did his rounds, the husbands were embarrassed and left the wards, and after rounds they didn't dare ask the doctor about anything and merely gazed into the doctor's eyes ingratiatingly, like a beaten dog.

Masha ran through the empty corridors, over the buckled and, in places, torn linoleum. There was soup spilled on the floor near a door, but the aide was in no hurry to wipe the puddle up. At the nurses' station, several emergency lights were on at once. But the nurse was in no hurry to go to the patients who had pushed the emergency button over their beds and were awaiting help. She was yakking with her friend. A man was lying on a gurney on the stairs. He had been brought in with acute pain from renal colic, but no one had come to look at him. And the doctor—Masha finally found him—was sitting in the lounge of the next department eating cake. In reply to Masha's request to come immediately and help her grandmother, the doctor just waved his spoon, which was loaded with sponge cake and half a cream rose, in the air. And he said the young woman was not allowed in the lounge.

It was the summer of 1996. President Yeltsin had just been elected to a second term, even though he was disastrously unpopular. Posters calling on people to vote for Yeltsin hung throughout the city, at nearly every step. The slogans for this campaign were "Vote with your heart" and "Vote or lose." The state did not trouble itself with explanations. You were supposed to vote simply because that is what the bosses had decided. Because God forbid the bosses should get angry if you didn't vote the way you'd been told. Masha was sixteen. She couldn't formulate her thoughts, but she felt that the voter's submission to the state and the patient's submission to the doctor were cut from the same cloth.

Contact with her father, which had been non-existent while Masha had been in Bolivia, was gradually restored. For her sixteenth birthday, Yegor Gaidar gave his daughter two of his books: *Economic Reforms and Hierarchical Structures* and *State and Revolution*. After her adventures in the hospital, Masha thought better of going to medical school, as she had planned, and decided to study something in economics or sociology. Her father advised her to choose the Higher School of Economics.

Later, when she was a student there, Masha asked her father whether there wasn't some youth organization engaged in fixing the world around them. By that time the hospital was no longer the only institution in Russia whose arrangement Masha didn't like. Yegor Gaidar replied that in the Union of Right Forces, where he was a member of the political council, there was a man by the name of Mikhail Shneider. "He's about sixty," Gaidar said, "and if anyone is involved in youth politics, it's Shneider."

Shneider gave Masha a hearty welcome. He said he just happened to be creating a public youth organization at that very moment and he invited the young woman to a meeting of the action group. The meeting was more like a party. They argued until they were hoarse. They spent the first half of the evening brainstorming a name for the organization (Shneider suggested Graal, for *grazhdanskaya alternativa,* or "civic alternative," and the second half divided up the map of Russia, in the sense that they decided which of the young people would be responsible for the Central Black Earth region, who for the Volga region, who for Siberia, and who for the Far East. Masha didn't understand why a person needed to be responsible for the Far East if that person had never been in the Far East, was doing nothing, and didn't even know anyone in Khabarovsk or Yuzhnosakhalinsk.

However, Masha liked the young people who had come to Shneider's. They continued to meet now in the office of Masha's friend on Kuznetsky Most Street. And they gradually came up with several projects. For instance, they defended the vocational schools when the Moscow government shut them down in the city center and moved them to Yuzhnoe Butovo. They thought, not without good reason, that vocational students, slackers who even in the center of town attended classes reluctantly, would not travel to the outskirts at all, would learn nothing, would not find work, and would either be poor or become criminals. The students themselves didn't care. The young people with a higher education, students at prestigious schools, went to the vocational schools to rally, so that the vocational schools wouldn't be moved to the back of beyond, but the vocational students themselves didn't care or take part in the rallies.

Masha's friends also assembled some reporters and, after reaching an agreement with the Interior Ministry, set up public monitoring of police work at train stations. The problem was that at the train stations, when policemen saw someone in the crowd rushing for the train, they would try to stop him to check his documents. They would check his documents so slowly that the person preferred to give the policeman a bribe so as not to miss his train. Masha and her friends watched the station policemen, but the people they stopped refused the public monitors' help, moved off to the side with the policemen, gave the policemen some money, and hurried on about their business.

Nonetheless, Masha felt she was doing something right, useful, and most of all positive. She worked as a manager at Video-International, married, and began an independent life. She called her social movement Yes and, foundamentally, she was proud of herself.

One day, on her day off, Masha went to her gym, changed into gym clothes, and started walking the treadmill. To keep from being bored, Masha put on earphones and turned on the television installed above the treadmill. She clicked the remote, looked for news on one of the channels and . . . the first item was the announcement that Mikhail Khodorkovsky, the owner of the Yukos oil company and the richest man in the country, a philanthropist and sponsor of democratic parties, had been arrested.

Masha kept walking, and when the news was over on one channel she switched to another to see the footage of Khodorkovsky and the commentary from his lawyers, the Yukos board, and political figures again.

Long before this arrest, her papa had told Masha what his old friend and fellow leader of the Union of Right Forces Anatoly Chubais had told him: Khodorkovsky would be arrested. But Masha hadn't believed it. She realized, of course, that the prosecutor's office might have questions for Khodorkovsky about just how legally he had privatized Yukos. Of course there might be questions. Masha walked on the treadmill and muttered under her breath. Of course there might be questions. But the prosecutor's office could have the same questions for anyone who had privatized anything in Russia after the collapse of the Soviet Union. Masha kept walking and switching channels. Arresting Khodorkovsky meant reexamining the results of privatization. It meant a redivision of the market, a revolution. Masha was still on the treadmill.

Or if not a revolution, then why did they arrest Khodorkovsky and not all the others, including President Putin, who also had something to do with the privatization of the mid-1990s? Masha kept walking. She changed channels, watched the same thing on different channels, and still could not believe it. When she finally did believe it, she turned off the television and stopped the treadmill. It turned out she had been walking for almost three hours and had gone almost twenty kilometers.

Later that same day, Masha and her friends made a sign, "Freedom for Khodorkovsky," and went to the building where the court had chosen to incarcerate the billionaire and had taken him into custody. The young people unfurled their sign. The sign was long: taped together from several pieces and attached to four poles, it took four people to stretch it out and hold it up. The picketers (besides Masha's friends, there were another two hundred people there) and passersby almost immediately started to come up to Masha and ask what was written on her sign. After the fifth person did this, Masha handed her pole over to one of her comrades, walked out herself to see what was wrong with the sign and why everyone in the world was asking her what this very simple slogan meant. It turned out that the syllables on the poster were all mixed up. Masha nearly burst into tears. All of a sudden it seemed as though the fight to defend the vocational schools, the "I Think" youth rallies, the fight against corruption in institutions of higher education, and public monitoring of the police at train stations were senseless, starry-eyed nonsense, just like this sign.

Then there was the Khodorkovsky trial. And also the terrorist acts: the Nordost theater, Beslan. And also the cancellation of gubernatorial elections. And the transformation of parliamentary elections into God knows what. Masha realized more and more clearly that even if her "positive" actions could fix the country, it would take two thousand years, whereas in no time, with each decree, the president was making Russia more and more unfree and more and more brutal. She couldn't remember precisely when she stopped wanting to say "Yes." She wanted to jump off a bridge, hang from a rope, unfurl a banner that said "Bastards, give the people back their elections!" and shout "No!"

ANGUISH

"Mashka!" Ilya was shouting from his rope. "Mashka, which way should we swim?"

"What's that?" Masha didn't understand.

"Which bank should we swim to? I think they're about to cut the rope."

Masha looked up. Several OMON men in their round black helmets were leaning over the railing now and two rescuers from the Emergency Situations Ministry in their dark blue and orange uniforms were fussing with some tools. There was also a woman. The policewoman was shouting down to them:

"Young people, can you swim?"

"I don't know which bank to swim to," Masha said.

"That one." She pointed to the bank opposite the Kremlin. "It looks closer."

"I think so, too," Ilya agreed. "But the current seems to be carrying all the trash to the other bank. Wouldn't it be better to swim with the current?"

Up above by the parapet the rescuers were clamping a sturdy metal cutter onto Masha's rope, and the younger rescuer fell hard on the lever.

"Mashka, take your shoes off in the water right away!" Ilya shouted.

Masha squeezed her eyes shut. She was waiting for the fall. She remembered that she had to keep her arms to her sides and look straight ahead, to enter the water like a toy soldier and not belly flop. But instead of breaking, the rope started creeping up. The rescuers' steel contraption was a winch, not a cutter. No one had any intention of letting Masha fall into the water. They were pulling her up.

As soon as Masha came even with the parapet, one of the policemen leaned over and ripped and wadded up the banner.

The rescuer put his arms around Masha and helped her climb over the railing, and as he was helping her he whispered in her ear: "What did you have written there on your banner?"

"Bastards, give the people back their elections." Masha was trembling from the cold.

"Good work." The rescuer smiled. "Next time, call us when you're going to hang from some bridge."

"Uh huh." Masha nodded, still shivering from the cold, although the rescuer had wrapped her up in a blanket.

"Afraid we'll report you?" The rescuer smiled. "Don't be. We won't. We're rescuers, not rats. We'll just pull you out faster so you don't freeze."

Masha sat in the police van for twenty minutes or so. The man in charge of the operation was wearing civilian clothes, but Masha could tell, from intangible signs known to any Russian, that he was a special services officer. On purpose, apparently, he held the rescuers back from raising Ilya quickly, to make sure the protestor hung a little longer and got good and chilled.

Half an hour later they were both taken to the police station. Masha's brother, Pyotr, followed them there. The policemen had not chased him off the bridge or arrested him. When they lifted Masha up and put her in the van, Pyotr called their mother and told her that Masha was okay. Later their mother recounted that when her colleagues found out what had happened, they began sympathizing with her for having such a wayward daughter. Masha never asked her mother what she had said to her colleagues in reply. She would have liked her to object, to tell them how proud she was of her daughter. But Masha was afraid to ask.

Masha had been in police stations before. Sometimes activists were arrested at Yes actions. After winding up at the police, after four hours of questioning, a trial, and a fine of five hundred rubles, some activists were so freaked out they never participated in actions again. But not Masha.

This time, however, they were questioned not by a police interrogator but by the FSB officer who had commanded the rescuers on the bridge.

He asked, "Are you members of the NBP?"

"What does the NBP have to do with this?" Masha, who had a fairly negative view of Eduard Limonov's National Bolshevik Party, said.

"Your action is in the NBP style," the special services agent insisted.

"Nothing of the kind," Masha objected. "We aren't seizing anything or smashing anything. This was a Greenpeac-style action."

"But sometimes the NBP—" the interrogator kept harping.

"Listen!" Yashin interrupted. "Her last name is Gaidar. Gaidar! What the hell could the NBP have to do with this if the girl's last name is Gaidar?"

After a couple of hours of questioning and a couple of hours of just sitting in lockup, so life wouldn't seem too sweet, Masha and Ilya were taken to court, fined, and released.

A few days later, in the evening, Masha and Ilya ran into the same special services agent on a street in the middle of town. He was coming out of a café arm in arm with a young woman and heading for his car.

"Hello!" Ilya bowed. "How's the fight against extremism going?"

"Sit in the car for a minute," the special services agent told the young woman.

"Wait! Wait!" Ilya was in a good mood. "Does your damsel know where her knight works?"

"Get into the car immediately!" the special services agent shouted at the young woman.

"Young lady!" Ilya continued. "Do you know? Your boyfriend harasses dissenters."

"Get in the car, I said!" the special services agent snapped.

It was a Moscow Friday night. Streetlights, a colorful crowd. A traffic jam consisting almost entirely of expensive cars. The special services agent's girlfriend walked meekly to the car, opened the door, and sat in the passenger seat, her hands folded meekly in her lap.

Masha saw the fear on her face. The poor thing was terrified of continuing her date with someone who, it turned out, worked for the secret police. But she was even more terrified of breaking it off.

CHAPTER 6
Ilya Yashin: Young Man in a Tweed Jacket

There was nothing but snow all around. White, like snow never is in Moscow. White as far as the eye could see. Even the road that plunged into the snow was white and could be made out in the middle of the field only because it ran along a slight rise. Behind Ilya, rather far behind now, the road was marked by ruts left in the snow by a bus. But the ruts suddenly broke off, getting muddled where the bus had turned around, heading back to Gryazi, where Ilya had come from. This intercity bus had been full of people in Gryazi, but then it kept going and going, and people kept getting off along the way in different towns and villages. For the last leg, to the village of Knyazhaya Baigora, Ilya was the only one left on the bus.

They still had about seventy kilometers to go, but after he had gone forty the driver suddenly stopped the vehicle and told Ilya, "Get out!"

Ilya got out. He thought the bus had broken down and the driver was asking him to get out and help fix it. But the driver closed the door, made a four-point turn on the narrow road, and drove off. Leaving Ilya there. In the middle of a field, in the snow, as night was falling. That the driver had thrown him off the bus and driven away without thinking about what would happen to Ilya here in the cold, without a hat, in his thin Moscow coat, was unfathomable.

There wasn't a soul in sight. No houses, no smoke. Naturally, his mobile phone didn't work; there was no coverage here. Ilya had no choice but to keep walking down the road judging from the kilometer marker, he was closer to Knyazhaya Baigora than to the village where the last passengers had gotten off the bus two hours earlier, a village whose name Ilya didn't remember.

He was up to his ankles in snow, trying to keep warm by walking. Snow filled his boots, which were now soaked through. No walking could warm his feet now. Ilya kept hoping that sooner or later a vehicle would drive past or toward him and pick him up. But he'd already been walking a good hour. In that time no one had driven by either toward or away from Knyazhaya Baigora.

After another twenty minutes or so, Ilya lost all sensation in his feet, and his shoulders began shaking hard. He thought he would probably die here in the open field and they would find him in the spring.

Fifteen minutes later he was warm and cheerful, the way a person gets warm and cheerful when he's freezing to death. The shimmering sun setting over the distant forest, turning the snow pink, became mixed up in his mind with scenes from his childhood and youth that were so vivid it was hard to call them memories. Snow and sun, and here's Ilya, still a little boy, running down the school steps, swinging his book bag; and sitting at the bottom of the stairs is the cleaning woman, Baba Katya. She's wearing a blue satin robe and a colorful kerchief on her head. On the floor in front of her is a dirty galvanized bucket and in the bucket is a gray rag made out of the same kind of robe as Baba Katya has on.

Snow and sun, and Baba Katya is talking loudly about the children running by: "Bastard children! Your mothers are whores! They should gather you all up, you little bastards, on Red Square, pour kerosene over all of you and set you all on fire!"

She repeats these words many, many times. Ilya runs by,

hears her, and, somewhere in his chest, a little higher than his solar plexus, the bitter insult turns in him, the way the milk used to turn in the bucket on the stove when they still got it from a cow, not from powder.

Snow and sun, and Ilya was practically running now up to his ankles in the snow, just trying not to lose the road, and at the same time he is sitting with his schoolmate at a computer, composing a proclamation entitled, "Fire Baba Katya!" If you didn't count the flamboyant heading, the proclamation was perfectly polite: "We respect people of labor, and we understand that Baba Katya has been working at the school for many years, but nonetheless, we do not think Baba Katya should use obscene words regarding us or insult us or our parents."

Snow and sun, and Ilya tripped, fell in the snow, and thought how nice it would be to stay here lying in the snow, but he got up and wandered on. And at the same time Ilya, still a boy, is sitting with his school friend in front of the computer arguing whether they should put their names at the bottom of the proclamation. His buddy says, No, don't, the petition demanding the school cleaning lady's dismissal should, in his buddy's opinion, appear in the school here and there anonymously, so that the school administration would think that a lot of children wrote the proclamation. "But if we sign it," his buddy says, "they'll realize right away that there are only two of us."

Snow and sun, and Ilya was smiling as he walked. Smiling because this buddy of his graduated from the FSB academy and was now working somewhere in the Kremlin guarding the president, while he, Ilya Yashin, was involved in opposition politics, had worked at the campaign headquarters for the Yabloko democratic party in the 2003 parliamentary elections, and lost over and over. He lost those key elections, before which there had been democrats in the Russian parliament and after which there weren't anymore.

Snow and sun, which was already touching the treetops, and Ilya was trudging through the snow and at the same time standing in the principal's office, and the principal is asking whether Ilya alone wrote this proclamation about Baba Katya, and Ilya is saying no, not alone, of course, but he refuses to say who his accomplices were.

Snow and sun, and the nearly expelled Ilya is walking to the coatroom, and at the bottom of the stairs where Baba Katya ordinarily sits with her bucket, there is no Baba Katya now. Nor is there the next day. Or the next. Or a week later. And Ilya, still a little boy, wonders whether he killed the old woman by putting up the proclamation he had printed out on his printer all over the school, whether something bad had happened to her heart, whether she was alive there in her Yasenevo or Biryulevo Tovarnoe, from which she commuted an hour and a half every day to mop the school floors.

Snow and sun, and the trees' blue shadows were getting longer, and Ilya was trudging through the snow. His memories were becoming even more vivid than the snow. Ilya could almost see himself, a university student, standing outside the State Duma in the ranks of people protesting the fact that Glinka's hymn had stopped being the Russian anthem and instead they were going to go back to the old anthem of the Soviet Union, music by Aleksandrov, words by Mikhalkov, very slightly changed, but still Mikhalkov's. There are about two hundred of them. They're shouting and above them are the banners of the democratic parties. And a little ways off, another two hundred or so people with red flags. The Communists. They, on the contrary, are opposed to the Glinka anthem and for the Aleksandrov. They are elderly people. Many of them resemble Baba Katya, and Ilya wonders whether something bad will happen to their hearts if they don't get back their familiar music and understandable words, "Russia, our sacred power, Russia, our beloved land."

Snow and a half-sun above the forest, blue shadows now lying across the entire snow-covered field, Ilya was trudging and at the same time knocking at the worn door of one of the Yabloko party offices in Moscow, on Khoroshevka. He asks the bored woman in the office whether the democratic party needs help with anything. The woman is surprised. "Well, you could pass out leaflets." She gives him a huge stack of leaflets to keep him away longer. And he passes out the leaflets. At high schools and institutes. He talks to university students and teachers. He says that the Yabloko party is opposed to the war in Chechnya. That if the plan proposed in the late 1980s by Yabloko leader Grigory Yavlinsky, the so-called Five Hundred Days, were approved now, it would be a much gentler way of shifting from socialism to capitalism. After passing out the leaflets, Ilya returns to the office. The woman in the office is surprised. "You're back? I thought you'd never come back."

Only a sliver of sun remained above the black band of forest. The trees' violet shadows now stretched all the way to the road, and Ilya trudged, stepping from time to time on the shadows' edge. At the same time he is unloading an eighteen-ton truck at a warehouse on the very edge of Moscow. On pallets in the truck are packets of campaign leaflets, because it's the elections. The year is 2003, elections for parliament. Ilya is already a member of Yabloko and even heads up the party's youth wing, twenty or so young men and women who are also here and are also unloading the truck. The loaders have scattered. As it turned out, the money the party had allotted for the loaders wasn't enough to hire anyone but the homeless and the drunks assembled right there, in the courtyards near the warehouse. Those drunks turned out to be unreliable workers. So now Ilya himself has to unload the truck and reload the leaflets in several smaller trucks, which would take them . . . God knew where they would take all these leaflets with their calls for freedom, democracy, and human dignity.

Ilya's mobile phone rings in his pocket. The voice of the Moscow party headquarters coordinator says, "Ilyush, one more truck will be coming at three in the morning, and you'll have to unload it fast." Ilya is listening, and the hand holding the telephone to his ear is shaking from all the stress. It's hard, but it would be even harder for him to work at headquarters and see where the money allocated for the elections is being spent and how.

The sun fell behind the forest. A violet twilight. The white of the snow went from warm to cold, and maybe for that reason he instantly felt the cold. Ten degrees below zero, in fact. Ilya kept trudging, but he had lost all hope. Just as he lost all hope when on election night, on the Central Electoral Commission's tally board, the result for Yabloko got as high as 4.1 percent and stopped. Just moments before, Ilya had run up the stairs at Yabloko headquarters and met the party's leader, Grigory Yavlinsky; he couldn't stop himself from asking whether the party would get into the Duma, whether it would pass the sacred 5% bar. "Don't worry, Ilyush." Yavlinsky patted him on the shoulder. "It's all going to be fine. I know for a fact." Five minutes before this President Putin had called him and congratulated him on the party getting into the Duma. Yavlinsky had believed Putin. Yashin had believed Yavlinsky. But at some point closer to morning, it became clear to the Central Electoral Commission that the ruling party, United Russia, would not get two-thirds of parliament, a constitutional majority. And at closed election precincts they started adding to the already processed ballots—in favor of United Russia.

So Yabloko's percentage declined. Toward morning Ilya watched with desperate hopeless bitterness as the party's results stopped at 4.1%. He felt the victory had been stolen from them, that they had simply been tossed out of politics, the way children are shooed out of a room when the grownups have to talk about something serious. He went home, dashed around his room, and then packed his backpack and left, taking commuter and long-distance trains, hitchhiking, traveling through Russia trying to understand what kind of a country it was where not even 5% of the people would vote for a party that offered peace, freedom, democracy, human dignity, and honesty.

He rode commuter trains. He looked out the little window at the snow-covered plains, at the abandoned villages, the half-destroyed or burned-out houses. He reached the town of Lipetsk and went from there to Gryazi, and from there boarded a bus for Knyazhaya Baigora, where, if he was to believe the Internet, an ancient church had been preserved. And halfway there the bus driver had simply tossed him out in the middle of a field, and there was no possibility of reaching any dwelling, and night was falling, and he faced freezing to death.

The twilight deepened. Ilya looked around. In the distance, down the road, a boat was slowly approaching him. A horse's head was carved on its prow. Its wide sides cut through the snow, and the snow flew to either side. Standing on the boat was a man, or if not a man then some monster wearing either a horned helmet or a crown. Ilya couldn't make sense of it because in the twilight the ship, and the prow, and the man were mere shadows.

A minute later, when the boat was close enough for him to get a good look, Ilya realized, finally, that it wasn't a boat but a horse-drawn wagon, and in the wagon, driving the horse, sat an old man wearing a huge sheepskin coat and a huge hat with three flaps, which in the semidarkness had looked to Ilya like a crown.

When he drew even with Ilya, the old man reined in the horse and asked, examining the young man from head to foot, "Where the fuck you goin'?"

He had to say something. Ilya said, "Hello, I missed my bus. I need to go to Knyazhaya Baigora. Will you take me?"

"Get in!" the old man said, as if not answering but continuing his previous thought. "Wrap up in a sheepskin. You'll freeze."

A RUSSIAN SONG

The horse moved swiftly. After about an hour they reached Knyazhaya Baigora. It was pitch dark. The old man dropped the reins to let the horse find its way home by instinct. Sensing the approach of home, the horse galloped faster and faster until, finally, the black silhouettes of houses appeared, lit by the sole streetlight for the entire village and by the moon peeking out from behind the clouds. Dogs started barking. The shaft knocked against something wooden, judging by the sound. The old man jumped down from the wagon, opened the gates, and the kind of mongrel known in the Russian expanses as a *kabyzdokh* flew out of the gates toward him. The dog barked, jumped, and spun around for joy like a wolf cub until his master gave him a gentle kick with his felt boot and commanded, "Fuck off!"

The trained beast obeyed, went into his doghouse, and from there continued to observe lovingly as the old man removed the harness and led the horse through the yard. Meanwhile Ilya was standing on the threshold, holding, besides his backpack, the old man's purchases as well, which Ilya had been ordered to collect from the wagon by a nod of the head.

"What're you standin' there for? Go on in!" the old man shouted, apparently irritated that the dog had understood his command at once, but he had to keep repeating it for the "student."

The old man's house was large and long, like a ship, because gathered under one roof was a hut for living with a ground floor for chickens and cows and a stable. Ilya walked into the cold enclosed porch. It was a spacious room made of thick split logs. Hanging on the walls were brooms, galvanized tubs, a couple of worn horse collars, and a gigantic tool of a purpose unknown to Ilya. Besides the front door, there were another four doors in the porch, so that the young man was confused as to which one to use. It took him a few minutes to get oriented. The right door, it turned out, led down, to the livestock. From there the warm smell of manure hit him. A cow was breathing loudly, and a pig was snorting without a care. The two doors opposite the entrance led to storerooms. The first storeroom held mainly lard; the second, unidentified boxes, most likely containing groats and elbow macaroni.

Leading to the warm living quarters was the left-hand door, and when Ilya opened it, trying not to drop the purchases, he smelled warmth and buckwheat groats steaming in the oven. He stood in the warm porch on a pile of small, round, hooked rag rugs and didn't know how to remove his frost-coated boots without using his hands or where to put the bags he was holding. The only bench in the porch was taken up by two pails of water.

Ilya was led out of his confusion by the old woman, who appeared from the room at his knock. The woman was wearing a woolen skirt, a knitted top, and a quilted vest. On her feet were felt boots cut down to the ankles, although the house was heated.

"Hello," the old woman bowed slightly or maybe she just leaned forward to take the bags out of Ilya's arms.

"Hello, I missed my bus . . ." Ilya began explaining his appearance.

But the old woman didn't wait to hear. She turned around and went into the room.

"Let me by!" The old man, who had just come in from the cold, gave Ilya a shove.

But the old woman was walking toward him carrying a milk

pail, and so for a moment all three were in the warm, crowded porch at the same time and couldn't disentangle. The old woman didn't kiss her newly returned husband, didn't hug him, and apparently didn't even nod to him. Actually, Ilya didn't see. He hurried to squeeze past the old woman and into the room as fast as he could so as not to create a jam and get a box on the ear from the old man.

A bleached but cracked Russian stove reigned in the middle of the room. Plank platforms extended over the door. They had been painted light blue, but about twenty years before. To the left of the stove a small kitchen had been set up: a table with a plastic cloth, a dish drain, and a few shelves on the wall. In addition to the shelves, there were photographs of a boy and girl hanging on the wall. And a yellowed, Soviet-era newspaper clipping. Behind the stove was the living room area, if you could call it that. The handsome timber walls there had been wallpapered, there was a bulky, flowered, noticeably sagging couch and a cheap television on a wobbly stand. The television was turned on and had been murmuring softly the whole time. But as far as Ilya could tell, though the televisioned remained on that entire evening and all the next morning, the old people paid no attention to it whatsoever.

"Sit!" The old man directed Ilya to a stool next to the kitchen table.

Presumably the old man had been silent the whole way not because he was afraid of the chill or the cold wind but simply because he believed that one should converse calmly and properly, that is, sitting at the table. He took an open bottle of moonshine from a little cupboard, informed him that it was tormentil moonshine, and was quite pleased when teetotaling Ilya refused the alcohol. Then the old man lowered his hand into the tub under the table, scooped up a handful of mushrooms, and plopped them into a bowl. He poured himself a glass, put a glass in front of Ilya too, just in case, but didn't pour for him, evidently following the northern notion that you could put a bottle of vodka in front of a guest but you could not pour for the guest because he might not appreciate its strength and get drunk, go outside, fall down, and freeze to death—and it would be your fault.

"Well," the old man said, downing his glass and taking a bite of mushroom. "Where are you from?"

"Moscow."

"Moscow itself?" the old man echoed, the way people always do in remote places for no apparent reason. "How's Moscow?"

"What do you mean how?" Ilya had already had experience dealing with voters, but now he was having a hard time keeping up his end of the conversation. "You know, we just had elections."

"What elections?"

"For the State Duma?"

"What the hell?"

The old woman came back with milk. She poured milk into Ilya's mug. The milk was fresh and warm, not like warm milk that's been heated on the stove, but the living warmth, the almost nauseating warmth of a cow's body. The old woman poured the rest of the milk into a bowl and whipped up a thin pancake batter. She took the iron burner off the stove with a poker. The fire leapt beneath the burner. She replaced the burner with an iron skillet and began cooking pancakes as translucent as the winter sun, quickly, one after the other.

"Did you vote?" Ilya tried to keep the conversation going.

"Oh, dearie." The voice of the old woman, speaking for the first time, was kind and delicate. "For us to vote, we have to ride seventy kilometers. And we don't even know who to vote for."

"There are different parties." Ilya livened up, having managed to steer the conversation to a subject dear to him. "They have ads on television. You do watch television."

"Yes, but we don't know the parties. They show lots more about murders there than parties."

The old woman put a bowl of pancakes in front of Ilya, added butter to the pancakes and buckwheat groats. She put a small saucer of lard on the table. She brewed tea, tossing a tiny pinch of tea into a huge teapot. As she served all of this, the old woman was silent, probably unable to talk and do things simultaneously. After she finished serving, she went back toward the stove and sat down on a stool, so as to take part in the conversation but not the meal.

"Well then, what kind of parties are there?" The old man had chimed in meanwhile.

"Different ones," Ilya replied. "Communist, United Russia, Yabloko . . ."

The old man shook his head and clicked his tongue, as if trying the *yabloko*—"apple" in Russian—said nothing for a bit, and concluded, "I don't know."

"What do you mean you don't know?" Ilya was amazed. "You don't know a single party?"

"You eat and stop jabbering." The old man smiled, took a pancake from the bowl, put it on Ilya's plate, plopped some buckwheat groats in the middle of the pancake, put butter and a piece of lard on top of that, rolled it up, and repeated, "Eat and stop jabbering."

Ilya took a bite of the pancake. He thought this simple food was incredibly delicious. But even more incredible was the fact that old people who had a television in their house didn't know a single political party.

"Who do you know?" Ilya continued with a full mouth. "Do you know the president?"

"Putin, I think?" the old man said uncertainly. "Yeltsin's over?"

Ilya was struck that the old man spoke about the president

as a natural phenomenon. As if a president, like the rain or a snowfall, had happened and was now over.

"Which president do you like more?" Ilya was feeling more comfortable and now served himself a pancake and wrapped up the groats in it himself. "Yeltsin or Putin?"

"Let them all burn!" The old man's voice suddenly rose.

"Hush, hush!" the old woman responded from the stove.

"Why burn?" Ilya asked as he tucked away a pancake.

"Because we had a kolkhoz here, a pedigree herd, a thousand head—"

"Hush, hush!" the old woman joined in, as if the old man's words were a soldier's song and the old woman was singing the descant.

"Young people worked, at the MTS, on the farm," the old man sang his part, referring to the machine-tractor station by its acronym. "And now—"

"Hush, hush!"

"Now there are three crooked old women and no young people left."

"Do you have children?" Ilya wedged into the conversation the way a second voice wedges into the first voice's part in a polyphonic song.

"A boy and a girl." Here the old woman's part began, and she carried her own sadly and simply from the stove. "My girl, thank the lord, married a good man who doesn't drink in Lipetsk. And our boy was in the army and is in prison now, he'll come out in six months, so we have to find him a place."

"Where are you going to find him a place, mother?"

"We have to. So he doesn't go back to prison . . ."

Ilya listened, and the old man and woman talked. About how there once was a good kindergarten here and the school wasn't bad, but now burned-out huts were left, and howling wild dogs. Ilya listened, and if he had known Russian folklore, the old people's story would have seemed to him just like a song you sing, your drunken head resting on your hand, at the table, or on the frozen road from Baigora to Gryazi, driving your horse on lightly, with no say in your fate, fearing no misfortune.

"All right," the old man summed up, pouring the rest of the moonshine into his glass. "Let's have one more drink and go to bed."

And with these words he drank up, gave Ilya a pat on the head, and said, "Oof, lad!" and he climbed onto his platform. The old woman bustled around, made up a bed for Ilya on the stove, went out into the cold porch, latched the door, and when she returned lay down on the couch without undressing.

Ilya didn't undress either. Through the couple of blankets and the mattress the stove wasn't exactly hot, but it was too hot to fall asleep, Ilya thought, but he did so instantly, and the heat soaked into, penetrated, and permeated him through and through.

Before dawn Ilya heard a rooster crow under the house. He leaned over the stove and looked out the window, but there was no hint of light outside. The cow mooed. The old woman arose and went out for water. It was completely quiet. Ilya heard the old woman's felt boots creaking over the snow, the water pouring into the bucket for the cow, the milk gurgling on the bottom of the milk pail, and the old man groaning on his platform, trying to vanquish with sleep either the chemical formula of moonshine or the magic formula of life, which assumes that a rooster crows, but the day does not begin.

At about seven the old people woke Ilya up, served him tea, gave him a loaf of bread for the road, and told him to hurry because, owing to the fact that they hadn't had mail service for many years, the bus was heading to town. It was still dark outside. Walking down the path trampled in the snow and glancing one last time through the old people's window, Ilya saw the television on. Apparently they didn't even turn it off at night. On the screen a young, well-coiffed woman wearing a sparkly, open dress was saying something soundless, probably about electronic gadgets, the latest consumer goods, or women's sexuality.

"Fool!" Ilya thought.

DOGS FOR MOTHERS

The bus incident and the night spent in Knyazhaya Baigora by no means discouraged the young man from his idea of traveling through his homeland and learning about it. Ilya traveled between provincial cities on commuter trains, which were cold and noisy, both from the driving carriages and the endless hawkers walking from car to car selling everything on earth— pencils, work gloves, newspapers that didn't write the truth, and ice cream in the middle of winter. Where there were no trains, Ilya hitchhiked, chatting with the drivers as they rode. None of the drivers knew anything about the parliamentary elections, just as they didn't know how long it was to the next town, actually.

"How long until we get to Lipetsk?" Ilya asked.

"Don't piss your pants, we'll get there," the driver answered. Hardly anyone in those parts could estimate the time more precisely than that.

When the day finally came to go home, at a small station Ilya boarded a passing train that was gray from the dust that had frozen to its sides. The train was on its way to Moscow from Grozny, the capital of Chechnya. It was a second-class sleeping car. There were mostly women and children traveling in the car. Men were rare, and if they were traveling, accompanying wives, sisters, or mothers, they looked as though they were doing so reluctantly.

Ilya took his seat, put his backpack on the luggage rack, and removed his coat, which he rolled up and dispatched to the luggage rack after the backpack. Then he removed his sweater. Under his sweater Ilya was wearing a T-shirt with a portrait of Comandante Che Guevara. He liked all kinds of revolutionary symbolism. He had decorated the room set aside for young people at *Yabloko*'s Moscow headquarters with slogans and posters. He had held the youth organization's meeting in a basement restaurant not far from headquarters called Apshu, where the food was bad but instead of club cards they gave out keys to the door, where smoke swirled under the vaulted ceiling, and the whole atmosphere reminded Ilya faintly of the Sorbonne in 1968.

He straightened his Che Guevara T-shirt. The woman across from him, who was feeding her child dumplings, forgot about the dumplings and threw up her hands. "Ooh! Hattab!"

Hattab was the name of a famous terrorist, and the woman spoke his name in fear, but also with respect.

"Why Hattab?" Ilya smiled. "This is Che Guevara."

"Listen"—the woman's eyes were playfully sly—"on the platform in Moscow, when they frisk you, if you want I'll say it's Che-Guevara-Me-Guevara. But I've lived twenty years"—she could have passed for forty—"I've lost two brothers, and I know what Hattab looks like, damn him."

"Hattab took your brothers?" Ilya asked, climbing onto his berth and sitting Turkish-fashion.

"The federals took my brothers." She was referring to the federal soldiers quartered in Chechnya after the second Chechen war.

"Why do you think that?" Ilya was amazed at the ease with which this woman started telling him, a stranger, about people disappearing in Chechnya, the kind of disappearance that had always been a taboo topic.

"Because the federals themselves came to my father and offered to let him buy back my brothers."

"What do you mean, buy back?"

"For five thousand dollars. I was listening." The woman continued to feed her child dumplings. "They offered to let him buy them back for five thousand dollars today alive or for a thousand dollars tomorrow dead."

"What happened?"

"Listen, we want peace. If Kadyrov or Putin can bring peace to Chechnya, I'll say glory to Allah for them."

"But what happened to your brothers?"

"My father didn't have five thousand dollars. He bought them back dead."

"How's that?"

"He bought them back and buried them," the woman told him, the way people might tell a sad but ancient legend.

Ilya nodded at the child. The child was about five.

"Maybe you shouldn't?"

"Shouldn't what?"

"Tell this story in front of the child."

The woman shook her head.

"He knows. He's a Chechen."

It was noisy in the car. People were sitting with their legs on the berths, talking loudly, and the children were running down the aisles, bumping into the women's knees but not touching the men. It was actually cheerful until a soldier stepped into the car at the next station.

Everyone fell silent at once. It was just a soldier traveling, probably, from his unit's deployment on leave. A soldier who had probably never been in Chechnya. But the minute he walked in, everyone in the car fell silent at once. The soldier walked through the car, and from each compartment he was accompanied by looks full not of fear—no, hate.

The soldier reached his side berth at the end of the car, climbed up, put his duffel under his head, and lay down facing the window. But even then no one in the car uttered a word.

Everyone traveled in silence and everyone watched the soldier pretending to sleep and obviously feeling the eyes on his unprotected back.

Only the child of the woman across from Ilya said something in Chechen. Ilya asked the woman to translate, but she only smiled. Ilya never did learn that the child had asked whether it was true that the federals had dogs for mothers.

At the station in Moscow the Chechen train was met by stepped-up police patrols. They checked the documents of everyone in succession, except for Ilya and a few other Russians. In one of the cars they were carrying an old man who was so sick that he couldn't walk on his own and was carried out on a stretcher. The policemen ordered the stretcher to be left on the platform until a special doctor could come and testify that the old man was actually sick and had not been injured in battle. The old man lay on the platform for twenty minutes, and the relatives accompanying him squatted around him.

When he got home, Ilya called all the leaders of all the youth opposition organizations: the SPS, the Communists, the Limonovites, the Vanguard of Red Youth . . . He proposed assembling young oppositionists for a rally calling for a boycott of the fast-approaching presidential election. It seemed to him that they had all been deceived, one and all. So one and all should protest. Together.

CHAPTER 7
Sergei Udaltsov: Young Man in a Leather Jacket

I t's true, he's unbaptized, an atheist, and a Communist,"
Nastya whispered.

True, she was a Communist herself. Eighteen years after
her birth in Cherkassy, she had joined the Ukrainian Communist Party, which had split off from the Communist Party of
the collapsed Soviet Union. She hadn't joined because her family lacked the money for the pretty dresses so important to
an eighteen-year-old girl. There wasn't any money for dresses,
sure, but Nastya joined the Communist Party because of a boy
in school.

She had studied at Lenin School, where there was a plaster
bust of Lenin on the first floor. In the late 1980s, when the talk
in Ukrainian kitchens was mostly about independence, one
boy, inspired by grownups' kitchen conversations, came to
school and threw a can of paint at the bust of Lenin. This boy
knew what he had done but did not know what would happen.
The paint ran down the plaster leader's bald head like blood.
The school principal shouted that Ukrainian nationalism was
impermissible in the fraternal family of Soviet peoples. She
then shouted that communism was the shining future for all
humanity. The principal then called the boy into her office,
where the slogan "Marxist theory is all-powerful because it is
true" hung under a portrait of Lenin. She chewed the boy out
under that slogan. She then summoned the boy's parents to the
school and threatened to go to his father's place of work and
say that the father had taught his son anti-Soviet propaganda

and Ukrainian nationalism. She then convened school-wide assemblies in the auditorium and chewed the boy out in front of all his schoolmates and forced the children to tell their friend that he was a traitor. She then dragged the boy to the Young Communists' city committee, where they also chewed him out and demanded that he name his accomplices. And then to the municipal KGB. After one of these meetings this boy got into his father's car, sped off, and rammed into a tank truck at full speed. The truck caught fire, the fire spread to the pile of scrap metal left over from the car that had rammed into it, and inside the car, what was left of the boy was reduced to ashes. This was a few months before the beginning of perestroika and a couple of years before Mikola Veresen pulled down the Soviet flag at Government House in Kiev and ran up the Ukrainian yellow and blue. Twenty months before the principal of Cherkassy's Lenin School turned in her party card and quit the Communist Party, cursing Communism, which had deprived Ukraine of its independence.

That was when Nastya decided that if that bitch was leaving the party, then she should join. She was accepted into the party by friends of her grandfather, who had been driven out of the party when Nastya was just a baby and who, nonetheless, considered himself a loyal Communist his whole life. They were the sweetest old men, these friends of her grandfather. They thought that now that the party had lost power they had to stay in it and had to continue to believe in "Communism, the shining future for all humanity."

That was how Nastya became a Communist. But she was a baptized Communist and a believer. She stood at confession and told the priest about the man she planned to marry. She asked for his blessing for this union without a religious ceremony because her beloved was an atheist and not baptized. The priest listened to her, his head bowed, and didn't rush her, although behind Nastya stood a whole line of people eager to confess, including close-cropped men in leather jackets whom the father knew were criminals and were waiting in line to confess the murders they'd committed. The darkened sanctuary smelled of incense and shabbily dressed people. The inevitable babushkas, in whom it seemed a demon had deliberately settled in order to disturb those praying and confessing, shuffled around, noisily scraping the wax from the candleholders, snuffing out and carrying away candles that had just been placed for someone's health or someone's eternal rest. Nastya got distracted. She wanted to tell the priest something important, something very important about the handsome and brave man she loved and with whom a life, therefore, could not be a sin. But the words sounded clichéd and flat, while the thoughts jumping around in her head would not take on words but only flared up as vague scenes. It seemed to Nastya that if she could see these scenes more sharply the Kingdom of God would come, or Communism, where her fiancé's faith would join with hers and there would be no Jew, or Hellene, or Communist, or liberal. An angel with a fiery sword would take the world in his palm, turn the world on its axis a little, and say, smiling, "Look, children, see how simply everything is arranged." Nastya thought that but could not convey her thoughts to the priest.

For instance, how do you tell him about the trousers? The trousers that, in the early 1990s, the mother of Nastya's fiancé, Sergei Udaltsov, decided to alter for Sergei from an old pair of his father's. Sergei was a handsome, slender scholar, and he needed good trousers, damn it. But there was no money to buy trousers. His mother decided to alter the old pair herself. She worked on them for several weeks. Then she triumphantly presented her finished work to Sergei and asked him to try them on. He did. He stood in front of the mirror in the room. His mother kneeled in front of him. She adjusted the creases. But no matter how she straightened the creases, the trousers still fit terribly and bagged. She began to weep. How can you explain that someone becomes a revolutionary not because he doesn't have trousers but because his mother, a university history professor, wept after failing at sewing trousers? The candles flickered softly. Nastya frowned. The priest quietly tilted his head to one side and slowly fingered his rosary. Nastya was saying something, but her words were powerless. How could you tell him about the assault on the White House in 1993? A cloudy night. Her fiancé, Seryozha Udaltsov, is still a little boy, a schoolboy. He goes to the White House just to get a look at the uprising and assault, out of curiosity. Some shabbily dressed people are running around. There are lots of soldiers. A *spetsnaz* officer with a smiling, childlike face stops them.

"What are you doing here, kids? Come on, let's go home! Step lively!"

The officer's name is Anatoly Yermolin. He commands the Vympel reserve detachment. He likes the boy with the bold, open face. But the officer is not involved in scouting yet. And the boy is not involved in politics yet.

"Home, and step lively!" the officer orders the boy, and the next time they meet, fifteen years later, it is at a Dissenters' March.

Naturally, the boys do not go home. They only pretend they're heading for the subway. At the subway some scruffy guy is using a pay phone to call a businesswoman he knows and shouting, "Your day is over. Get it? Over! Take what you've managed to steal and run."

The boys fan out to avoid the officer who has driven them away and keep walking, in the midst of the confusion, and somewhere shots are heard, and the shots cheer them up, and suddenly one of the boys in their group falls and is lying wounded, screaming, shaking from pain and puking from shock and fear simultaneously. The next day it turns out that the father of one of the boys, who had gone to the White House in search of his curious son, had also been caught by a stray bullet—and killed.

Nastya tried to gather her thoughts, tried to explain what a boy wounded by a stray bullet had to do with the fact that she was planning to marry without a wedding, but she couldn't. Just as she couldn't explain about the music or the books. About Viktor Tsoi or Yegor Letov. The priest had probably never even heard of the songs "Our Hearts Demand Change" or "Everything's Going According to Plan." But Nastya had gone as a twenty-year-old girl to Moscow from Cherkassy to meet the musician Yegor Letov, the writer Viktor Pelevin, and the writer Eduard Limonov. And since she was a pretty twenty-year-old, that was easily done. She met Letov, the musician, literally a couple of days later at a press conference after one of his semi-underground concerts. He wore torn jeans and a stretched sweater, and he was saying that he was wearing the same sneakers he wore as a student, that you have to be outside the system, because any system is slavery. But when Nastya asked him to come give a concert in Ukraine, he refused. Nastya said that she and her friends would pay for his train ticket and would feed him all the time he was in Ukraine, but Letov asked for a thousand dollars in addition, an amount Nastya's friends not only did not have but could barely picture.

"I get it," Nastya stammered. "Show business."

"I have children to feed," Letov parried.

"You don't have children."

"I have a cat. I have to feed her."

"A thousand dollars?"

Here is how Nastya met the writer Pelevin. A friend got her Pelevin's phone number, Nastya called, left some girlish oohs and aahs on the answering machine, and Pelevin unexpectedly called back. They met. They chatted in a café. After that Nastya called from time to time, left a message about what she wanted, and Pelevin called back. Pelevin did not call back, however, on the day Nastya asked him to sign a letter in support of the writer

Limonov, who had been put in prison. He didn't call back the next day or the next. He never called back again.

Nastya met the writer Limonov at the Bunker. That's what they called the cellar on Frunzenskaya rented by the National Bolshevik Party Limonov had created. All you had to do was go into the Bunker, say you wanted to meet Limonov, and a sullen young man led you straight to Limonov through a labyrinth of cellar offices where there were stacks of the *Limonka* newspaper on the desks, where opened but unfinished cans of fish lay about, and where a freshly cleaned hazmat suit with a gas mask hung in the washroom. Somewhere way in the back Limonov sat talking to his comrades, teasing the young women who flocked like moths to the light, to this wholly romantic underground.

If there was a rally on Vasilievsky Slope right by the Kremlin walls, then a merry crowd of Limonovites would return from the rally to the Bunker down the embankment, stopping to rest at the square by the Krymsky Bridge, and Limonov would buy everyone beer out of party funds. That was what the revolution was like. And Nastya liked it. She joined Limonov's party. She started participating in actions.

They went to the liberal parties' congresses and shouted, "Stalin! Beria! Gulag." And nothing happened to them. They didn't shout like that because they actually liked the Gulag but because the liberal congresses' presidiums consisted of people who, in Nastya's opinion, were just like the school principal who first drove a boy to suicide over his anti-Soviet propaganda and then became the biggest anti-Soviet in town. They shouted because the words "Stalin! Beria! Gulag!" were the only words that made the new liberal masters of life, yesterday's former Communists, shrivel and foam at the mouth. They shouted, drank beer in little squares, and flirted in the Bunker until Limonov was arrested and convicted for possession of firearms and nearly for planning an armed uprising in Kazakhstan.

Then Limonov was betrayed. Half of the merry young people left the party as soon as they realized that for revolutionary activities the clumsy police could not only chase you, young and agile, through the alleys, but also put you in jail.

The candles flickered and the priest sighed and rustled his stole. He straightened the crucifix lying slightly crooked on the lectern. And Nastya didn't know how to tell him that everyone betrays everyone, and how this fact was connected to the fact that she had to marry without a religious ceremony. And what the man depicted there on the cross, who became the most famous victim of betrayal in the world, had to do with this. This man on the cross had nothing in common with the writer Limonov except that both were betrayed.

The candles flickered. Nastya didn't know how to tell the priest about the 1996 presidential elections. When the Communists' leader, Gennady Zyuganov, had a rating of nearly 40 percent and President Yeltsin didn't have any rating at all. When the country's richest people pooled their capital to support Yeltsin and keep Zyuganov out of power. When the first falsified campaign was unleashed in the new Russia, the candidates still approached the elections in such a way that Zyuganov was either supposed to win and prove that the Communists could in fact govern the country fairly or else discredit the Communist slogans, as in Eastern Europe. Zyuganov won. But the elections were falsified. Nastya was certain of that. And Sergei Udaltsov, who was not yet her fiancé then, was certain of it. The whole nation was certain of it. People, regardless of their political views, told each other a joke about how Yeltsin calls the chairman of the electoral commission, who tells him, there's good news and bad news. The bad news is that Zyuganov has gotten 60 percent of the vote; the good news is that Yeltsin is leading.

It was summer. It seemed to Sergei Udaltsov that given this kind of voter support, Zyuganov could, in response to the falsification of the elections, lead hundreds of thousands of people out onto the streets. That people could live for weeks in tents, shutting down the center of Moscow and other major cities. That this would be a crowd to be reckoned with. That justice would be restored, that even his mother, the history professor who had sewn him the absurd trousers, and his schoolmate wounded by a stray bullet on the street of a peaceful city, would demand justice. That there would be a velvet revolution. But there was no revolution. After the elections Gennady Zyuganov did not summon his supporters to the square but somehow gave in immediately, somehow accepted the results of the falsified elections immediately and agreed to be the leader of the opposition, which was tantamount to having power without taking responsibility for any reforms.

The candles flickered. The babushkas scraped the wax off the holders. The people behind Nastya shuffled, waiting impatiently for their turn to confess. Nastya got distracted. It was hard for her to explain what a civil marriage had to do with the fact there was always someone being betrayed and someone washing his hands of it.

March on Moscow

After the 1996 presidential elections, Sergei Udaltsov went to the very first Communist rally just to look Zyuganov, the Communists' leader, in the eye, and understand why the hell he had summoned people to the square not after Yeltsin's falsified victory but three months later, on November 7, to mark the anniversary of the October revolution and conduct the "workers' fall offensive," that is, wave flags and shout, "Put Yeltsin's gang on trial."

As always, Zyuganov delivered his angry speeches in a thick voice. But next to Zyuganov Sergei saw a short man in a threadbare jacket, and this little man was shouting something wild. Something sufficiently radical for Sergei to like it. The little man's name was Viktor Anpilov, and he headed up the Labor Russia party, radical Communists who did not want to become members of parliament and who insisted that the Soviet Union should be restored to its former greatness, with all its attributes—an extremely noble idea but about as realistic as trying to stick a burst soap bubble back together. He, Anpilov, did not like any of the new Russia's achievements—the little restaurants, the foreign cars on the streets, the reporters clamoring discordantly on the various television channels. He rode the subway or drove his old proletarian-red Niva. He spoke with everyone worker style, informally, familiarly, and suggested to everyone but the very young Udaltsov that they address him in similar fashion.

He leaned over the tribune and said to Udaltsov, "What's up, kid?" And having listened to the not entirely intelligible explication of Udaltsov's radical views, he said, "Come by! We're going to organize a march on Moscow."

The next weekend Udaltsov and his friends went to the outskirts of the city. There, at the address Anpilov had given him, was a dilapidated house of culture that during the Soviet era had belonged to some factory and now didn't belong to anyone because the factory had been shut down. Anpilov arrived in his red Niva. He got out, shook Sergei's hand, and led the young people into the central hall, where mainly elderly people were already sitting on ripped-up red armchairs. There were about twenty people. He didn't need to go up on stage and stand at the lectern to speak before them. But Anpilov did approach the lectern. He banged his fist on it and said they had to organize a march on Moscow, the way Subcomandante Marcos had organized a march on Mexico City.

Anpilov's head was chock full of revolutionary romanticism. He mixed up names and dates, republican Spain and revolutionary Cuba, Cuba and Angola, and Angola and Chiapas. But the total effect was fiery: "Courage knows its goal, Cuba became a legend, Fidel once again speaks inspiringly, courage knows its goal." He talked about how Subcomandante Marcos, who led the Zapatista revolutionary army in the Mexican state of Chiapas, undertook the march on Mexico City alone, left his village of Aguas Calientes alone, and as he walked to the capital was eventually joined by a million people, and they entered Mexico City and surrounded the parliament or the house of government, or the presidential palace, or whatever is most important there in Mexico, and demanded health care reform, and free education for all, and the government was forced to . . . Courage knows its goal . . . That's how they, Anpilov said, would march on Moscow, in three columns, from Tula, Ryazan, and Vladimir. They would pass impoverished Russian villages, unfortunate little towns where the factories had been shut and people had no work, villages of scientists where the Homeland's nuclear shield had been forged and there was now desolation . . . And in each village more and more new comrades would join their march so that by the time they got to Moscow they would be a million strong, too, like the Mexican Indians and Subcomandante Marcos, and they would surround the Kremlin . . . Courage knows its goal!

Anpilov waved his arms about. You could see a tear under the arm of his worn jacket, but Sergei liked this eccentric old guy, and it was decided to organize a March on Moscow. True, organizing a march in Russia wasn't as easy as in Mexico. First of all, you had to wait for winter to be over because you can't walk from Tula to Moscow in the winter. Second, you had to reach an agreement with the police. At that time, in the mid-1990s, the police were kind, they didn't beat demonstrators, but you still had to come to an agreement with them because it's much easier to walk down a highway than to make your way down village roads without accurate maps. They had to find tents. They had to stock up on medicines because most of the march participants were elderly.

Sergei dealt with all of these issues right up to the summer. He even got a hold of a truck with a megaphone on the roof, the kind of truck that should lead a column, encourage the demonstrators with revolutionary songs, and sometimes give lifts to those who were worn out.

The March began in July 1997. While people were gathering, Sergei sat on the main square of Tula in the truck with the megaphone shouting out slogans: "Put Yeltsin's gang on trial," "Down with minister capitalists," "No to predatory privatization." He enjoyed shouting slogans into the megaphone so much that he didn't even stop when the truck door opened and someone's firm hand dragged him out by the collar. The four policemen threw him down on the asphalt and he was still shouting about Yeltsin's gang. They searched him briskly, picked him up briskly, and shoved him briskly into a police van.

Only then did he say, "What happened?"

But the van was already driving through the streets of Tula, and the policemen escorting Sergei did not talk to him. They took him to the station and put him in lockup, a metal cage where several of his comrades, march organizers, already were. They were all cheerful and talking loudly. When people are arrested, they often experience a certain euphoria.

Sergei grabbed onto the jail's iron bars and shouted to the policemen keeping watch in the corridor: "Guys! Are you serving the oligarchs? Policing capitalism, right?"

In response to his shouts, a policeman walked in from the corridor carrying a truncheon. He ran the truncheon over the bars, nearly hitting Sergei's fingers, and said, "Stop your hollering! I should be catching criminals, and here I am dealing with you, idiot."

"Then tell me," Sergei parried. "Who has better weapons,

you or the crooks? Eh? Can you keep up with a crooks Mercedes in that heap of yours? Tell me. Do they pay you an okay salary, or do the crooks get paid more?"

"A little more, of course." The policeman smiled.

"We're demonstrating for you. And you lock us up."

"I have my orders." The policeman shrugged. "And if it weren't for them, I might go with you to demonstrate myself."

"Well then, at least give me some water." Sergei smiled, too. "I've shouted myself hoarse."

Five minutes later tea with sugar appeared. The policemen surrounded the cell, passed marmalade and crackers to the prisoners through the bars, and yakked about how unfair life was. Half an hour after that two Tula deputies from the Communist Party arrived. They too joined the tea drinking, and they asked the policemen to release the prisoners. But they couldn't. They were obligated to write up a report on each person, take each person to court, and fine each person for disturbing the peace.

At first Sergei refused to sign the report. He said he had done nothing illegal. But his new policeman friend said, "Seryozh, do you need this? We'll be sitting here 'til the middle of the night. Why don't you sign it quickly, then quickly go see the judge, and that'll be it."

About four hours later the column of demonstrators with their Communist and antigovernment slogans was moving from Tula's central square toward Moscow. There were about two hundred people. They were escorted by a police car. The highway lane closest to the shoulder had been set aside for them, and their truck with the megaphone drove in front, belching Soviet songs.

They made about thirty kilometers a day. In the evening they would stop in some field, pitch tents, lay fires, and cook macaroni and canned meat. Sergei was as hungry as a wolf. After the macaroni Anpilov usually spun out some revolutionary song:

"We marched to the rumble of the cannons . . ." People would join in: "We looked death straight in the eye . . ." The nights were warm. The sky starry. "Spartacists' brigades, daring fighters, advanced ever onward . . ." These lines were hollered with particular rapture by fans of the Spartak soccer team, of which there were many among the demonstrators. They hollered so loudly that even the nightingales in the hazel grove by the side of the road were briefly silent. Sergei fell asleep to the nightingales' song and awoke to the song of the lark, though he didn't know it was a lark.

After about a week the column reached the Moscow Ring Road. Naturally, no one had joined them along the way. This wasn't Mexico. Not in the impoverished villages, not in the unfortunate little towns that had fallen into desolation, and not in the settlements of scientists who had forged the Homeland's nuclear shield. There was nothing like the million people Anpilov had spoken of from the lectern of that Moscow house of culture. There were even fewer of them now than in Tula because many of the elderly had not withstood the trip's hardships and had taken the train home.

But here, on Moscow's border, they joined up with the brigades that had come from Ryazan and Vladimir. From a distance they saw the tents and the red flag waving over them. "Hurrah!" Anpilov shouted. He took a banner from someone and started running for the tents. He was met by the leader of the Officers Union, Terekhov, also running with a banner, a rather sullen nationalist who turned out to be not a bad muzhik when he was among comrades. The banner carriers embraced. The camp grew. The macaroni and canned meat for dinner were somehow festive. More than a thousand people in all had assembled in the combined brigades of demonstrators. Maybe even two thousand.

The next morning they folded up their tents and entered Moscow in an orderly column. But on Sevastopolsky Avenue, near the very first subway station, OMON personnel barred their way. An OMON officer told Anpilov politely that although the march had been permitted, as had the rally in the center of the city, the demonstrators could not walk through the city because that would interfere with traffic.

"Take the subway," the officer said.

It was an obvious ruse. Half of the march participants were from out of town. They would get lost in the subway, be late for the rally, and confuse the names of streets and underground stations.

"We won't take the subway!" Anpilov screeched. "We will shut down traffic on Sevastopolsky Avenue."

With these words he sat down on the asphalt. The other demonstrators spread out over the thoroughfare and sat down as well. Traffic stopped. The OMON officer shrugged. He turned away and said something into his radio. In those days OMON did not habitually beat up demonstrators. This OMON officer ordered two street sprinklers to be driven over. Not water cannons to disperse the demonstrations, just street sprinklers. They didn't douse the demonstrators with water. They just poured water on the asphalt, and the water flowed down the pavement, because Sevastopolsky Avenue is on a slight incline. Five minutes later all the demonstrators were on their feet. And had freed up the thoroughfare. And many felt sick. Literally sick at heart, so mortified were they at having been so easily dispersed.

Sergei looked for Anpilov. He was walking across the lawn where elderly people were lying here and there on the grass and a nurse was running among them with smelling salts and nitroglycerine. Anpilov was sick at heart too.

Sergei found him lying on the grass, his shirt unbuttoned, sucking on nitroglycerine and sobbing, "Bitches! Bitches! Water! So I'd have wet pants! So it would look like I'd wet myself! Bastards! Bastards!"

That's when Sergei thought that all these people were too old for even a velvet revolution. Too feeble to protest.

COME TO THE PLENUM

The candles flickered. The priest listened, breathed heavily and with concentration, inasmuch as he was a man with the sizable belly traditional for Orthodox priests. Nastya was completely muddled. It seemed as though the priest understood absolutely nothing of her incoherent stories. Behind her in line people were coughing, hinting to the father that it was time to let the young woman go and hear everyone else's confessions. This flustered Nastya even more.

She wanted to tell him about their first date. But she didn't know how to. She and Sergei Udaltsov had known each other long before their first date. They had met at Yegor Letov's concerts. At birthdays of mutual friends. On one of these birthdays Nastya was especially cheerful and looked especially pretty. She flirted recklessly with everyone. She especially wanted Sergei Udaltsov to like her. That evening she especially liked his handsome and brave face. But he told her she was a flirt. Or maybe he didn't say it—Nastya didn't remember—maybe she just thought he considered her a flirt. So one day, learning that Sergei Udaltsov had created a youth organization known as Vanguard of Red Youth within Anpilov's Labor Russia Party, Nastya decided to go see Sergei at a rally. She liked the name. The name was militant. Vanguard of Red Youth—AKM—an abbreviation like that of a Kalashnikov, a modernized Kalashnikov. She liked the name but Nastya went to the demonstration biased. She was a Limonovite, a radical revolutionary woman, and she could feel only pity for Anpilov's party, which consisted of nothing but pensioners. Even Labor Russia's youth organization must be for retirees, Nastya thought. Not only that, Sergei Udaltsov considered her a flirt. But the rally was fun. Cheerful and lively. How could she explain to the priest how a lively young people's rally differs from a pensioners'?

At the end of the rally Sergei Udaltsov saw Nastya to a taxi, opened the door for her, and whispered, "Come to our plenum tomorrow."

And to Nastya it felt as if Sergei was asking her out on a date. How was she now to explain to the priest why her chest tightened so and why her palms itched when the man invited her to the plenum in a tone of voice he would use to invite her out to dinner? The candles flickered. The altar boy ran up. He whispered something into the father's ear.

The father nodded. Then he asked Nastya, "Have you been with him already?"

"Yes," Nastya answered honestly.

And suddenly she realized that it was as if everything had already happened. She still didn't know how to marry Sergei Udaltsov, but it was as if everythng had already happened. She didn't know they would have two children. That she would join the Vanguard of Red Youth. That she would become press secretary for the Vanguard of Red Youth. That every evening when her husband came home they would talk about party matters over dinner. But it was as if it had already happened.

She didn't know that one day she and her husband would discover a snitch in the AKM ranks who was informing the FSB about all the upcoming picketing and actions. That they would expel that person. And that Anpilov would stand up for him and say, "It's good there's a snitch. Let the FSB have a good look and see you're not up to anything." That after these words they would have to leave Labor Russia.

She didn't know that Seryozha's mother would come by in the morning on rally days to babysit and say, "Careful, Nastya. Bear in mind that if they arrest you I won't babysit for you anymore and let you go to rallies."

She didn't know that one day at an Anti-capitalism demonstration they would arrest her, throw her on the metal floor of the prison van, pile a heap of other arrested people on top of her, start beating her on the head with their boots, turning her face into one big bruise, and tear her hair out in clumps.

She didn't know that one day one of their comrades, a chemistry student, would assemble a homemade bomb and try to detonate it at the entrance of a government building. And that Sergei would be imprisoned over this failed blast as the mastermind, a criminal rather than an administrative charge. Although Sergei would have no idea about the bomb. Although the bomb would be more of a firecracker than ammunition. And she would have to explain to their son why his papa was in prison.

She didn't know that cruel times lay ahead. That even an unsanctioned picket would be considered a criminal rather than an administrative offense, extremism.

She didn't know that every time, every Dissenters' March, her husband would be arrested first and released last. And every time she would run from police station to police station and ask whether anyone had seen Sergei Udaltsov.

She didn't know any of this, but suddenly she realized that it was as if everything had already happened. The candles flickered.

The priest straightened his stole and said, "You are already his wife. One flesh. Help your husband. That is your cross. Be beside him always."

He wanted to add, "In grief and joy, in health and sickness, until death do you part." But he didn't. He simply blessed her. He covered Nastya's head with his stole and absolved her of her sins—witting and unwitting.

CHAPTER 8
Maksim Gromov: A Smoker Who Pockets His Butts Rather Than Throw Them Away

If you're in a punishment cell, you're in prison three times over. On the outside is the prison zone: towers, barbed wire. In the middle of that zone is the camp prison for convicted prisoners. And in the middle of the prison is the punishment cell for prisoners convicted in prison.

A solitary punishment cell is narrow, like a pencil box. After you get up, the guards make you prop the bed, which is knocked together from wooden laths, against the wall. The bed attaches to the wall with an iron shackle the way raised berths in second-class sleeping cars attach to the wall. They make you slip the foam rubber rug that serves at night as both mattress and bedding between bed and wall. All that remains of furniture is a very narrow concrete column in the middle of the cell—a stool. And a slightly wider column—a table. You can sit on the stool only with one buttock. You can't lie down. Even on the floor.

A bright lamp burns in the ceiling. Sunlight does not fall through the barred window, which looks out onto the prison's inner yard and is covered with a solid wooden board. No air comes in from the outside, either. On the other hand, music pours in. Loud music. Children's songs or taped muezzin's cries. This is called the music box—a type of torture. For ten hours straight, a ringing child's voice shouts out, "I don't care if there's snow, I don't care if it's hot, I don't care if it's pouring rain, as long as I have my friends," and you're alone in your cell. Or an adult voice shouts in Arabic, "Arise, prayer is better than sleep," and you would be happy to lie down but there's nowhere to do so.

Maksim perches on the hard concrete stool and, trying not to let the children's songs into his consciousness, tries to remember a poem:

Carrying buckets of ripe grapes,
Pouring the clusters into a trough.
Oh, they're not carrying grapes—
It's the young men being chased
To the black grindstone, to press the wine.

Who is this? Maksimilian Voloshin? Yes, Maksimilian Voloshin. Maksim sways slightly from weakness. This is the tenth day of his hunger strike. But besides weakness, fasting also brings an amazing clarity of thought, and poems are easily recalled. In the two years he has spent in solitary, Maksim has recalled many poems. In solitary it turns out that poems once read and forgotten can in fact be remembered. They can be extracted from the memory's secret recesses with the same happy feeling as when a prisoner extracts from his boot the knife he has carried through three searches.

Maksim also remembers where and when he bought that small volume of Maksimilian Voloshin's poems. In 1992 at the book bazaar on Novy Arbat in Moscow. Along with Eduard Limonov's *It's Me, Eddie.*

Maksim had not had a hometown, a town in which he lived on a permanent basis and to which he was attached, since he was a child. Nor had he had a profession. He probably couldn't have said whether he was a milling-machine operator or a trumpet player. He was born in Lipetsk, spent some of his childhood in Cheboksary, and entered music school there, but one day he went to visit a friend in Cherepovets, met a girl named Svetlana at the Cherepovets Music School, fell in love at first sight, and stayed in Cherepovets, even though the girl he stayed for did not love him back. After studying to be a trumpet player for a year in Cherepovets, Maksim went to the recruitment office and asked to join the army. Otherwise Maksim would not have had the strength to break the knots of unlucky love on his own. The Cherepovets military commissar was a retired *spetsnaz* officer who had lost a leg during military actions in Egypt. He was amazed that Maksim had come to him of his own accord: a young man registered in Cheboksary but living in Cherepovets—the army would never have found Maksim if he hadn't come to the army himself.

The military commissar marveled, gave Maksim a fresh issue of the Communist newspaper *Zavtra*—Tomorrow—and said, "Here, read this. You'll see it's all ass backward."

After the army Maksim worked as a courier, paved roads, and pumped water at the municipal pumping station in Cheboksary. The only thing that never changed was that he was constantly reading books. He would buy books every time he passed through Moscow on his way between Cheboksary, Lipetsk, Chelyabinsk, and Cherepovets. Then, in April 1992, the Maksimilian Voloshin poems he bought at the Moscow book bazaar sank deeply into his memory, and the book by Eduard Limonov, also bought there, seemed brilliant.

Later Maksim joined the Chuvashsky Tractor Factory in Cheboksary as an apprentice miller. He married and had a daughter. He became a good milling-machine operator. He followed in the newspapers as Eduard Limonov organized his National Bolshevik Party in Moscow. Reading the newspapers, Maksim sometimes recalled the Cherepovets military commissar, smiled, and muttered to himself: "I do see. It's all ass backwards." And one day Maksim got the idea of writing to Limonov that he, Maksim Gromov, was prepared to form a branch of the National Bolshevik Party in Cheboksary. "Come here," Limonov had replied. "We need to talk in person."

A certain unease had always driven Maksim around the country, from town to town. Limonov's letter was enough to make him take a couple of days off from the factory, kiss his pregnant wife, and board the train. Limonov met Maksim in his basement "bunker" on Frunzenskaya and said that the main task of a regional branch was to distribute the newspaper *Limonka* and dispel the myths about the National Bolsheviks. "You have to explain to people that we are not Nazis or racists or scoundrels," Limonov said. "How could we be Nazis if half the people in the party are Jews? How could we be racists if the leader of the Riga branch is black? How could we be scoundrels if you work as a milling-machine operator and I as a writer? Do you understand? We will work, and we will live!" Limonov concluded his briefing with his famous closing phrase, and Maksim headed back to Cheboksary with a huge stack of newspapers in an oilskin tote bag. It was 1998.

After that, Maksim's life changed. He didn't join the other muzhiks for a beer after work or go home to his wife to read books; rather, he went to the university for the student debates that were then coming into fashion. His first recruits were student philologists, philosophers, and historians. They even called themselves National Bolsheviks already, but to turn this club of radical windbags into a militant party cell required action, direct action, through which people would achieve something, not just blabber about their accomplishments.

At that time the Republic of Chuvashia was probably the first region in the new Russia where the Soviet practice of punitive psychiatry had been revived. Three human-rights activists and writers—Zotov, Malyakov, and Imindayev—had been incarcerated in a psychiatric hospital with a diagnosis of schizophrenia after Chuvashian president Fedorov decided he didn't like those men's books.

In response to their forced hospitalization, Maksim suggested to his comrades that they organize a protest action on the main square of Cheboksary: chain themselves to the Lenin monument and sew their mouths shut with rough thread, the way it was once done (Maksim had seen it on television) by either terrorists or human-rights activists somewhere in Thailand or the Philippines.

The student philosophers agreed to chain themselves to Lenin but refused outright to jab their lips with a needle and sew their mouths shut with thread. They agreed that only Maksim would sew his mouth shut and the rest of the Chuvash National Bolsheviks would simply bandage their mouths shut.

And so on the appointed day the young men ran onto the main square, crossed it in front of the usual thick-headed policemen, surrounded the monument, wound a chain around it, handcuffed themselves to the chain, and unfurled a banner that said something about the need for freedom of speech and the inadmissibility of punitive psychiatry. The policemen ran up and pulled on the chain, as if hoping to break it. They shouted, "What are you doing? Why are you here? Who gave you permission?" But the student philologists had bandaged their mouths shut and made no reply even to the questions of the reporters photographing the protest action and shooting videos.

All that remained was for Maksim to sew his mouth shut. He took a specially prepared needle and thread from his jacket lapel and jabbed the needle into his lip. It was unexpectedly painful. How could the Thai terrorists have sewn up their mouths if it hurt so much? Under the needle—Maksim saw it out of the corner of his eye—a drop of crimson blood formed and ran down his lip. An instant later Maksim had a salty, nauseating, bloody taste in his mouth. Worst of all was that the lip wouldn't puncture. The needle nicked the soft flesh meant for kisses but just wouldn't come out the other side. He had to twist the needle, drill it, and it took several minutes to make just one little hole and pull the painfully rough thread through that hole. Things got even worse with the lower lip, which now had to be stitched to the punctured upper. The lower lip was even softer and more tender. Maksim stabbed from the inside, his mouth filled with blood, and he had to swallow the blood, but he couldn't get the needle through his lip. Looking down, Maksim could even see the lip protrude under the needle's pressure and the needle's steel tip shine through the skin. There was only a little way to go, but the lip wouldn't puncture. Maksim had to tear the skin with his nail and pull the needle's point through to the other side. And then pull the thread through. And that was just one stitch.

Maksim realized he was crying. The tears were streaming from his eyes involuntarily, not even from mortification or embarrassment that he couldn't repeat the feat of the Thai terrorists, but simply from pain, like a child. Letting the needle dangle on the thread sticking out of his lip, Maksim reached into his jacket pocket, took out his sunglasses, and put them on, so the reporters and his comrades wouldn't see his tears. And he tried to sew again. Once again he jabbed the needle and drilled. Now the blood was flowing not just into his mouth but down his chin, down the front and back of his neck. Saying, "What are you doing!" a policeman turned away. Maksim went on sewing. Blood was running over his tongue and down his throat and tears over his palate. Altogether, it took him at least a quarter of an hour to make just five stitches and appear before the reporters with a truly sewn mouth.

Right then the emergency crew arrived, clipped the chain with hydraulic shears, and undid the handcuffs, and the policemen loaded the protestors into the van and took them off to the station.

At the station the emergency physician who had been called in to treat the wounds on Maksim's lips said, "You dope! How did you manage to plow up your entire mouth?"

"I couldn't get the needle through" Maksim lisped in reply.

His lips had swollen up and it hurt to talk.

"Dummy." The doctor smiled. "You have to hold the lips taut when you sew. With your fingers. Then they puncture easily. You should have called me. I could have triple-sewn your lips shut in thirty seconds."

PORTRAIT OF A PRESIDENT

After that bloody debut, direct actions came more easily to Maksim. One day Cheboksary's authorities prohibited a Naitonal Bolshevik rally on the Day of Reconciliation and Accord. So Maksim and his comrades climbed the highest tower in the city and threw leaflets out over the city. He was immediately arrested, taken to the police station, and given his first fifteen days for hooliganism.

Another time, when the Lithuanian authorities introduced visas for Russians taking the train from Moscow to Kaliningrad through Lithuania, Maksim and his comrades seized a Moscow-Kaliningrad passenger train. They boarded the train at Belorussky Station in Moscow. They gave their passports in law-abiding fashion to the Lithuanian consul passing through the cars and sticking transit visas in Russian passports. The consul put the visas in. But as soon as the consul left, the young men tore the visas from their passports and burned them. At the Lithuanian border they handcuffed themselves to the metal handles in the cars and shouted, "This is Russian territory!"— and the Lithuanian authorities were forced to detach the car, arrest the protestors, and put them in a Lithuanian prison.

Maksim liked the Lithuanian prison. Compared with Russian prisons, where he had already had to spend several days, the Lithuanian prison was a resort. The cells had electrical outlets and television stands in case relatives brought the prisoner a television. But first and foremost, you could lie around on your bed as much as you liked and sleep the whole day. Maksim simply slept through his month-and-a-half sentence. He even became famous in the narrow circle of revolutionaries and policemen. In Russia he started landing in prison not for participating in National Bolshevik direct actions but while these actions were still in preparation. Two young toughs might approach him on the street, ask for a cigarette, start a fight, and as soon as Maksim started defending himself, officers from UBOP, the department fighting organized crime, would seem to pop up out of nowhere, arrest Maksim, accuse him of starting the fight, and lock him up for fifteen days.

After the fifteen days had passed, Maksim had only to pass out of the prison gates when two young toughs would come up to him again, ask for a cigarette, and start a fight . . . Maksim would go back to prison without even managing to get home.

Maksim came up with the idea of hunger strikes in response to these kinds of provocations. The minute he ended up in prison he would declare a hunger strike to protest his illegal arrest. Fifteen days later he would emerge from prison gaunt and transparent from hunger. Policemen were afraid to beat him and afraid to put him in prison again, afraid he would die, so they would let him fatten up. This was enough time to go to Moscow to see his friends, for instance. To sit it out and wait for the next anti-National Bolshevik campaign. It was even fun.

Everything changed when Eduard Limonov was arrested in Moscow on firearms possession and for planning an armed uprising. On the day of Limonov's arrest, late in the evening, the doorbell rang at Maksim's Cheboksary apartment. Maksim opened up. On the threshold stood investigators from the organized crime department, and they had a search warrant. He had to let them in. Maksim watched carefully to make sure the investigators didn't plant a packet of drugs or a box of submachine-gun cartridges. First, Maksim asked the investigators to examine the washroom and toilet, in the presence of witnesses. If an investigator wanted to plant anything, he would shyly go into the toilet to take care of business, hide cartridges there, and then find them himself, but not in the presence of witnesses. This time, though, the investigators did not try to plant anything. They apparently took Maksim seriously—whether as a hardened criminal or as a law-abiding citizen who might really help them solve a serious crime.

Maksim's two-year-old daughter was asleep in the nursery. She was ill. She had a high fever. The investigators asked Maksim to pick up his daughter so they could search the child's bed more easily. Maksim obeyed. He picked up the child and kissed her forehead, which was dry and hot.

Maksim's wife wasn't home.

After the search the investigators said, "You're going to have to come with us to the office for questioning."

"I don't have anyone to leave my child with."

"We'll take you for questioning with the child and bring you back."

"The little girl is sick."

"It's warm in the car. Don't worry."

They questioned Maksim for a long time. The little girl slept in his arms throughout the entire interrogation. He answered calmly so as not to disturb the child. After the interrogation, the UBOP officers did in fact take Maksim and his daughter home and held the doors for him so they wouldn't slam and wake the little girl up.

From the moment of Limonov's arrest, the life of the National Bolshevik Party became rather serious and restrained. Many members left the party, and those who remained began looking more serious. The endless hanging out in the Bunker drinking beer ended. Intra-party romances were reduced to a minimum. Now that Limonov was in prison, Maksim realized that leaving the party or even stopping serious party work would be a betrayal. He read the newspapers carefully. He and his comrades found fault with every step the government took. He came up with protest actions that were increasingly decisive and increasingly desperate.

Maksim carried out his most desperate and most decisive action in 2004. Limonov was already at liberty. In the Bunker, Maksim's eye came across a bill being discussed in the State Duma on benefit monetization. The essence of the law, which had been drawn up by Health Minister Zurabov, was that the state would no longer fixed cover treatment for the elderly and disabled, allocating only a fixed sum of money to treat each disabled and elderly person in the country. The disabled could receive the assistance due them in monetary form and purchase their medicine themselves. They could also get free medicine, but only up to a certain designated amount. Moreover, the Health Ministry was assuming that not all the disabled really needed medicine; consequently, the money allocated for healthy disabled people could go to sick disabled people.

"What bull!" Maksim said, not to any of the comrades with him in the Bunker at that moment but seemingly to the sky. "Zurabov wants to apply the principle of medical insurance to the disabled. Ten people pay insurance. Two of the ten are sick, the eight who are healthy pay for them, then these two get well and they start paying for whoever has gotten sick. But that doesn't happen with the disabled! All ten of them are sick! All ten of them are sick, understand? Always!"

His comrades didn't even argue with Maksim. Many didn't even want to examine whether Zurabov's benefit monetarization law was fair or not. They just felt that this law unquestionably demanded protests, and that it would be easy and simple to protest in defense of the elderly and disabled, to protest being deeply confident of their own rightness.

All they had to do was come up with an action.

The law was supposed to have its first reading and discussion in the State Duma on July 2. The night before, Maksim bought a few giant pieces of fabric. By six in the morning he and his comrades had sewn these pieces into a giant canvas on which they had written "Canceling benefits is a crime against the nation." At nine in the morning they arrived at Okhotny Ryad and climbed to the roof of the Moskva Hotel, which was then being demolished, and the construction site was walled off with huge billboards advertising an expensive BMW. They climbed up and waited for the stroke of ten, when discussion of the benefits law was supposed to begin in the Duma, to hang their canvas over the expensive BMW. The banner was revealed in all its glory right across from the deputies' windows. The Duma guards began rushing about. Taking advantage of the confusion, Maksim and his comrades fled, so that not one of them was even arrested.

However, the law was approved on first reading, and the members of parliament, as well as the parliament's accredited journalists, preferred not to make note of the banner hanging across from the Duma.

The law was supposed to be approved on second and third reading on August 2. The night before, Maksim went to a bookstore. He purchased two portraits of President Putin. At two hundred fifty rubles apiece. Wildly expensive.

On the morning of the 2nd, a few National Bolsheviks wearing the uniforms of Emergency Ministry rescuers walked up to the Health Ministry building.

"Emergency training exercises! Fire drill," Maksim politely told the guards at the entrance, and he smiled. "All employees must gather outside and sign the list."

With these words he headed decisively into the building and the guards didn't stop him. The other costumed National Bolsheviks strode behind. They went up a couple of floors and into an office with windows that looked out on the street, in order to give the previously alerted reporters a good shot, and Maksim again politely told the women working in the office,

"Emergency training exercises! Don't worry. We're working out a fire evacuation route. You just need to go downstairs and outside, sign the list, and that's it. Forgive us for the disturbance." The women collected themselves and headed for the exit. One forgot her purse, and Maksim called to her.

"Madam citizen, don't forget your purse, anything might happen, you know . . ." The woman smiled. She went back for her purse. She smiled again. She seemed to like the firefighter in the Emergency Ministry uniform.

When the employees had gone out, Maksim and his comrades barricaded the doors and flung the windows open.

"The building has been seized!" Maksim shouted to the street, and in response to his cries camera shutters started clicking and flashes flashing below. "We are protesting the criminal monetization of benefits."

While Maksim was saying this, one of his comrades pulled out of a folder one of the portraits of Putin and threw it out the window. There were portraits of Putin hanging on the office wall, of course, but the National Bolsheviks purposely decided to toss out their own, not the ministry's, so that they couldn't be accused of defacing state property those portraits, that is, ministry assets.

From the outside, from the reporters' point of view, it was supposed to look as if the National Bolsheviks had seized the ministry and were ripping portraits of the president off the walls and tossing them out the window. In fact, it didn't look like that at all. Maksim's comrade threw the portrait in such an inept way that no one noticed it was a portrait of the president and not another leaflet.

Then Maksim took a second portrait, poked his head out the window with it, and waited for all the reporters to focus their lenses on him before letting the portrait fall. It fell handsomely, that portrait, and glided spectacularly. A few hours later, all the world news agencies had sent out photographs showing National Bolshevik Gromov throwing the president's portrait out the ministry window. That is basically where the action ended. The police entered the building. The National Bolsheviks themselves opened the door so that the guardians of order wouldn't have to break it down and damage state property. An hour later all of the action's participants had been taken to the station. Four hours later papers had been filled out on them. Six hours later the district judge convicted them of hooliganism under an administrative article and fined each one a thousand rubles. And they were released to their homes.

AN ESPECIALLY DANGEROUS CRIMINAL

But the photographs of the flying portrait came out too beautifully. Too many newspapers printed them. The next morning there was a knock at the door of the apartment of one of the National Bolsheviks where the action participants had gone to spend the night. Maksim went to the door.

"Take this subpoena from the prosecutor's office," said a male voice behind the door.

"I won't open up," Maksim replied.

"What am I supposed to do?" the voice insisted. "I have orders for you to take the subpoena and sign for it."

"Maks, open it," the father of their comrade who lived in the apartment, the apartment's owner, told Maksim. "The subpoena is for me. About my dear son. I'll sign."

Maksim opened up. About twenty OMON men burst through the door, knocked Maksim to the ground, twisted his arms behind his back, and handcuffed him. Maksim didn't see what happened to his comrades. All he saw was an OMON colonel leaning over him, removing his passport from his jeans' back pocket, taking three hundred rubles (all his money) out of the passport, and pocketing it. And following arrest procedure, handing the passport to the escort.

Then one more OMON officer walked over to Maksim as he lay on the floor. He slowly put one heavily booted foot on Maksim's face and threw all his weight on it. Maksim thought the skin was going to come off his cheekbones and his eyes were going to pop out. But the officer stood on Maksim's face in his boots and lightly bounced, as if taking a little jump.

"A heroic deed!" Maksim rasped from under the officer's soles.

The officer stood there a little longer and stepped off the arrested man's face. They picked Maksim up, put him not in the usual van but in a black UBOP Mercedes, and took him alone to Petrovka to the remand prison.

They barely beat Maksim on Petrovka. It was frightening enough that the investigation of their case was being handled by a special investigations team made up of twelve men led by Lieutenant Colonel Alimov, an investigator tipically assigned to especially important cases, robberies and murders. The investigation was completed in a week.

During the trial Maksim was moved to Matrosskaya Tishina, where there was a huge common cell that held fifty people twenty more than it should have. There were two tiers of cots along the walls, and the prisoners sat on the cots naked because the stuffiness and heat were unbearable otherwise. The moment Maksim entered the cell, one of the prisoners said, nodding at Maksim's criminal case, which Maksim had to study before his trial, "You a political?"

The file (Maksim was holding it under his arm) was fat: too many pages to be a simple crime.

The trial was just as speedy as the investigation. Without a doubt, someone's supreme will was driving the state prosecutor and judge on because usually they were in no hurry. State

Prosecutor Tsirkun rushed, lumped the charges together, accused the National Bolsheviks of damaging state property and conspiring to overthrow the state—he accused them of all sorts of things. Once, right during the trial, Maksim called State Prosecutor Tsirkun by the offensive nickname Tsirkach, or Acrobat, which was what everyone on trial called him behind his back. The judge ordered the bailiffs to take Maksim out. They took him to a cell set up at court and beat him.

That evening, when they brought Maksim to his Matrosskaya Tishina cell, the prisoners were playing cards. Maksim put his things on his cot and asked, "Excuse me, could you move over a little?" It was his rule to be emphatically polite with his cellmates.

"Who are you telling to get fucked?" one of the card players snarled.

Maksim realized it was all over for him. The escort at the courthouse was unlikely to beat him to death, but the prisoners in his cell might. If the prison administration promised them release or a relaxed sentence, they might kill him and the whole cell would keep mum, covering up who'd killed him. Maksim realized it was all over.

"Who are you telling to get fucked?" The burly cellmate continued to advance on Maksim. According to thieves' principles, that word was a deadly insult.

"No one," Maksim replied quietly. "You've got something confused. I generally don't use obscene words."

"Who are you telling?" A few notes of bravado, thieves' hysterics, slipped into this prisoner's voice, and a homemade knife was retrieved from his boot.

"No one." Maksim shut his eyes and prepared for the knife thrust, the dull grinding of his flesh, the warm pain in his pelvis—and death.

The cots over Maksim's head creaked, two bare feet hung down, and a man Maksim had never seen before dropped heavily to the concrete floor. He was wearing track pants and was naked to the waist. His whole chest, back, shoulders, and arms were covered with tattoos, testifying to an entire life spent in prison. His eyes were cold and expressed not even a hint of compassion. This Great Urka, so respected by the cell that for several days he had not even had to come down from his cot and appear before Maksim, now gave a brief wave of his hand. Maksim thought this was the knife thrust. But no, it was a gesture of contempt. With this small gesture, as if he were brushing a tick off his collar, Great Urka drove the shouting cellmate away from Maksim. And he said, "He didn't swear." And to Maksim, "Don't be afraid. No one's going to touch you. We don't touch politicals. Live, Revolution. If you have problems, complain to me."

From then on, the nickname pursued Maksim from prison to prison: Revolution.

The next day, when the judge pronounced his sentence, State Prosecutor Tsirkun, a.k.a. Tsirkach, was standing at the courtroom door. Suddenly he was surrounded by the defendants' mothers and fiancées, who started shouting right in his face that he was an executioner. At first Tsirkun was taken aback, but then he himself started shouting, waving the women away.

"You Bolsheviks were in power. You stood my great-grandfather up against the wall for being a bourgeois! And no one blinked an eye! I hate your Bolshevik power! Understand?" he shouted, as if the National Bolsheviks, not he, State Prosecutor Tsirkun, represented the state. "I hate you! Damn Communists! What did you do to the country? When you slashed the bellies of pregnant women with your sabers? Did you feel sorry? You fighters for the class idea! Yes? Well! Shoot me! Hang me! I hate you, damn Commies! Understand? I will always trample you underfoot!"

He had trampled National Bolshevik Gromov as best he could, this Prosecutor Tsirkun. For entering a ministry office and throwing a portrait of the president out the window he had demanded five years of hard prison time for Maksim. And the judge had agreed.

A couple of days later Maksim was transferred from Matrosskaya Tishina. They took him to the train station in a van and loaded him on a second-class sleeping car for prisoners. The sections of this car were separated by bars. And if free people rode in a section like that in fours, then prisoners rode in eights.

The train rocked over the rails for a week. Sometimes, besides gruel, the convoy guards gave the prisoners hot water to brew tea. But there was plenty of bread. Sometimes, when it suited the guards, the prisoners were taken to the toilet one at a time. There was no door to the toilet. The prisoner did his business and the guard watched him the whole time.

A week later they brought Maksim to Ufa, to one of the model colonies where the justice minister took EU commissars and reporters on excursions if he had to. To the famous "bitch zone," where 98% of the prisoners were stoolies—that is, they collaborated with the administration. That is, they had signed a commitment to inform on their comrades.

Right after Maksim had warmed up and taken a shower, the camp's deputy chief, Prokhorov, ordered Maksim to sign a commitment to work at least two hours a week. Maksim refused. The commitment to work could always be used against a prisoner, they could always impose a penalty on the prisoner for committing to work and not working. Then Prokhorov suggested Maksim sign a statement asking to join the "discipline and order section." That is, the informers' section. Maksim refused.

So he went to a punishment cell. For refusing to inform he spent two hundred days in solitary. Then another fourteen months in the camp prison. He did not see the sun for two years. Then Moscow human-rights activists took up his cause, and for a short time, just before the end of his sentence, Maksim was moved to general population. This was prison, too, of course, but you could walk outside from barrack to barrack, you could see daylight, you could breathe air.

From time to time Maksim was called in by Deputy Chief Prokhorov and was ordered over and over to become a stool pigeon. Each time Maksim refused, realizing that by evening he would be in a punishment cell. A formal excuse was always found. Guards would come into Maksim's cell and say, "Gromov, tell us, where's your dirt?"

"Look under the basin." Maksim bared his teeth as usual.

And the guards wrote down that prisoner Gromov was not keeping his cell clean.

"What other violation shall we write down for you?" The guard laughed.

"Write that my rag is crumpled." Maksim bared his teeth.

And he put his hands behind his back. And he headed for solitary—because there was dirt under his basin and his rag was crumpled—for fifteen days.

So it went this time too. He had little more than a month left until his release.

Deputy Chief Prokhorov called Maksim in and asked, "Gromov, you're going to go free soon, and then what? Are you going to write about me in the newspapers?"

"Of course I am," Maksim replied. "You know me, citizen chief. I wasn't silent here, and I won't be silent at liberty."

"You will, Gromov." The chief's look was leaden. "You will be silent! Because before you get out of here you're going to piss yourself." He jerked Maksim by the collar of his prison jacket, tore the collar, and barked, "A violation of the uniform, fifteen days!"

That was how Maksim ended up in the punishment cell for the last time. He declared a hunger strike in protest. For ten days straight his head swam from the screaming, incessant children's songs. He tried to remember the poem: ". . . It's the young men being chased to the black grindstone, to press the wine." And through the children's songs he still heard the feeding slot rattle in the cell door, the guard shout, "Gromov coming out," and the key clanking in the lock. He stood up, put his hands behind his back, and started walking.

They led him to the torture chamber, threw him on the floor, and started kicking him. Systematically. Maksim had already been beaten this way several times. Maksim knew the guards beat the prisoner either until he agreed to carry out the administration's demands or until the prisoner started defecating involuntarily. Maksim knew they didn't want to kill the prisoner, they beat him "until he shat himself," but Maksim also knew that the guards didn't have the sense to understand that after a ten-day hunger strike prisoner Gromov simply couldn't shit himself. They beat Maksim, and he realized his organism was incapable of giving his executioners this signal— which they understood and which humiliated the person being beaten—to stop. Maksim realized they would beat him to death. And in his head burned the words that by that time had become the National Bolshevik motto, borrowed from the English "Yes! Death!"

These words became more and more vivid in his mind and then they went out. All the lights went out. Everything disappeared. Maksim plunged into darkness. But then he suddenly surfaced from the darkness and opened his eyes. It wasn't death yet. It was loss of consciousness.

Seeing that the prisoner had come around, the guards continued beating him. Yes! Death! The world around Maksim went out again. The darkness was complete. There were no more guards, no more prison, no more Deputy Chief Prokhorov, no more President Putin, no more writer Limonov, no more Maksim, no more little daughter, and, most important, no more pain. Yes, death.

But this wasn't death yet either. Maksim opened his eyes and felt the cold. A cutting into his wrists and cold. Water was being splashed in his face and running into his nostrils and not letting him breathe. Only when they took the water away did Maksim realize that while he was unconscious they had hung him from the prison bars by his handcuffs and beaten him in the face with a fire hose nozzle. That was what the pain in his wrists was. And that was what the water in his nostrils was. Maksim lost consciousness again and woke up in his cell. Alive. Alive, judging by how his body hurt and especially how his wrists, rubbed raw by the handcuffs, burned.

A month later, when it came time for Maksim to be released, his wounds had almost healed. Usually prisoners are released at ten in the morning, after being allowed to shave and take a shower before being sent home. But politicals are released at dawn, so that human-rights activists and reporters don't meet them at the prison gates.

It was a warm summer morning. Right at dawn. A red sun risinig. The gates cracked open. Maksim stepped outside. The road leading away from the camp looped around. A few little houses and copses. People ran out toward Maksim from the nearest copse, three people, two men and a woman. For a second Maksim thought they were provocateurs, but a second later he recognized in these running people his comrades, who knew that politicals are released at dawn and had been keeping watch there since midnight.

They embraced and started walking with their arms around each other, past the copses toward the Belaya River. Maksim took off his clothes and walked into the water. He sat on a dock-tailed rock in the middle of the river. And the young woman who had met him handed him a razor. Maksim scraped his cheeks, and the razor was sharp, and the water was cold, and the sun was warm.

And you don't know what happiness that is.

CHAPTER 9
Natalya Morar:
A Beautiful Brunette with Brown Eyes

I'm denied entry into Russia! Ilya! I'm denied entry into Russia!"

The Israeli flight arrived late. The hall at Domodedovo airport where the passport control booths were and the symbolic line of the Russian border was drawn across the floor in red paint was empty. Not a soul. Therefore her cry reverberated.

"I'm denied entry into Russia! Ilya!"

Ten hours earlier, Natasha Morar had been strolling with her fiancé, Ilya Barabanov, along the sea in Caesarea. They'd been on a business trip, a business trip more like a vacation or an excursion. They lagged behind the group of Russian journalists who had been invited to Israel to learn something about the Holocaust, and they were strolling, arm in arm, along the beach. It was December 2007 and 20 degrees Celsius. The wind ruffled Natasha's long hair. The wind tore the flag from the flagpole of the seaside hotel and pulled it in the direction of Lebanon. The wind drove the waves to lie on the sand at their feet, and Natasha ran from the waves and laughed when her sandals got wet. But it was unbearably sad. They had spent an entire happy year together and now it was as if they were saying good-bye. It had been so sad ten hours earlier, as if they had known they really were saying good-bye.

Four hours earlier, they had boarded a plane in Tel Aviv, and the plane had set its course for Moscow. Through the window Natasha had seen the sea, gloomy at night, and the little lights of the steamers and yachts sprinkled over the sea. They dozed in each other's arms, wasting two whole hours on sleep before their parting.

Forty minutes earlier, when the plane landed, they were walking down the concourse in the chaotic and bustling crowd, such as only Jews know how to create if they are led somewhere as a crowd. "Sonechka, where's your basket? . . . Children, children, hold hands, you'll get lost, children! . . . Yasha, wrap up your throat, you have a pacemaker! . . ." They stood in line for the passport control booth, close to the very back of this chaotic crowd. Finally, Natasha walked up to the border guard, held out her passport as a citizen of Moldova, and said hello. The border guards in these glass booths are typically stern and never say hello. They just look sternly at the photograph in the passport, at you, and back at the photograph. Like any foreigner crossing the Russian border, Natasha felt like going into explanations, telling them that her documents were in perfect order, that Moldova and Russia did not require visas, that the Russian Federation's constitution guaranteed freedom of movement . . . But Natasha held her tongue, realizing that the border guard was not smiling or saying hello simply out of habit and it had nothing to do with the fact that she had seen a Moldovan. The gloomy woman examined Natasha's passport for a long time, stuck it in a scanner, tapped the computer keys—for such a long time that the neighboring lines ran out, and Ilya passed through passport control at another window and went to wait for their suitcases, which were supposed to tumble out of the airport's womb onto the conveyor belt and circle, in search of their owners.

He had passed through passport control, and there was no one left near Natasha on the Russian border. And when there was no one left, the border guard asked, "Are you Natalya Grigoriyevna Morar?"

That scared Natasha. Because Moldovan passports don't have patronymics. The border guard could not have learned her patronymic from her passport. She had probably learned it from the computer, from some letter or order. The faceless state machine for some reason turned out to be looking for Natalya Grigoriyevna Morar and had entered her into its memory while she was strolling with her beloved on the beach in Caesarea. Nothing good could come of that question.

Natasha replied, "Yes, I am Natalya Grigoriyevna Morar."

A senior border officer appeared. He called Natasha aside, led her to a room, asked her to show her press card, asked her to show her ticket, asked her whether she had any other documents attesting to her identity, and then finally said, "Natalya Grigoriyevna, you are denied entry into Russia. You will now fly back to Israel."

"Why? On what grounds?" Natasha babbled. Then she took herself in hand and said, "First of all, introduce yourself."

"I have the right not to introduce myself," the officer lied. "The basis for your deportation is an order from the central apparatus of the Federal Security Service of Russia"—a piling up of prepositional phrases, she felt like sleeping, sleeping in Ilya's arms, and then waking up, smiling, and going to make coffee . . . "I'm just carrying out orders. I don't have the right to explain anything."

Snatches of thought flashed through Natasha's mind. She imagined her uncollected suitcase circling endlessly on the conveyor belt. She imagined returning to Israel.

"Wait a minute, why Israel? I don't have a multiple Israeli visa. They won't let me into Israel!"

"I don't know." The officer shrugged. "You could be flying between Moscow and Tel Aviv your whole life. That's no concern of ours."

Natasha freaked out. She looked around. There was no one in the hall. A fluorescent light blinked overhead, imitating the sound of moths beating against a lamp. Moscow, where Natasha had spent the last six years of her life, was right there, beyond the frosted-glass walls, but she couldn't go there. What about the apartment? Natasha thought. I am renting an apartment, after all. And my things? I don't even have a change of clothes.

Right then Ilya peeked out from behind the passport control booth. According to the rules, after passing through passport control he was supposed to go get his suitcase, but he'd returned because Natasha still hadn't come.

There were twenty meters of empty space between her and Ilya, but Natasha shouted, "I'm denied entry into Russia! Ilya! I'm denied entry into Russia!"

And Ilya started shouting, too. From behind the red line, without crossing the border, he shouted to the border guards that they had no right, that there were at least two television cameras here at the airport, that an Ekho Moskvy radio correspondent was on his way . . .

But the border officer told him, "If you really want to help your girlfriend, go buy her a ticket home, to Chisinau. Otherwise I'll be forced to send her to Tel Aviv."

The journalists Natasha had traveled to Israel with dashed off and bought her a ticket to Chisinau. Despite the late hour, Ilya called Yevgenia Albats, the deputy editor-in-chief of his magazine. He said they wouldn't let Natasha into the country, and as he said this, his voice was quaking.

Albats, who strictly forbade any office romances, didn't know that Natasha and Ilya were involved. When Ilya called her in the middle of the night, her first thought was that a person's voice wouldn't quake like that if a mere colleague wasn't being allowed into the country.

In less than an hour, Albats arrived at the airport. She brought a lawyer, the Ekho Moskvy radio correspondent Irina Vorobyova, croissants, and a bottle of water. The lawyer was useless. Every half hour Vorobyova went on the air with the news about how Natalya Morar, a journalist for the opposition magazine *The New Times*, had been denied entry into Russia. But that was useless as well. The croissants were useful. Natasha was hungry.

By some miracle they allowed Albats to pass through the "green corridor" to see Natasha briefly. Through a labyrinth of frosted-glass panels and past a machine that saw through suitcases. Albats was going to give her the croissants. She was shaken. She told Natasha not to worry. A few days would pass and the misunderstanding would be resolved. But she was shaken.

They also allowed Ilya to go through the "green corridor" to see Natasha. To bring her suitcase and Air Moldova ticket. They said good-bye standing on opposite sides of the symbolic red line that designated the Russian border. Standing next to them was a border officer. Natasha asked the officer to go away for a moment and leave them alone, but he refused.

Natasha suddenly remembered the presents bought in Israel for Ilya's mother that were in her suitcase, and the presents for her own mother in Ilya's. She opened the suitcases and started transferring the gifts. Salt from the Dead Sea, a piece of the white limestone Jerusalem is built from, a cypress cross, light blouses, summer dresses . . . And it also became clear that many women's and men's items were jumbled up in the suitcases. Natasha started transferring, separating, their things.

At this the officer said, "That's it! Let's go."

The young people kissed across the red line.

Ilya said, "Don't be afraid, we'll get you out of this."

Natasha picked up her suitcase and started to follow the officer. What she felt was a kind of euphoria. The way an injured person thinks for several minutes that he can still walk. She walked and thought that the next day a scandal would erupt over her in the media. She thought lawyers would get involved. Her human-rights activist friends . . . Then she looked back. Ilya was standing on the red line watching her.

Tears poured down her face for the first time, bitter, childish, powerless tears.

The officer led her to a tiny room. Two by three meters. The room had an outlet, a bench with four plastic seats, and not a single window.

"They're deporting me?" Natasha asked gathering her thoughts. "Deportation requires a court decision."

"You're not being deported," the officer parried. "You're denied entry."

"Then why do I have to be in a room for people being deported? Why can't I sit in the waiting room, in the bar?"

"Go in!"

The officer gave Natasha a gentle shove into the windowless room and shut the door behind her.

THOUGHTS OF AN EXILE

Natasha sat in that tiny room and all kinds of thoughts bounced around in her head. When did this start? Why? When? In school? How did she come to be the invariable instigator of all the children's mutinies and revolutions back in school? Why? She wasn't supposed to be. She was supposed to be quiet and grateful. A girl from the little town of Hincesti, the kind of provincial hole where there isn't the slightest chance not just of a good education and career but even of a decent marriage. Because all the men worth anything deliberately left Moldova to make their living in Moscow. A little girl from a nearly destitute family, where for a whole week there might be nothing but plain beans or plain macaroni for supper. Where the only luxuries they bought were flowers and newspapers. Because flowers are beautiful, little girl, and the newspapers write about the great shining world where you will never go, poor little girl.

All Natasha's mother could do for her was move to Chisinau and put her little girl in a Russian school. Maybe someday, somehow . . . But the school was pretty bad. There was no point dreaming about going to university with that education. And then Natasha got lucky. A physics teacher from Gaudeamus, the best private school in Chisinau, came to their pretty bad school to make some extra money. For some reason this teacher decided that Natasha was a math genius, and she persuaded the director of the private school, where tuition was a hundred dollars a month, an unbelievable sum for Moldova, to take the girl for free.

Natasha was supposed to be quiet and grateful. But one day this same teacher forbade her to shut the window during the lesson. Natasha's classmate—not even her friend—Lyuda was sitting next to the window. Lyuda had a cold that day. It was chilly by the open window. She was shivering. Suddenly it seemed to Natasha that there was nothing in the world more important than that window and ill Lyuda, and she shouted to the teacher, "That's not right!" When one child shouts, you know, the others do, too, and they shouted that she should close the window, and the teacher gave them all bad marks. The children rebelled, left the classroom, and complained to the principal. The next day the teacher drew up a letter on the children's behalf saying that there had been no window or unfair bad grades, just bad children. In class the teacher demanded that the children sign the letter. She turned first to Natasha Morar, her pet, her protégé, who was supposed to be quiet and grateful.

"All right, Natasha, sign."

Natasha stood up because school etiquette required that you stand when the teacher spoke to you. She walked up to the teacher's desk since she was already up. She looked at the false letter on the desk and said, "No, I won't sign."

And she headed for the door. That "no" meant the loss of

her protector and expulsion from Gaudeamus. "No" meant that, for the sake of her ill classmate Lyuda, Natasha had let her only chance slip. The girl walked up to the door, flung it open, and strode out of the classroom, like St. Simeon into the deaf and dumb arms of death. But while St. Simeon had baby Jesus gurgling behind him, Natasha's exit was followed by the rumble of chairs being pushed back, murmuring and the stomping of feet. The whole class followed her out. Without even looking around, Natasha realized what this was, how this could happen when people supported you, when people, damn them all, followed you. No one expelled her from Gaudeamus. In eleventh grade, having become passionate about sociology rather than mathematics or physics, contrary to expectations, Natasha wrote her thesis about the possibility of subliminal psychological influence on young people, and the school principal proudly entered Natasha's paper in a competition for best pupils' theses in Moscow.

Click! The door to the deportees' room opened. The same officer led in a wordless and frightened Tajik. The Tajik sat on the edge of his seat, and the officer went out and locked the door again.

"Hello." Natasha smiled. "Are they deporting you, too?"

The Tajik did not reply. He didn't seem to know Russian or else had a rule never to say anything in this foreign country but simply obey without demur. He was a frail man in ragged clothing. It looked as though they'd beaten him before deporting him. He was silent anyway.

Maybe I should adopt the rule of always remaining silent, Natasha thought. Maybe I should have been silent from the day I arrived in Moscow.

She'd arrived in Moscow for the thesis competition when she was seventeen. She even won a prize. But that wasn't the point. Moscow was the first big city Natasha had seen in her life. The colorful lights, the colorful people, the big, shiny world Natasha had only dreamed of seeing before, if only a glimpse. She went to the museums, whose visitors all seemed smart. She went to theaters, one better than the next. She did not go into the expensive stores on the streets, but the expensive stores' customers seemed unbelievably beautiful.

The competition was held at the university. When Natasha stepped onto the university grounds, the huge classroom buildings surrounded her, grasping her like stone hands. And she thought that more than anything in the world she wanted to study here. That summer she returned to Moscow to enroll in the sociology department.

In Moldova, when children go to Moscow to compete for the university, their parents usually go with them. They go for a whole month and take lots and lots of provisions. They stay with their Moscow relatives. They bring food: jars and jars of red bell peppers, oozing ripe sheep's cheese, irreparably sour wine. A month later, when their child does not get into the university owing to poor preparation and the lack of money for bribes, they go home and tell stories for a whole year about how they went to Moscow, how everyone rushes and shoves there, and how the police detained them for not registering their presence in Moscow.

Natasha insisted on going alone. The trip with her mother would have been twice as expensive, and Natasha knew her mother was going to have to borrow the money even for one ticket to Moscow and back. The night before her departure, her mother was watching a show on Russian television, *Man and the Law*, about bribes at institutions of higher education. On the program they said that the bribe for being admitted to the sociology department at Moscow State University was $25,000. More than their Chisinau apartment cost.

"Don't go anywhere," her mother said. "It's no use."

But Natasha went anyway. Of all the matriculants, only

four received an "excellent" on the mathematics exam, and Natasha was among them. Of all the students admitted for a free education, only one-fourth got in without bribes, and Natasha was among them. Her great dream had come true. Even stranger, less than five years later Natasha quarreled with her academic advisor, incited a student rebellion against the chairman of her department, and organized a sit-in in the chancellor's waiting room.

She wrote her term papers and thesis in the political science department. Her academic advisor headed up the campaign headquarters of one of the leaders of the United Russia Party who was running for the Moscow City Duma. One day he told all of his students to go to the headquarters for practical experience: to answer the phone and run small errands. Everyone but Natasha did. The next day, in front of all the students in the group, the professor flung Natasha's term paper so that the pages flew all over the classroom. He shouted that Natasha would never get a better job than serving her boss coffee. He demanded that Natasha come see him in his office after the seminar.

She did.

"Why weren't you at headquarters?" the professor asked.

"It goes against my convictions," Natasha said distinctly. "I wouldn't lift a finger for United Russia to come to power again. If I need practical experience in a campaign headquarters, I'm working with Ilya Yashin at the Yabloko campaign headquarters and also at the campaign headquarters of Viktor Shenderovich, who's running for the State Duma. I'll bring you a note. And an evaluation."

The professor rubbed his temples with his fingers, stood up, paced the two steps to the wall and back.

"Child . . . I recognize my younger self in you. I was just as uncompromising." It was as if he were trying to justify himself. "But you'll grow up. Life is more complicated. I'm not helping

United Russia, I'm helping a specific person, and he's a good person."

Natasha smiled and the professor continued. "All right, he is a member of United Russia, but that doesn't mean anything."

The next day, at the department meeting, this professor said that all of his students were doing decent work and there was just one student Natalya Morar, who wasn't amounting to anything. Natasha had to change departments and write her thesis on a nonpolitical topic that didn't interest her.

Matters were even more desperate with Dobrenkov, the chairman of the sociology department. This Dobrenkov had his own interviews hung up all over the department, interviews given to various newspapers, all in a loyalist vein, in each of which he invariably said that Vladimir Putin had been a stroke of luck for the country. All the teachers who had any oppositionist views whatsoever were gradually fired by the department chairman. On the other hand, someone who had written a book about Jews, who, he wrote, were exterminating the Russian people in order to grab living space for themselves, began teaching a special course.

"Forgive me," Natasha's fellow student Ilya Azar asked in the seminar. "I liked your book very much, but what am I to do, what am I to do, professor, if I'm a Jew?"

Natasha also learned for a fact that Chairman Dobrenkov had given his own son the license to run the department café. It was an expensive café. Soup cost three hundred rubles, salad two hundred fifty, meat and potatoes five hundred, while at other student cafeterias in other departments you could eat your fill of not very tasty but perfectly nourishing student food for fifty rubles.

"We want to eat!" That was the slogan with which Natasha and her friends organized their first picket in the sociology department. They didn't even demand that the expensive café be shut down. They demanded that another cheap one be opened. The hungry students' protests easily struck a chord among reporters, who dreamed of writing about student riots but had a hard time provoking anger in the president and State Duma deputies to whom Chairman Dobrenkov wrote letters about how the OD-group represented a threat to the political order, was funded by the Central Intelligence Agency of the United States, propagandized homosexuality, and was turning youth toward an orange revolution, as in the Ukraine. The chairman wrote about homosexuality because Natasha was involved with a young woman at the time. He wrote about the orange revolution because the Kremlin feared an orange revolution. But by order of the chancellor the café was closed anyway, and Dobrenkov's son lost that business.

The OD-group is what the students who organized these protests called themselves. Journalists were inclined to decode the acronym "OD" as Otvet Dobrenkovu—Response to Dobrenkov. In fact, "OD" meant Otryad Dambldora—the Dumbledore brigade. The students had been reading Harry Potter.

They didn't stop with a less expensive café. They demanded the return of dissenting teachers. They demanded an independent commission that would hold a competition to fill professorships. Twenty people burst into the chancellor's waiting room, sat down on the floor, and made a commotion, and they wouldn't leave until the chancellor came out to see them and listened to the demands of students, who, apparently, wanted to study as well as eat.

Actually, by the end of her time at the university she had so dreamed of attending, Natasha knew that all you do at university is take exams; your real studies happen outside university lecture halls. At the entrance to the main building she tore off a sticker with a portrait of Mikhail Khodorkovsky, who had recently been put in prison. She felt sorry for Khodorkovsky. He had founded Open Russia, a philanthropic project providing education for provincial children, and she, a little girl from

Hincesti, knew all too well what a miracle one of the schools organized by Khodorkovsky would have been in her small town, if her town had been Russian and not Moldovan.

At rallies in support of Khodorkovsky in Moscow at the Basmanny Court, Natasha battled her burning shame when she had to unfurl a sign for the first time and stand with it in full view of everyone. She met Marina Litvinovich at these rallies and became friends with young human-rights activists. Together they started organizing I Think, a youth movement, the goal of which was to think. They organized rallies on the one hand, and on the other, lectures at the Higher School of Economics, to which they invited the best economists in the country, like Andrei Illarionov, and favorite writers like Viktor Shenderovich.

At one of the I Think rallies, Natasha met the journalist Yevgenia Albats, who began inviting Natasha and her friends to dinner at her house every Tuesday. They would talk. They would eat the delicious Jewish concoctions Albats prepared—forshmak and ginger cakes—and talk with opposition politicians, journalists, and economists whom Albats, using her journalistic connections, would invite "to speak with the children."

One evening Aleksandr Osovtsov, one of the leaders of Open Russia and a regular at these Tuesday gatherings, called Natasha aside and asked, "Would you like to work for Open Russia?"

"Well"—Natasha attempted to stay calm—"I'd probably find it interesting."

"Then come to Kolpachny tomorrow and we'll talk," Osovtsov concluded, and he walked away, leaning on his famous cane with the silver handle. Natasha went out on the staircase, waited for Osovtsov to leave, and banged her forehead against the wall about fifty times out of joy, because working for Open Russia was a dream come true, even greater than that of studying at Moscow University.

Click! The door of the transit room at Domodedovo airport opened, the border officer brought in yet another Tajik being deported, and again locked the door. The Tajik was wearing training pants, a T-shirt, and slippers, despite the December cold. Natasha thought, "Oh no, I don't have any warm clothing! I left all my warm clothing in Moscow!" Just in case, she smiled at the Tajik and said hello to him. But he was silent. And Natasha returned to her thoughts. "I'll freeze."

The office of Yukos, Mikhail Khodorkovsky's company, was on Kolpachny Lane, and so was the office of Open Russia. And Ilya Barabanov was freezing on Kolpachny. He had fallen in love with Natasha back during the I Think rallies, fallen head over heels during the Tuesday gatherings at Albats's, and was now freezing under the windows of Open Russia, waiting for Natasha to finish work. Natasha refused to see that Ilya was in love with her. She considered him just a friend. She came out of the office, went with Ilya for coffee, and told him, friend to friend, about the serious romance she was having at that time with a famous oppositionist politician. Ilya listened, dying from despair. But he still kept coming to Kolpachny, still kept freezing, and still kept listening to Natasha's revelations, as if he were her best friend.

A couple of months after Natasha's job began, Open Russia's accounts were frozen. The state was systematically devouring Yukos, and finally reached Yukos's philanthropic program. Osovtsov told Natasha flat out that there wasn't going to be any more money. He suggested she leave or, if she could, see the education projects through to spring, to the end of the academic year. Simultaneously Osovtsov said they were preparing a Civic Congress, an international conference with opposition politicians and human-rights activists, and she could work for the Civic Congress as press secretary. The Other Russia coalition grew out of the Civic Congress. A few months later, Other Russia split into political and human-rights wings. Politicians

Kasparov, Kasyanov, and Limonov started organizing the Dissenters' Marches, and human-rights activists grumbled that they couldn't participate in marches with Limonov as long as the proletarian hammer and sickle, which resembled a swastika, appeared on his banners and his 1993 program was posted on his party's site, saying in black and white that liberals should be hanged.

At one of the Other Russia conferences involving Kasparov, Vanya Ninenko—Natasha's old friend from their days of picketing in support of Khodorkovsky—got up and asked Kasparov outright whether he really liked swastikas and whether he shared Limonov's desire to hang liberals since he marched alongside Limonov.

Kasparov gave him hell. He told Vanya Ninenko—who defended Khodorkovsky, organized rallies in support of political prisoners, and organized the I Think lectures—that he, Ninenko, had been specially hired by the Kremlin, that the question was a provocation, and that the Kremlin had paid Ninenko well for that question.

For Natasha, Vanya Ninenko was like that classmate Lyuda shivering by the open window. Only dearer. Natasha and her classmate Lyuda hadn't spent nights drinking in the dorm discussing Baudrillard, hadn't organized the Dumbledore Brigade, hadn't broken bread together. But she had drunk, discussed, organized, and broken bread with Vanya.

She stood up and said, "Garry Kimovich, excuse me, you have just insulted a good person. He is my friend. I can swear that he has never once been hired by the Kremlin. He just wanted to ask, and it seems to me that you could answer, what day and age this is that you can march under swastikas with people who have suggested that someone, anyone, be hanged."

The conference ended. In the lobby Marina Litvinovich, who then worked as Kasparov's aide and a member of the Other Russia political council, walked up to Natasha. Walked up to her and said that basic discipline does not permit Other Russia's press secretary to speak out so harshly against a leader at a public conference.

Her friends told Natasha that after that speech of hers and before finding Natasha in the lobby Litvinovich had shouted, "Who does she think she is, this Morar! How dare she! I'm going to do everything in my power to kick her out of Other Russia."

That evening Natasha told this story to her friend Ilya at the Bilingva Café, which was noisy and cheap, had bad food and a bookstore, and attracted people who cared that it was cheap and had a bookstore. Ilya came up with a plan, a strategy, then and there: the next evening he had a drink with his boss, Yevgenia Albats, the deputy editor in chief of the opposition magazine *The New Times,* and just happened to mention that Morar was leaving Other Russia.

"Natashka!" Albats phoned Natasha immediately. "Natashka!" Albats has a way of adding diminutive suffixes to all names (Natashka, Ilyushka, Barabashka). "I have a brilliant idea! Come work for us!"

"But I'm not a journalist." Natasha was taken aback.

"That doesn't matter! We'll teach you! You see"—Albats has a way of going into explanations immediately—"journalism is the kind of profession you have to try to tell whether you're going to do it your whole life. Come on! Try it!"

And Natasha did. She simply had nowhere else to go. People who had worked for Khodorkovsky's Open Russia, to say nothing of Kasparov's Other Russia, were not going to be given any jobs other than at the last oppositionist magazine, *The New Times,* or the last oppositionist radio station, Ekho Moskvy.

Natasha didn't know how to interview, ask questions, come up with topics, check facts, or string words together. Nonetheless, every Monday she had to announce her topic for the next issue at the editorial board and by Friday she had to have written an article on that topic. Ilya, who sat at the next desk over, helped her. He was an experienced journalist, though he was a year younger than Natasha. The inimitable atmosphere in the rooms where people are putting out a new magazine, where people work without sleep, argue until they're hoarse, and are constantly coming up with ideas together—it was the kind of atmosphere in which people fall in love, especially if those people are twenty-somethings. One evening, when Albats, who usually drove Natasha home, had gone on a business trip, Ilya took it upon himself to see the young woman home. In the back seat of the taxi he just took Natasha by the elbow and drew her slightly toward him. But it was like a flash of electrical current. Velvet lightning.

At the time Natasha was doing research on the Kremlin's "black till." About how, if a political party found itself a sponsor, the sponsor first had to send his donations to the Kremlin and from there the money would be reallocated to the party after a 20% cut. Before this Natasha had researched the Kremlin's ties with Raiffeisenbank and the Kremlin's ties with VTsIOM—the All-Russia Center for the Study of Public Opinion on Social and Economic Questions.

They were riding in the taxi and kissing. They weren't thinking that in a couple of months an acquaintance in the president's administration would tell Ilya confidentially over a mug of beer that they were very unhappy at the top with Natasha's research. They were kissing and not thinking that ten months later, after reading another one of Natasha's articles, the president's deputy chief of staff would say, "Fuck this Morar!" They were kissing and not thinking that a year later Natasha would be denied entry into Russia. If they were worried about anything, it was only how to hide their romance from their boss.

Click! The Chisinau airplane takes off at dawn. The border officer had unlocked the door of the transfer room, led

Natasha out, escorted her through the still empty airport, comprising her convoy, and put her on the plane. The flight attendants were sleepy. The pilot, however, was a daredevil, or possibly upset over something. In the middle of the runway he pulled back on the steering column harder than usual, and the plane shot up like a Roman candle.

RETURN

Ilya went to see her in Chisinau a couple of days later. Then again a week later. Then a week after that. At first Natasha was in a state of euphoria, giving interviews every day, writing inquiries to the consulate, submitting complaints to the court. But the euphoria passed, and Ilya started noticing an anguish in Natasha's eyes. Anguish comes in different forms. There is the inimitable expression of anguish in the eyes of people who have been in prison. And another expression of anguish in people who are seriously ill. But Ilya had never seen the kind of anguish in Natasha's eyes. He had never before seen the eyes of an exile.

Naturally, Natasha was unable to return to Moscow in a few days, as Ilya had promised at the airport, or in a week, or in a month. The pages of Ilya's passport quickly filled up with stamps for crossing the border between Russia and Moldova.

Other Moscow friends besides Ilya came to visit Natasha in Chisinau, including Nikita Belykh, the leader of the oppositionist party Union of Right Forces, a blond who resembled a huge bear and who abstained from alcohol on principle so he wouldn't hurt anyone while drunk, but in Chisinau he let his hair down and cheerfully danced and drank the night away with Natasha in bars. The journalist Oleg Kashin came. He didn't dance, but he and Natasha talked for a long time, and when he returned to Moscow he wrote in a magazine financed by the regime that Yevgenia Albats had purposely set Natasha up for deportation in order to create a scandal that would give *The New Times* a boost.

After about three months, on another of Ilya's visits, they went to a bridal store, bought wedding rings that were too big for their slender fingers, and registered at the district Registry Office without any fuss or white dress or limousine or bridal bouquet.

Ilya was certain that now they would let Natasha into Russia because she was the wife of a Russian citizen. Natasha was certain they weren't going to let her in anyway, but a few days after their quiet wedding she and Ilya went to the airport and boarded the plane from Chisinau to Moscow. Because now she was this man's wife and was therefore ready to go with him to the ends of the earth. However, the fact that they weren't flying alone, that journalists had come flocking from Moscow to fly and cross the border with them dismayed her. The journalists said it might be a good idea to warn the lawyers and human-rights activists in Moscow, but Natasha, who was friendly with many human-rights activists, objected categorically.

"When we want to conceive a child," Natasha said, "are we also going to have to warn the human-rights activists about that?"

In Moscow, at Domodedovo airport, Natasha was the first of her group to approach the passport control booth. She held out her passport, said hello, and smiled. The somber border guard made no reply and did not smile back. A senior border officer appeared immediately and told Natasha that she was denied entry to Russia and that she must leave the country on the same plane she flew in on.

"You will pay a five hundred ruble fine for every minute you delay the plane," the officer said to intimidate her.

But no one believed him. Natasha, Ilya, *New Times* correspondent Armina Bagdasaryan, Ekho Moskvy correspondent

Vladimir Varfolomeyev, and two other correspondents from
RTVI television sat on the benches in the transit hall and began
demanding that the officer take their statements on this violation
of the right to freedom of movement, that they let the lawyer
waiting outside come to them, that he bring them water . . .
But their statements weren't accepted and the lawyer wasn't
allowed in. The television reporters went out for a smoke, but
they were subdued in the smoking room and dragged across
the border by force. Armina Bagdasaryan went to the restroom, where she was caught and also taken across the border
by force. Vladimir Varfolomeyev never left Natasha and Ilya's
side. Policemen approached him, twisted his arms behind his
back, and took him across the red line. Natasha and Ilya were
the only ones left.

Passengers kept walking past them to the passport control
booths. The plane to Chisinau took off. Now the young people
faced spending at least twenty-four hours in the airport, unless
of course they discounted the miracle of Natasha being let
into Russia. Ilya still had hope. His friends called him and
said that Putin was following their story and that the issue
was now being "decided at the very top." Natasha did not
have hope. How could she hope that Putin would feel sorry
for a Moldovan girl?

They hadn't taken any books with them. For lack of anything to do they read the discarded migration cards lying on
the floor. One man, for instance, hadn't known how to write
his name in Russian letters and had written and crossed out
"Aroyan" and then "Aronyan" several times.

They were hungry. The only food was the coffee in the
vending machine. But late in the afternoon the border guards
took pity on them and brought Natasha and Ilya a plastic tray
of airplane food—one for the two of them. The journalists and
friends standing on the other side of the border were not
allowed to pass the newlyweds any food.

As the evening wore on, a Turk sat down next to them on the bench. They weren't letting him into Russia either. He had flown to see his beloved girlfriend, whom he had met at a Turkish resort, but instead of a tourist visa he had accidentally gotten a work visa. And they wouldn't let him in. He had a whole sack of food. He gave Ilya and Natasha food, watched them eat, listened to why they couldn't get into the country, and failed to understand.

Natasha and Ilya lay down on benches in the transit hall. It was cold. Cold and hard. By morning they were thoroughly frozen.

An officer came up to them and said that Ilya was free but Natasha was detained and would be forcibly deported from the country as soon as the Chisinau airplane arrived. Just in case, Natasha and Ilya had belted themselves to each other and then belted themselves to the bench. For this the border guards had forbidden them to move the benches, so they couldn't lie down.

They passed the time with word games. They would choose a long word and in five minutes try to come up with as many small words as possible. Natasha always won. When the word was *politikanstvo*—politicking—the first word that both Ilya and Natasha made was *toska*—anguish.

The second day passed. A detail was assigned to them. A male and a female border guard. There was no more talk of arresting Natasha. It no longer made sense to belt themselves together. The female border guard took Natasha to the restroom. The male border guard took Ilya to the restroom. In the toilet stall Ilya quietly smoked. They wouldn't let him go to the smoking room. Once, sitting in the stall with a cigarette, Ilya heard a man and a woman go into the next stall. The woman was laughing, and the man, who had a Caucasus accent, was telling the woman that he wouldn't insult her and would definitely give her a hundred dollars if she would give him head. Ilya left his stall and saw the two of them: the man was evidently a passenger from some southern flight, and the woman was one of those somber border guards who sit in the passport control booths and never say hello or smile.

When Ilya returned, Natasha complained that her kidneys hurt. There was something wrong with her kidneys. Ilya called a doctor. The doctor examined Natasha and said, "You really need to eat and drink properly. And you can't be in the cold. But what can I do? All I can do is ask that they feed you."

Meanwhile, their journalist friends had flown to Kiev with bags of food and water so that they could return and hand over the food and water to Ilya and Natasha in the airport transit hall.

The third day began. Sleep was impossible. It's very hard to sleep when it's cold and you're sitting on hard chairs. Toward the middle of the third day Ilya started having something like hallucinations. Suddenly he started seeing his own eyelashes. His eyelashes swelled and burst.

Natasha's kidneys hurt. Very badly now. Natasha also said the presidential elections in Russia were two days away.

"If we sit here until the elections," Natasha said, "it will look like we got married and are sitting here as a sign of protest against the elections."

And Ilya said, "We're leaving."

He called the officer on duty. They allowed him to buy a ticket to Chisinau. Three full days in the airport had passed when they boarded the plane to Chisinau.

Behind them in the plane sat a man of such unobtrusive appearance that he screamed FSB agent. The flight attendant went up to them and started speaking in Moldovan to Natasha.

"We were rooting for you. We debated how many days you would last. We're proud of you. If you need anything, call for me."

An hour after takeoff the captain addressed the passengers. He said, "We have cleared Russian airspace!"

That's all he said, but his tone suggested what he was really saying was, "We are in the free world!"

CHAPTER 10
Viktor Shenderovich: A Man Who Laughs
and Gestures Because He's Sad

At age seven, Valentina learned the writing on a poster by heart. It said: "Viktor Shenderovich: It's Raining in Gadyukino." This was her papa's first book. The poster announced the book's launch at the Estrada Theater. It was a funny book. The Estrada Theater laughed. People were dressed in their very best, which still was wasn't very good, and when Valentina's papa stood on stage and read excerpts from his book they laughed at the absurdity of their own life.

Seven-year-old Valentina, a brown-eyed girl with a shock of thick, black hair that was amazingly thick and black even for a Jewish child, memorized not only the book's title and the theater's name but everything written on the poster in fine print: the printing press order number, the print run, the offset stamp . . . The little girl very much liked the fact that her papa was a writer and also a funny theater man. And that he might take her by the hands, show her three times how to describe funny pretzels with her feet on the parquet floor, and then dance with her, even though she mixed up the steps. The little girl was sure that she had a very special papa and that no other papa was like him.

He may in fact have been an unusual person, this Viktor Shenderovich, Valentina Chubarova's papa. That's why people get involved in the theater, why they put words together on a typewriter—in order to be unusual. In order not just to get up at six in the morning and drag themselves to the dairy canteen, not just to stand there in a line of gloomy fathers with medical notes certifying that they have babies and that their babies need milk. Not just to stand in that line in the freezing cold but rather to teach muzhiks to dance the letkajenkka. Not just to fill up with gloomy, desperate rage over why the hell there wasn't any milk in the country, even for children. Not just to imagine that, in response to a notice that there won't be any milk, you'd go off and kill first the dairy canteen dispenser, then the director of the dairy factory, then all those people in gray who worked in the provincial and city Communist Party committees, and then the Politburo led by moribund old men. . . Not just to poison your own heart with these venomous thoughts, but—

One, two, put on your shoe!
Still asleep? Shame on you!

Come on, muzhiks, come on. It's dark, goddamn it, the sun's not up. Ankle-deep in snow, the turners dance, and so do the bakers, engineers, teachers, policemen, and soldiers—people who understand full well that the Soviet state is deceitful, helpless crap. Come on, muzhiks, come on.

Glorious and lovely, the hilarious letkajenkka
He's asked us to dance!

Of course he was an unusual person. For ordinary people life just happened, but he, Viktor Shenderovich, also noticed and jotted down his observations of the life happening around him—until those notes took shape as a satirical book that had no beginning, middle, or end but comprised a collection of gags. He noticed, for example, that one day the commuter trains became silent. At the turn of the 1990s, people stopped talking in Soviet commuter trains. There was total silence. Because in every car someone would turn on his transistor radio and the entire car—turners, bakers, engineers, police-men, and soldiers—would listen to the broadcast of the Congress of People's Deputies, which had announced great changes in their seemingly petrified country. Little Valentina, sitting on her papa's lap and chewing a hematogen fudge bar, the only sweet to be had, didn't have a clue that people ordinarily talked or read books on commuter trains. She thought it was normal behavior on trains to listen, stock still, to the radio.

Of course he was an unusual person. As an artist on stage he sensed the moment when he had grabbed the hall's attention and brought the audience along with him, the way a writer senses that the words he has cobbled together have begun to ring true, the way Viktor Shenderovich suddenly felt in the early 1990s that all those gloomy turners, bakers, and engineers had suddenly combined the efforts of their multidirectional wills and become capable of changing life with a united effort of will. Half a million strong, they came out on Manezh Square and, submitting to their will, the Soviet army quit the Baltic countries. They demanded the abolition of the one-party system, and the one-party system was abolished. They went to the White House, and the tanks that had orders to kill President Yeltsin went over to President Yeltsin's side. It was magic. The same magic that happens in a theater or on the pages of a book. The magic of a story coming together. And of course he was an unusual person, Viktor Shenderovich, since he made this magic his profession. Little Valentina simply sensed this. Simply sensed that her father was a magician. As if he could start a fire in the palm of his hand.

But every writer knows how a story is put together. Something in it has to break for it to move. Hamlet had to encounter the Ghost and learn that his father had not simply died in his sleep but had been killed. Anna Karenina had to fall in love with the officer Vronsky, otherwise she would have gone on living relatively happily with her big-eared, elderly husband and there would have been nothing to tell. On December 31, 1994, Viktor Shenderovich had to turn on the television and learn that federal troops had entered Grozny, that sitting in those New Year's tanks were boy draftees, that the rebels had fired grenade launchers at them all, and that a person who burns up in a tank looks like a charred log. Valentina didn't see this because she was sent to bed. In her bedroom they turned on the New Year's tree so she wouldn't be afraid alone in the dark. She slept while her father and mother talked in the kitchen for a long time about who in the democratic government of the new free Russia could make such idiotic decisions and issue such cruel orders.

To keep from going crazy, Viktor Shenderovich had to imagine the politicians as pig-headed monsters and had to watch the battle reports from Chechnya on NTV—Independent Television—in order to find among the reporters people who shared his shame and fury at the decisions of the pig-headed monster politicians.

Every writer knows how a story comes together. If in one episode the hero is struck by what pig-headed monsters the politicians are, and in the next episode the hero watches NTV correspondents' reports from the Chechen war, then all of that is there so that in the third episode NTV can propose to the hero that he create a program about pig-headed monster politicians.

Valentina remembered her papa coming home one evening and saying, "I've been offered a job. They're going to pay me a huge amount of money, and you can use the money to bury me with pomp."

"Why bury you?" The little girl was frightened.

"No, no"—Valentina's father stroked her head—"I'm joking. It's just that the job is on television. A weekly show. Jokes served up to order every week." She had grown up some by then, his little girl, she already went to school, so she ought to understand. "It's just that it's very hard work, that's what I meant."

NTV had offered Viktor Shenderovich a satirical program, *Puppets,* in which political figures were represented as ridiculous and fairly repulsive rubber blockheads who spoke not malicious foolishness, as in real life, but funny foolishness, which was easier to bear.

The very next day her papa took Valentina with him—there was no one to leave her with—to the dacha of his producer Grigoriyev. Valentina roamed under the pines all over the huge property, while her papa and three other men sat on the terrace of the huge house endlessly discussing something. Valentina was bored. She tried playing with the puppet she'd brought, but it wasn't working. Her papa kept talking on the terrace with those three men. He was right there, but for the first time Valentina wasn't having a good time with her papa. To the little girl, the television project seemed like a waste of magic, like boiling the kettle on the fire you could start in the palm of your hand. The little girl liked her papa's books, but she did not like television, to say nothing of politicians, and basically she didn't understand what the point of politicians was.

The three men sitting with her papa on the terrace were the producers Vasily Grigoriyev and Aleksandr Levin and the director Vasily Pichul. These men started coming to her home, and Valentina heard her papa arguing and laughing with them in his study, and sometimes he would run out of his study laughing and shout to her mama, "Did you hear? Did you hear what Chernomyrdin said? 'We wanted to do better but it worked out as usual.' Ha ha ha! You couldn't make that up if you tried!"

Valentina now knew that Chernomyrdin was the prime minister. She didn't watch the television news or read the newspapers, but she now knew all the politicians from her papa's programs, which she watched once a week. She didn't know what politicians said or did in fact. She knew what they said on her papa's programs. That's how she pictured them, as rubber blockheads who resembled neither people nor toys, and she believed she was none the worse off for ignoring the news, that her papa would tell her about everything important in his funny—that is, not frightening—way.

Valentina was certain her papa was stronger than his puppets. In any case, when the Yeltsin puppet tried to sue her papa for insulting the honor and dignity of the president of the Russian Federation, nothing bad happened to her papa, he just became famous. On his days off, reporters started coming to the apartment to interview him and even Valentina, and at school they started asking Valentina whether she was really Shenderovich's daughter.

LITTLE ZACHES

We know how a story comes together. It's stronger than you. It isn't the author who comes up with the metaphor to better explain to his audience where things stand. The metaphor occurs to the writer and leads him on, the way a horse is led by the bridle or a bull by the ring through its nose. As a rule, the author does not intend the meanings that his metaphor lets him discover. Often the author is frightened or doesn't want to believe what he's written, carried away by the metaphor. But language is wiser. Its very grammar and syntax hold a knowledge of life accumulated over centuries. Grammar and syntax seem to tell the author, "Yes, little one, that's the way life is. You merely put words together according to the rules, and you see how they line up. That's the way life is." The writer's daring consists in trusting his own metaphors, just as a scientist's daring consists in trusting the results of his experiments. No matter how awful the conclusions.

In winter 2000, when President Yeltsin had just stepped down and the little-known, brand-new prime minister, Putin, was left to carry out his duties, it occurred to Viktor Shenderovich to do a *Puppets* program about the prime minister based on motifs from E. T. A. Hoffman's tale "Little Zaches."

The program began with the Yeltsin puppet rocking the Putin puppet to sleep and griping about what an ugly heir he had. The Berezovsky puppet hovered over them, promising to comb the Putin puppet's hair with his magic television comb so that everyone in the world would like the ugly fellow.

Valentina was a big girl now. She was already graduating from high school. She was interested in the social sciences, poetry, and love. She had no interest at all in Putin, Yeltsin, or Berezovsky. But she knew all about Berezovsky from her papa's program. He was a cunning millionaire, the actual owner of all kinds of things, including Channel One. He—clearly to play a nasty trick—had selected from among politicians someone who suited his purposes, made him prime minister, and now was making him president, too. That is how Valentina saw the political lay of the land. Serious newspapers and serious analytical programs could not say this in so many words; they needed facts. But a satirical program could easily say it metaphorically, and Valentina now knew what the people involved in politics whispered about in their quasi-secret conversations.

Later in the program all of the puppet politicians started admiring Little Zaches, and only puppet Yavlinsky was free of this delusion. He tried to make everyone see reason and shouted that Little Zaches was an ugly, evil dwarf. That is how Valentina saw the political lay of the land. She considered Yavlinsky noble and smart, though he too was a puppet, full stop. It never occurred to her that when it came to Yavlinsky her papa was misleading her. At that time NTV had reached an agreement with Yavlinsky, was supporting him, promoting him, and taking money to support and promote the Yabloko party, which Yavlinsky led. Viktor Shenderovich may sincerely have known nothing about this or not wanted to. In any case, he misled his daughter by presenting Yavlinsky as a visionary who did not share the general rapture over Putin.

If Valentina had watched any programs about politics besides her papa's, she would have seen that Yavlinsky had wholeheartedly joined the universal chorus of glorifications bestowed on the prime minister, who was swiftly winning points for the victorious second Chechen war. That was when she would have asked her papa a question, as adolescents like to do. Her papa would have been embarrassed and mumbled something like, "Just try to get by without glorifying the person who, thanks to Berezovsky's television propaganda, is just about to become the country's new president." Then Valentina would have asked him directly, as adolescents like to do, "Papa, don't you make fun of Putin and Berezovsky because they're enemies of your Gusinsky, who owns NTV?" And her papa would not have known what to say. In any case he would have been silent and thought about how to wiggle out of this.

At the end of his program, when puppet Putin arranged a concert, stood on stage in his underwear, and sang, "A croc came walking down the street," while all the politicians in the audience thought they were hearing him singing in a magical voice "O sole mio," puppet Yavlinsky managed to make his way to the ugly fellow, rip his magic television hair from his head, and reveal his ugliness to one and all. Valentina really did think that Yavlinsky would be the person to bring about order. In fact, Yavlinsky achieved no such feat, ran an inept campaign whose budget was mostly stolen by its implementers, including people from NTV, and was barely able to drag his party into the Duma one last time. But Valentina didn't understand this. Viktor Shenderovich himself probably didn't either.

He understood that something terrible was happening when, arriving at work one day, he learned about the resignation of one of NTV's directors, Oleg Dobrodeyev. For good reason Shenderovich had considered NTV the country's best television channel: the best news, best films, best reporters, a unique journalistic collective nurtured by Dobrodeyev. And now Dobrodeyev was leaving to head up the state television channel Rossiya, which Shenderovich had considered, with good reason, a gaggle of fatuous toadies. Shenderovich could not understand how one of the most respected journalists in the country could of his own free will switch from the category of people who laughed at the puppets to the category of the puppets themselves. Dobrodeyev became a state official. Given a certain confluence of circumstances, a puppet could be manufactured in his image and likeness and launched to clown around in the satirical programs Shenderovich dreamed up.

"What's the matter with you, Oleg?" Shenderovich stormed into Dobrodeyev's office. "They're using you! They're discrediting you!"

Dobrodeyev didn't agree. He said that, on the contrary, he was attempting to propagate the standards of high-quality, free journalism in state television. When he left, he brought with him an entire cohort of illustrious NTV reporters who, for double the salary, also agreed to be transformed from people into puppets.

The journalists were leaving. Arkady Mamontov left. Shenderovich had been proud of his reports from Chechnya but didn't yet know that Mamontov would start filming reports on orders from the Lubyanka and one day would shoot a film about human-rights activist Lyudmila Alekseyeva being an English spy. Ernest Matskyavichus left. He had drunk with Shenderovich at the Petrovich Club, joked around, and been photographed, and Shenderovich didn't yet know that Matskyavichus had had his picture taken as a memento because he had accepted Dobrodeyev's offer and that there, at Rossiya, he would anchor the election debates—which were dishonest and not free, even though all the politicians were given equal time.

There, at the Petrovich Club, an NTV editor had come up to Shenderovich, called him a genius, and said she knew all his programs by heart, and Shenderovich, embarrassed, had smiled at her. She too had been hired on at Rossiya and was prepared to think that Putin was a stroke of luck for the country.

After writing his script about Little Zaches, Shenderovich reread it and thought, "Is this too extreme?" But he didn't think that for long. As always, the metaphor was wiser than its author. After he became president, Putin began saying in earnest the kinds of things Shenderovich might have ascribed to him in his satirical script. The president was by no means joking when he said about terrorists that he would "whack them in the toilet" and in addressing officials he was by no means joking when he said, "Quit your sniveling." The public liked the way all the puppet politicians on Shenderovich's program liked the boorish Little Zaches.

The metaphorical reality of *Puppets* seemed to have jumped out of the television set only to destroy the television channel from which it had burst forth.

One night—Valentina was already a student at the university and coming home late—her papa came out of his room and told his daughter that NTV had been seized. For the first time Valentina turned the television on not to watch her papa's program or a film. For the first time she turned it on to watch the news. But by then it was too late. Instead of news or films, NTV was broadcasting a black screen on which was written that the journalists were striking in protest against the channel's seizure. On other programs they showed the NTV building being stormed by armed masked men. And a new director, Alfred Kokh, appointed by the Kremlin, was entering with them. Kokh had been a deputy prime minister a few years before the events described. When he was deputy prime minister, his puppet had actually existed. Valentina knew puppet Kokh by face. Now the puppet come to life had arrived at NTV and declared that the leadership of the television channel was changing.

The journalists organized rallies. Valentina even tried to write newspaper articles about the rallies. Rebellious journalists seemed so romantic that for a short time she herself wanted to become one. Then Valentina saw how, in a last-ditch attempt to save their channel, NTV journalists had asked for an audience with President Putin. On television Valentina saw ten famous TV personalities, including her papa, go to the Kremlin and ask—who? a puppet!—not to shut them down. Valentina saw the president talk with the journalists with the same boorish pushiness that her papa might have ascribed to the puppet in his next script. If Shenderovich had wanted to create a special services puppet, he probably would have had it turn documents face down. On television Valentina saw the way Putin turned documents face down. He told the journalists he had compromising materials on NTV owner Vladimir Gusinsky, but he didn't show them the documents.

Did Shenderovich fight? Yes. When it became impossible to work at NTV he moved to little TV-6 along with a group of reporters who refused to join Oleg Dobrodeyev or had not been invited to. TV-6 had a brief life and was also shut down. Remnants of the journalistic team migrated to the very tiny channel TVS. One of the news anchors joked at the time, "Pretty soon we're going to be broadcasting over the intercom." But Shenderovich would not surrender. He couldn't do *Puppets* anymore because the rights to the idea belonged to the producer Vasily Grigoriyev, who did not share his oppositionism. He came up with new satirical programs, sometimes funny ones, but they never had the success of *Puppets*. When TVS was shut down, Shenderovich started broadcasting a satirical radio program on Ekho Moskvy. It wasn't quite the apartment building intercom, of course, though it was getting very close.

But still he fought. Valentina remembered her papa coming home one day, sitting her and her mama down at the kitchen table, and saying he was going to run for State Duma deputy. This was awful. Valentina pictured her papa in an official suit sitting in the State Duma and driving around the city in a black BMW with a flashing light. "Oh no, you don't understand," her papa said. "Of course I'm not getting into the Duma." She was grown up now, his little girl, and she had to understand. "That isn't the point."

Valentina listened and it gradually dawned on her what her papa had dreamed up. Now he, a real person, was going to vie with puppets for a seat in the State Duma, and it would be obvious to anyone who witnessed this competition that we were ruled by rubber blockheads. Valentina calmed down. She even found the idea amusing.

But then her papa said, "You'll have to prepare yourselves for having mud slung at you as well as me."

"Oh! I'm prepared for that," Valentina said with noncalanche.

Which was a mistake. She wasn't prepared. When her papa registered as a candidate for deputy, when Marina Litvinovich, the head of her papa's campaign headquarters, started coming to their home with her little son, Savva, her papa changed. He still joked at dinner, but more and more of his jokes were about the tabloids, where they were printing phantasmagorical slander about him. He brought these tabloids home and read paragraphs from them, and for a long time Valentina didn't understand that he was looking for support. He was used to praise, if not fame. For a long time Valentina didn't understand that it was hard for him to read vile things about himself, and she absolutely did not understand why he was reading vile things about himself as if bewitched.

One day Valentina heard her papa calling some editorial office.

"You write in your newspaper," her papa said into the receiver, "that I'm impotent. So I am prepared to offer a rebuttal to your editors by fucking the journalist who wrote this crap, assuming the bitch is young and pretty, of course." A newspaper lay on her papa's desk. Published in it was a letter from some woman who called herself her mama's best friend. Valentina knew of no such friend. The friend called her mama Lyudochka, although Valentina's mama, Lyudmila, could not stand the nickname "Lyudochka," preferring "Milochka." The friend wrote that Lyudochka was unhappy. That Shenderovich was impotent and beat Lyudochka, taking out his impotence on her. That Valentina wasn't his real daughter . . . It was a lie from start to finish, but for some reason she couldn't just set the paper aside and not read to the end. Valentina read, and every word exacerbated the insult. At dinner they joked about the article, repeating each line many times, and suddenly Valentina realized that slander if was unbearable if you didn't repeat it yourself two hundred times, laughing each time.

Another day, shortly before the elections, her mama and papa came home in the evening in a somber mood. Valentina knew they had gone to speak with producer Aleksandr Levin, with whom her papa had started *Puppets*. A new project maybe? Maybe they hadn't come to terms? But her papa told Valentina that Levin had spent an entire hour jabbering about all kinds of nonsense. No proposals, no ideas. Toward the end of the conversation, though, he had suddenly said, "Be careful. Mila's at the wheel. You could be in a car accident." This was a threat that the puppets were conveying to her papa through his former comrade. After telling her this, her papa took Valentina's hands, but instead of dancing with her, as in her childhood, he very seriously asked her not to come home late and not to travel around town alone at all.

Of course he fought. Except that, if in the past everything

had worked out for him, now he kept losing. And Valentina could see that he, so used to success, was finding it harder and harder to be without it. Of course, there were still books. Of course, there were still radio programs, theatrical performances, and stage appearances. Every week her papa spoke about the injustices that were multiplying everywhere you looked. About the lawyer Aleksanyan, who was being held in prison, despite a terminal illness. About President Putin, whose name was literally being used even for canned goods— a kind of sauerkraut in cans. He still spoke humorously about all this. But now with a sarcastic anguish that had replaced his former carefree gaiety.

One morning Valentina saw her papa get up, mobilize himself as if for war, dress very warmly, and leave the building. It was the day of the first Dissenters' March in Moscow. Naturally, no Dissenters' March was shown on television. But that same evening Valentina saw many photographs of her father in the blogs. There he was on Pushkin Square, where OMON soldiers were beating people up and arresting them. There he was on Sretensky Boulevard. OMON soldiers were advancing on him in a chain, and he was lecturing them about walking on the benches, which were meant for romantic trysts with young women, not for being trampled by their combat boots. There he was on Chistoprudny Boulevard. At the podium. Speaking. Next to former prime minister Mikhail Kasyanov.

Next to his former puppet.

Hostage

Valentina did not share her papa's opinion about going to the Dissenters' March. Her papa told his daughter that if the poets Rubinshtein and Gandlevsky were going, then it would be shameful for him not to. Valentina said that, on the contrary, it was shameful to march in the same column with Limonovites, who had what was practically a swastika on their banners and whose program said that liberals should be hanged. Her papa didn't argue. On the contrary, he secretly rejoiced that his mature daughter was not going to place her head before the OMON truncheons. Even if it was a Dissenters' March. Because Valentina went to other rallies of a liberal and human-rights persuasion much more often than her papa would have liked.

That's the way life is. You live by your conscience, as the saying goes, you protest when you need to protest and you don't bow or grovel before the powerful. And one day you see that you have taught your little girl to protest. That she belongs to the Oborona—Defense—youth movement. That her young man is a human-rights activist. That one day she mobilized herself the way you had for the Dissenters' March and went to picket in support of someone named Oleg Kozlovsky, who, don't you know, had been conscripted into the army illegally. What the hell? Let them go on taking all the young men into the army illegally. Why did your little girl have to march for them against OMON truncheons? But you did join the Dissenters' March. How could you explain to your little girl now that you were scared to death when she was out there picketing?

The picketing in defense of Oleg Kozlovsky in late December 2007 did, in fact, end badly for Valentina. It was an authorized picket. The police protected the picketers until Police Lieutenant Colonel Inkin from the Arbat Internal Affairs Administration saw among the protestors Sergei Konstantinov, whom he had arrested before and who had written a complaint against the lieutenant colonel that had cost the lieutenant colonel his bonus.

"You're here, too?" the lieutenant colonel said, using the familiar "you."

Konstantinov parried, objecting to the familiar tone, and ran, realizing that they were just about to arrest him.

Konstantinov wanted to lead the police, who resented him personally, away from his comrades, who had done nothing illegal. He ran into an underground pedestrian passageway. The police caught up with him there, threw him to the ground, twisted his arms behind his back, and dragged him past the picket line to their van.

"They've got Serzh!" someone next to Valentina said when he saw a dozen police carrying someone by who was twisting and turning like a worm on a fish hook.

Those words were enough. The picketers rushed to free Sergei, and from that moment their picket ceased to be authorized and turned into a "failure to obey the legal demands of the representatives of power," the kind of failure to obey that entails fifteen days in jail, as everyone knows.

The trial was the next day. They convicted Sergei Konstantinov and three other young people detained along with Sergei because it was silly to arrest one person rather than several at a picket.

Valentina and four comrades went to the court as witnesses for the defense. She was supposed to tell the judge that Konstantinov had not broken any laws, but that Lieutenant Colonel Inkin had. Valentina told them everything. Nonetheless, the judge sentenced Konstantinov to fifteen days in jail. It was late December. Konstantinov would be spending the holidays in prison; Valentina had done could for her comrade.

All she could do was remain in the courtroom as a witness and watch them try Konstantinov's three accomplices, members of the banned National Bolshevik Party, a young woman and two young men, about whom Konstantinov later said that the woman was a nationalist, one of the young man men was a Communist, and the other was an anarchist. No common ideology whatsoever. Valentina didn't like the National Bolshevik

Party, but her group of young human-rights activists believed that if a person is tried, witnesses must be found who could lighten his sentence. The National Bolsheviks didn't do that. The National Bolsheviks weren't afraid of prison. They had a cult of imprisonment, and they did not help comrades who ended up in court because doing time was a mark of valor for them.

Nor could Valentina help these National Bolsheviks. Yet she decided to stay to observe the judicial process and later describe the trial in her blog. Her resolve to stay grew when the judge demanded that Valentina and her friends leave the courtroom.

"Declare this a closed trial," objected this young woman, a petite brunette with a still childish face, to the judge. "Your Honor, until you declare the trial closed, we have the right to be present and we're not going anywhere."

Without thinking very long, the judge ordered the policeman and bailiffs on duty in the courtroom to take that girl and her little friends out and to the police station and charge them with "interfering with the work of the court"—up to two years in prison.

It was almost night when Viktor Shenderovich got a call from Lyudmila Alekseyeva, head of the Moscow Helsinki Group, a human-rights activist whom everyone tenderly called "Babushka."

"Vitya," Babushka said. "Do you know your daughter is at the police station?"

Shenderovich did know his daughter was at the police station. Valentina had called her father, but this had happened before. Shenderovich was beside himself with fear, of course, but he restrained himself, thinking that the four hours for holding without cause for arrest would pass and they would release his little girl.

"Vitya," Babushka said. "Do you know they want to shut her up?"

"What do you mean shut her up?" Shenderovich didn't understand the human-rights slang.

"Shut her up, Vitya, means putting her in prison."

"For what?" Shenderovich shouted.

"Interfering with the work of the court. Up to two years. They're at the Presnensky station. Get there as fast as you can." They drove fast. Shenderovich's wife, Mila, was at the wheel. Her hands were shaking. The likelihood of having an accident was much greater than before the elections, when the producer Levin had warned them of the danger of driving a car. Mila ran a red light, but Viktor didn't notice. Hunched over in the passenger seat he kept calling and calling and calling, not even aware he was calling the puppets. He called state officials he barely knew, he called police bigwigs he barely knew, he was prepared to grovel at their feet, beg them for mercy, sign any renunciation they liked, as long as his little girl didn't go to prison for two years. After so many years of oppositionism, he was prepared to surrender, only he didn't know how or to whom. Daring and refusal to compromise are explained fairly often by the fact that you simply don't know whom to surrender to or how.

The only more or less official person who answered Shenderovich was Nikolai Svanidze, a television anchorman, documentary filmmaker, writer, member of the Public Chamber, and despite his involvement in state television, a decent human being. Theoretically, a Svanidze puppet could have appeared on Shenderovich's program if such a program were still on the air, but it would have been a decent puppet.

"I'm on my way," Svanidze said. "Where is she? Which station? Presnensky?"

And an hour later he did in fact arrive.

The appearance of a famous television anchor and Public Chamber member at a police station looked just like an episode from Shenderovich's satirical program. The policemen did everything in their power to behave politely, but they understood nothing about being polite, so they played the scene just like actors in Count Sheremetyev's serf theater performing a scene taken from French aristocratic life.

"What brings you here at so late an hour?" a police officer with a face that made you seriously wonder where he might have ever heard a phrase like that, bowing to the Public Chamber member.

An hour or so later Valentina and her comrades were released. Driving home, Svanidze said to Shenderovich, "I don't care about you. You can ruin your life any way you like. But why drag your child into that pandemonium?"

Shenderovich nodded guiltily.

But Valentina refused to leave. She was an adult. She had graduated from the institute. She was now teaching sociology and anthropology. But she still thought that people invested with power were puppets, rubber blockheads, and there was no reason to fear them. She told her papa that in the cell from which she had just been released there was a young woman who had been sitting there for three days without food or a warrant for her arrest and she had to be helped somehow.

"We have to find a lawyer," Valentina said.

"Please," Shenderovich said, "don't. Please, let's go home. One crazy person in the family is enough. I beg of you."

So they drove off. And Valentina doesn't know what happened to that young woman who had been in jail for over three days without food or a warrant for her arrest.

CHAPTER 11
Andrei Illarionov: A Man Who Takes
a Detached View of Everyone

On April 14, 2007, Andrei Illarionov went to Pushkin Square in Moscow just to see what it would be like. What these Dissenters' Marches were all about. A few weeks earlier, on March 3, a Dissenters' March in St. Petersburg had been a deafening success. Or at least the oppositionists, the march participants, had called what happened to them in Petersburg on March 3, 2007, a success. They thought everything was a success, no matter what happened.

There were plenty of provocateurs hired by the regime in the crowd of five thousand. These provocateurs unfurled banners and shouted slogans, "Bush, Help Russia," and "Berezovsky, we're with you," to scare off the patriots. Or, on the contrary, they unfurled banners and shouted, "Stalin, Beria, Gulag," to frighten off the liberals and intelligentsia. But the participants in the Petersburg march perceived the provocateurs' presence as a sign of the regime's fear of them, and that meant they were a serious political force.

During the Petersburg march, OMON soldiers had beaten up a local deputy, Gulyayev, and broken his arm. The official newspapers, if they wrote about this at all, blamed the march organizers for provoking violence. But the march participants perceived the violence against them as success, in the sense that real heroes had appeared in their ranks, heroes who had suffered for freedom and confirmed their love of freedom with their blood. The dissenters' leader, Garry Kasparov, quoted Mahatma Gandhi: "First they laugh at you, then they beat you, then you win." It turned out that the Ghandian nonviolent civil disobedience that the dissenters had introduced into Russian political practice had passed through the first stage, laughter, and entered the second stage, beating, which meant that the third stage—winning—was nigh.

The main success of the Petersburg march on March 3, 2007, had been that a crowd of ten thousand had broken through the police cordons onto Nevsky Prospect. Not a small group, as would happen several times after that, but such a huge crowd that Marina Litvinovich, climbing onto the pedestal of one of Klodt's horses on the Anichkov Bridge and looking to the right and left along Nevsky, saw a human river as far as the eye could see, her friends and comrades in arms, free, strong, and dissenting.

That is why Andrei Illarionov went to see whether this miracle would be repeated in Moscow. Somehow it was clear from the outset that it wouldn't. This Dissenters' March on April 14, 2007, was half-sanctioned by the authorities. The organizers filed an application to go from Pushkin Square down the boulevards to Chistye Prudy and hold the rally on Chistoprudny Boulevard. The authorities authorized the rally but didn't authorize going down the boulevards from Pushkin Square. The organizers responded that according to the law the application was not to ask the regime's permission for the march but simply to inform the regime where the march was going to take place, and they called on their supporters to assemble at Pushkin Square anyway.

When Andrei Illarionov arrived at the square, he saw there was nowhere for the march participants to assemble. Gray police trucks with metal bodies and headlight grilles formed a solid wall between the outside world and the square around the Pushkin monument. There was not a soul to be seen on that square. Across Tverskaya Street, on Novopushkinsky Square, where liberal rallies had traditionally been held, an emergency rally of the pro-Kremlin Young Guard movement had been called. The square was fenced off, and no one was allowed in except Young Guards with passes, which were superfluous, actually, because you could always tell a Young Guard by the special vacant expression of enthusiasm in his eyes.

Down Tverskaya and at all the intersections, and both up and down the adjacent side streets, there was also a solid wall of trucks by the sidewalks, so that you couldn't even see what was happening across the street. All people had left, basically, were the sidewalks. People were standing on the sidewalks, not knowing where to go, not seeing their banners or their leaders, and the police were telling people they should go home.

The police trucks had license plates from towns relatively close to Moscow and large enough to have their own OMON—Voronezh, Lipetsk, Tambov. Illarionov thought that these policemen from Lipetsk, Tambov, and Voronezh had to be able to explain to themselves somehow why they'd come to Moscow, why they'd barricaded a peaceful city on a Saturday, and why they weren't letting citizens walk down the streets. En route, the special service agents assigned to OMON had probably described to the soldiers how the people coming out on the streets in Moscow were enemies, accomplices of American imperialism, hirelings of the world's back rooms. And the soldiers believed it, because you can't rout peaceful citizens using special methods unless you believe these citizens are enemies.

Lots of people on the street were carrying small, pale roses. At one intersection, Marina Litvinovich was handing out these flowers to anyone who wanted one, as if wanting the Dissenters' March to be in harmony with Georgia's "rose revolution" or with the famous photograph from the counterculture era in which the young woman puts a flower in the barrel of a policeman's gun. Illarionov thought the OMON soldiers had probably been instructed about the roses as well. They were defending the city from provocateurs intent on starting a revolution in the Georgian or Ukrainian manner. Illarionov thought it would be easier for an OMON soldier to strike an unarmed person holding a rose than simply an unarmed person.

Near the Benetton store Illarionov finally saw Garry Kasparov, who was walking at the head of a small group of people. A hundred people maybe. And he was holding a rose. He approached an underground pedestrian crossing, but OMON soldiers had blocked the steps. Illarionov thought the soldiers must have some explanation for not letting people without weapons, banners, or slogans enter the underground passage. Could holding a rose be sufficient explanation?

"Please let me pass," Kasparov said politely, coming right up to the OMON chain.

"You can't go there," a soldier growled in reply. It had to be awkward for him to firmly refuse the famous chess player, the world champion.

"Let me pass," Kasparov insisted softly. "You have no reason to block the street. It's a Saturday, the middle of the city. We really don't have the right to walk down the streets?"

"Your demonstration is illegal!" the OMON soldier growled because the secret service agent assigned to them had instructed him in the bus that he would be dispersing an illegal demonstration.

"This isn't a demonstration," Kasparov parried. "We're not carrying banners or flags, we're not shouting slogans, we're just walking down the sidewalk. Or has an emergency been declared in the city and people can only walk around with a pass?"

Standing at a distance, Illarionov could see a shadow of doubt flicker across the OMON soldier's face. Illarionov heard an OMON officer behind them shout, "Carry out your order! Block the passage!" But he was not shouting with confidence either. Only the man in civilian dress standing in the street, only the man with the earpiece—the secret service agent—was sure of himself. He ordered the OMON colonel to keep citizens from walking down the city's streets. Illarionov thought that if Kasparov were a little calmer, if notes of nervousness didn't slip through in his voice, he would be able to convince OMON to open the street despite the secret service agent's confident prohibitions. And just as Illarionov thought this, behind Kasparov two young men (whether provocateurs or supporters whose nerves couldn't take it) threw up the black Limonov flag and started shouting, "We need another Russia!" And there was relief on the soldiers' faces. "Russia without Putin!" other young people shouted. With a clear conscience, the OMON soldiers took out their truncheons and cut into the crowd.

Now they had an explanation for beating unarmed people on the streets of a peaceful city. Now they were facing the very same dangerous enemies and underminers of the constitutional order that the secret-service agent had warned them about in the bus. They twisted arms and shoved into the bus first the young men with the flag, then Kasparov, although he wasn't shouting anything, then everyone nearby holding roses, then everyone else who wasn't . . . When they started cutting into the crowd and waving truncheons, Illarionov retreated a little more. Maybe because he was afraid. And maybe he was afraid because he knew something about the regime the others didn't.

PRESIDENTIAL ADVISOR

In the late 1980s, Andrei Illarionov had been part of the economic circle called the Moscow-Leningrad School, the goal of which had been to come up with ways to solve the economic crisis of the recently defunct Soviet Union. This circle included young economists: Yegor Gaidar, who, when the Soviet Union collapsed, became acting prime minister in the first Yeltsin government; Anatoly Chubais, who took charge of the economy and finances as deputy prime minister in the second and third governments of the Yeltsin era; and many other future government officials. These young economists spoke in general about the need for market reforms at the meetings of their circle, which were held in remote tourist camps and resorts. But they had different views about how radical the reforms needed to be.

Some said that industry had to be privatized entirely; others, that only light industry should be privatized but heavy industry, led by the oil industry, should remain in state hands. They wrote serious economic reports to back up their opinions. However, Illarionov noticed that a report's cautiousness was in direct proportion to the importance of its writer's position. They needed an explanation for their acts, just as an OMON officer needed an explanation to disperse unarmed people using special methods. You can't work in a Soviet economic institute if you think the Soviet economy is unviable by definition. Therefore you devise serious reports explaining that the Soviet economy is only in part unviable.

Then the Soviet economy collapsed. The Soviet Union fell apart. President Yeltsin brought the economists of the Moscow-Leningrad School into the government and basically gave them carte blanche to carry out economic reforms. Illarionov was not a member of the government and therefore saw that in their almost seven years in power Gaidar and Chubais did not carry out a single reform discussed at the meetings of the Moscow-Leningrad School. Economic growth did not begin, financial stabilization did not ensue, and the ruble continued to devalue. Gaidar and Chubais in the government had their own explanations for every step they took. Just as an OMON officer always has an explanation for breaking up a demonstration. Gaidar, for example, abruptly freed prices, which had been regulated in the Soviet Union, and prices soared, inflicting irreparable damage on Yeltsin's popularity and ruining Gaidar's own political career. Chubais carried out privatization, dividing up the country's wealth unevenly among its citizens and basically handing over factories and oil wells to the chosen few, creating a caste of oligarchs. Illarionov thought this was a mistake.

But Gaidar had freed prices in the face of famine and war. And Chubais carried out privatization at a moment of political crisis. He didn't merely divide up the oil wells and factories but divided them up in such a way as to create a class of the new rich who would support Yeltsin, which they did. These may have been mistakes. Profit for Chubais and Gaidar may have been part and parcel of these mistakes. But they had explanations. Everyone needs explanations for his actions, be he a prime minister or an ordinary OMON soldier.

In 1999 and early 2000, when Vladimir Putin first became prime minister and then acting president, Andrei Illarionov also had explanations for becoming a Putin economic advisor. Illarionov knew that Putin was KGB, of course, but at the turn of the millennium, Putin was usually compared with Pinochet, on the premise that a Putin-Pinochet was not that bad, that, after tightening the political screws, he would call in the "Chicago boys," young economists, carry out liberal reforms, and then voluntarily hand over power to parliament.

That was the usual way of looking at it. And Illarionov viewed it that way too, especially because just ahead of the elections Putin did in fact create an economic institute led by the liberal German Gref. Illarionov viewed it that way because Putin had invited him and taken a serious interest in reforms. Illarionov viewed it that way because one day he was talking to Putin about economic freedom, and Putin in turn began talking about economic freedom for Ivanovo weavers during one of his campaign trips. Putin's speechwriters started calling Illarionov and asking him what economic freedom was and how to insert it into the boss's speeches. And this—Putin's sincere and profound interest in reforms—was his explanation. Sufficient explanation to accept Putin's offer the third time around and become his economic advisor.

In April 2000 Andrei Illarionov became President Putin's economic advisor. The second Chechen war was under way, and it was repulsive and brutal. But at the same time the law on a flat income tax—one of the main liberal reforms Illarionov had proposed—sailed through the State Duma with an ease unseen in the Yeltsin era. Now rich and poor paid taxes equally, at a rate of 13 percent, no matter what their income. Although a little dubious of the government's sincerity, the rich stopped hiding their income. Huge fortunes emerged from the shadows. Huge manufacturing businesses stopped operating with unreported cash. Business in Russia stopped being completely criminal. Mikhail Khodorkovsky, head of Yukos, the largest oil company, started going to see economic advisor Illarionov and telling him he intended to make his company transparent and take it public. For this Illarionov was even prepared to put up with the repulsive and brutal Chechen war, in and of itself a criminal business.

In 2001 economic advisor Illarionov suggested to President Putin that he renew payments on the Soviet Union's debts and the Russian debts accrued in the Yeltsin era. At the time the suggestion seemed absurd. It seemed absurd to pay off debts if the whole world considered Russia a sleeping bear and lent the sleeping bear money not because it hoped to be repaid but because it was afraid of riots on the Moscow streets, an uprising, and the ascent to power of the nationalists, who would do God only knew what with their nuclear weapons. Illarionov insisted that if Russia started paying off its debts, the world would gradually learn to treat it like a civilized country and accept it into the G8 and other international economic organizations.

The proposal to revive the payments was much harder to get approved than the flat income tax had been, but it was. It was now logical to appoint Andrei Illarionov as the sherpa-negotiator to negotiate with the most developed countries of the world about including Russia in the Group of 8. Serious difficulties began for economic advisor Andrei Illarionov in 2002, when electricity reform was launched. Here Illarionov seriously disagreed with Unified Energy System chief Anatoly Chubais, whose goal was to destroy the company he led, end the state's monopoly on electricity, and thereby create the economic prerequisites for the country's free development. Chubais was an old pal from the Moscow-Leningrad economic school. Chubais had apparently invested considerable effort in 2000 to see that Andrei Illarionov became the president's economic advisor. But the scheme for privatizing UES proposed by Chubais assumed that only the power stations would be privatized, while the electrical grids would remain in state hands. Andrei Illarionov did not see any destruction of the monopoly in this. Who needed a power station if you couldn't plug it into the grid? What kind of destruction of the state electricity monopoly was it if the state and only the state decided who could and couldn't plug into the grid? At numerous meetings Illarionov expressed his point of view time and time again to President Putin, and Putin agreed. Nonetheless—it was like running up against a brick wall—electricity reform followed Chubais's plan and concluded according to Chubais's plan. The grids were still in state hands when Andrei Illarionov had already ceased to be the president's economic advisor.

The window of opportunity that the advisory position had afforded Illarionov narrowed by the day, by the month, until it was a tiny window, if not a crack. In spring 2003, the hard times began for Yukos. Criminal charges were brought against its directors, and Platon Lebedev, Mikhail Khodorkovsky's partner, was arrested. Illarionov realized that in the past there probably had been grounds for instigating criminal proceedings against Yukos, but at that time criminal proceedings should have been instigated against every single director of a successful company in Russia because in the 1990s no one operated according to the law because there were no laws. Illarionov thought it particularly absurd that the first blow had fallen on Yukos—the very company that had first attempted to become transparent and operate legally. The very company whose head, Mikhail Khodorkovsky, at a meeting with the president, had admitted that he had participated in corrupt schemes and said the following, referring to the collected leaders of Russian business: "The corruption began with us and we have to stop it."

It would have been more sensible politically to grant amnesty to the businessmen who became rich in the 1990s and not prosecute the one who was the first to want to work honestly. But Illarionov was an economic advisor. He used economic arguments to try to convince the president not to prosecute Khodorkovsky and Yukos. He said, "If you imprison Khodorkovsky, you'll be killing the goose that lays you the golden eggs. Oil production at Yukos is increasing at 12 percent a year. I don't know of another company that could offer such impressive economic growth."

The president agreed. He agreed with Illarionov's arguments, but on October 25, 2003, Khodorkovsky was arrested. That day, Illarionov was on a business trip. Upon his return, he ran into Vladislav Surkov, the president's deputy chief of staff. At one time, before the start of his political career, Surkov had been Khodorkovsky's partner.

Illarionov was sure that Surkov, too, if only out of old friendship, had tried to talk the president out of prosecuting Khodorkovsky. Illarionov said, "Why? The president agreed with us! Who is making the decisions? Why aren't you protesting?"

Surkov shrugged. "There are no limits to man's flexibility."

Just a week later, Aleksandr Voloshin, the president's chief of staff, was fired. He was considered to be close to Chubais, and his place was taken by Dmitry Medvedev, a lawyer from Petersburg; at the time no one could have guessed that in 2008 he would become the president of Russia after Putin.

One of Medvedev's first orders in his new post was a ban on free contact with the press for employees of the president's administration. Now, if some journalist asked Illarionov for an interview (and he received several interview requests daily), the advisor was supposed to direct the inquiry to the administration's press service. The press service would take a couple of weeks to examine the request, which in many cases—if, for instance, they needed a comment on late-breaking news—made the interview moot. Two weeks later the press service would reply to Illarionov and as a rule with a refusal. "This publication is unfriendly to us," a minor clerk in the press service wrote to Illarionov in all seriousness. Or, "This journalist has shown disloyalty . . ." Or, "Considering your economic views, it is undesirable that you comment in the press on the problem of inflation . . ."

Naturally, Illarionov sent these inquiries to the press service merely for laughs and met with journalists when he wanted to, organizing press conferences and friendly meetings over tea. And he said whatever he pleased. Chief of Staff Medvedev reproached Illarionov for this several times, and in July 2004 he issued a reprimand and took away his bonus. If you don't take bribes, bonuses are an important part of a state official's income. At the end of each quarter, if he has behaved well, an official receives a bonus worth two months' salary. Illarionov had his taken away to the very end of his advisorship.

However, the advisor did not lose heart. Illarionov framed the chief of staff's reprimand and hung it on the wall of his office among his many letters of commendation and gratitude from the president. And he continued to meet with journalists as he saw fit. Then Medvedev stopped signing off on the trips Illarionov intended to take on economic matters. Moreover,

Medvedev dreamed up utterly pointless trips for the obstreperous advisor. One day Illarionov came to work and the secretary handed him an order from the chief of staff that implied that the advisor was supposed to be present at three events in one day—in Petersburg, Novosibirsk, and Khabarovsk. Moreover, as Illarionov was able to clarify after phoning Petersburg, just the day before they had known nothing there about the important event involving the president's advisor and were now quickly preparing the event, obeying the order from Moscow.

"This is absurd. I can't be in three cities simultaneously," Illarionov told Medvedev. "I will not be party to this profanation."

And he received a second reprimand.

But Illarionov did not resign over bureaucratic pettiness or the nastiness of red tape. He says he resigned over Beslan. When terrorists seized the school in this North Ossetian town, presidential advisor Andrei Illarionov either took part in or was witness to several meetings. As a result of these meetings, a clumsy assault was organized. Children perished. A tank fired into the windows of the gymnasium where the hostages were being held. Federal soldiers fired flamethrowers at the windows of the gymnasium where the hostages were being held. Children perished. This happened because at the meetings to which Andrei Illarionov was witness certain decisions were made. Only Andrei Illarionov won't say what they were.

He says that during terrorist acts one has to think about rescuing hostages, not about punishing terrorists. But if you ask him, "Who, Andrei Nikolaevich, who made the decisions and what were they?" Illarionov is silent. He is probably afraid. He probably has reasons we don't know for remaining silent. One day he will probably tell us who made what decisions on September 3, 2004. But not now.

Now we only know that immediately after Beslan Illarionov submitted a other of resignation to the president, asking he be relieved of his position as sherpa. And we know that his request was turned down.

We know that on December 14, 2004, a group of National Bolsheviks seized the president's administration building, and in the investigation the National Bolsheviks testified that they had been going to a meeting with Andrei Illarionov. Later Illarionov asked the head of the Main Penal Administration if he could meet with the National Bolsheviks in prison and find out what they wanted. We know that this request of Illarionov's was turned down as well.

We know that on December 30, 2004, Illarionov made a show of attending the trial of Mikhail Khodorkovsky and that while Illarionov was sitting in the courtroom, having turned off his mobile phone, the president allegedly called him on an urgent matter. Illarionov's phone said "subscriber unavailable." That evening, Chief of Staff Medvedev told Illarionov that he had canceled his meeting with the president. "You've made your choice about who you're going to meet with," Medvedev said then. And we know that on January 3, 2005, Illarionov was fired from his position as sherpa.

Khodorkovsky was convicted, and Yukos's assets were transferred to a state company, Rosneft. It wasn't Khodorkovsky who came to presidential advisor Illarionov to discuss taking these oil wells public but Bogdanchikov, the head of Rosneft. Illarionov recounts that if one were free to discuss all the subtleties of going public with Khodorovsky, then it would be clear Bogdanchikov understood nothing about going public. The documents show that the money from taking the company public would go into the company's accounts, not the state's.

"This is like a guard selling property from a warehouse, but instead of giving the money to the warehouse owner, he pockets it for himself," Illarionov said. "Why should I agree?"

"Because," Bogdanchikov replied, "Rosneft never forgets who helps it."

The documents also show that the billion and a half dollars Rosneft received from the sale of shares on the free market would be distributed among the company's top managers as a reward for the successful IPO.

THE LIMITS OF FLEXIBILITY

And that was why Andrei Illarionov was now standing on Pushkin Square in a crowd on which the OMON fighters swooped down from time to time the way a raptor swoops down on a flock of birds. They would swoop down, scoop up whoever came to hand, and load him into their vans. He was standing in the crowd and babushkas he didn't know were defending him.

An OMON officer shouted from the pavement, "Muzhik, why are you hiding there behind the women! Come here, come here!"

And the babushkas shouted to the OMON officer, "Don't you know who this is? Can't you see that this is the president's advisor Andrei Illarionov?"

Over and over again the OMON soldiers swooped down on the crowd, and over and over again they snatched people from it. It was so hopeless that Illarionov realized that he and only he had to lead these babushkas and students who had recognized him and defended him from the truncheons away from here. He had to because all the leaders had been arrested and because, besides him, the people who had come to Pushkin Square did not see a single familiar face.

"Citizens!" Illarionov exclaimed. "Gentlemen! We are going to Chistye Prudy. There is an authorized rally there. Follow me to Chistye Prudy."

That was why he was leading a column of dissenters. How easy it is to lead a column if you know Moscow well, the OMON men blocking the streets, of course, were from out of town. Illarionov led the column from Pushkin Square to Chistye Prudy not down the boulevards but via back streets, looping around and turning first right, then left. People followed him because they were used to trusting people who appeared on television.

Illarionov hadn't appeared on television for a long time, but people still remembered him; to them he was still the president's economic advisor, and by his very presence he confirmed that these people walking down Moscow's side streets from Pushkin Square to Chistye Prudy were not enemies or terrorists but citizens who had come out on the streets to express their dissent.

At the intersection of one of the side streets and Tsvetnoi Boulevard, Limonovites suddenly jumped out from nowhere with their black flags and headed up the column. They lit firecrackers and shouted, "Russia without Putin!" Illarionov frowned. He just wanted to lead the students and babushkas alive and uninjured from Pushkin Square, where OMON had dispersed the rally, to Chistoprudny Boulevard, where nothing threatened them. He did not want to turn these people into a phalanx of radical revolutionaries. It made him sick that the Limonovites were exploiting people's confusion and herd mentality for the sake of an illusion of revolutionariness. A police cordon awaited the column on Rozhdestvensky Boulevard. Illarionov was ashamed. It turned out that it was he who had led the babushkas and students right to the truncheons. At the last moment Illarionov once again shouted, "Follow me!" and once again led the crowd into the side streets, up, up, across Rozhdestvensky, past the Sandunovsky baths, past the little gingerbread houses, past the shields and helmets. Up, up, just to save their heads, just to keep peaceful people from getting beaten.

Half the column continued down the boulevard and were

beaten up and arrested. The second half slipped through behind Illarionov down the side streets, joined up with the crowd ringed by OMON on Chistoprudny Boulevard, participated in the rally, and peacefully dispersed to their homes.

After this incident Illarionov himself accepted an offer from the Cato Institute in the United States. He left and began doing research. He did not want to be the leader of a revolutionary crowd. That's just what happened. That's what always happens if you know something about the regime that the crowd doesn't.

CHAPTER 12
Garry Kasparov: The Missing Man

Here, at a roadside café I've made up (no, I took it from another trip, another highway) because I still can't name the place where the meeting in fact took place, here, halfway between Moscow and Petersburg, one man is missing who should be here. I'm speaking of Garry Kasparov, the world chess champion and leader of the United Civic Front. He isn't here. He's in prison.

We're not too worried. He's not in prison the way National Bolshevik Gromov was in prison: just for five days, not for years. For "failure to obey the legal demands of law enforcement personnel," as the court's verdict indicates. In other words, for walking around town despite a police ban on walking. They're not torturing him, not handcuffing him to a window, and not putting him in the "music box." A lot of lawyers, human-rights activists, and journalists are keeping track of his fate. Foreign politicians have taken an interest. Apparently, even the American president has been told that Garry Kasparov is in prison. He's not doing so badly, but he's still in prison.

Tomorrow, in Petersburg, the Dissenters' March will be held, and the day after tomorrow in Moscow Marina Litvinovich will begin to organize solitary pickets across from the prison on Petrovka under a sign that says "Freedom for Garry Kasparov." Solitary pickets are the one form of street demonstration in Russia that does not require consent from the authorities. If you're alone, you can write any slogan you like on a piece of paper, go outside, and stand there with that sign.

But only as long as you're alone. If supporters show up, if some passerby wants to support you, the picket becomes illegal. Policemen then have the right to detain you, let you stew for five hours at the police station, and then take you to court, where you can get up to fifteen days. Just because someone came up and supported you.

And that is how they combat solitary pickets. The Federal Security Service must have a special department that hires homeless people to join solitary picketers, turning them into crowds, that is, illegal pickets, and giving policemen the right to arrest the picketers.

They also hire activists from pro-Putin youth movements. There, across from the prison on Petrovka, when Boris Nemtsov, the leader of the opposition party Union of Right Forces, will stand in a solitary picket with a sign that says "Freedom for Kasparov," a young man will come up to him with a sign of his own.

"What do you need, Putinoid?" Nemtsov will say, turning to the youth. "Get lost."

But the youth will only press up to Nemtsov, as if he wants to embrace him, and a brief embrace will be enough for policemen to run up to Nemtsov, grab him by the arms, and drag him away.

They will drag away another leader of the Union of Right Forces, Nikita Belykh, because a hired "supporter" with a sign will join him. And the writer Viktor Shenderovich and the leader of Yabloko youth, Ilya Yashin—all the picketers—will be dragged away in turn to the police station under the pretext that their picket is not solitary at all; rather, they're standing in a crowd of supporters.

On the fifth day, when the time comes to release Garry Kasparov, Marina Litvinovich will get a call from a stranger who will say that if Marina organizes a gala party and invites journalists, Kasparov will not be released. They will simply take him to the outskirts of town in a closed car and throw him out there, the way people throw a dog out of a car when they don't want it to find its way home.

So Marina will keep the time and place of Kasparov's release a secret even from friends. Journalists will be told to meet Kasparov in the courtyard of his building. At five in the evening. At five it's already dark.

Kasparov lives in the byways of the Arbat, in an ugly brick building of the kind built for the party élite during the Brezhnev era. At the sunset of the Soviet Union, after all, Kasparov was the world chess champion, practically like the party élite. Under Soviet power this was like being a high-placed official.

By five, about fifty journalists with cameras will gather in the small courtyard behind the iron fence, along with spies, also with cameras, from the special services, but fewer of them, about ten. And a police cordon will be set up along the fence, and a police officer will tell Marina Litvinovich, "Let's do this nicely. Just two questions. But if there's going to be a rally—"

"A briefing," Litvinovich clarifies.

"Well, or a briefing . . . I'm going to be forced to disband it. You know what I mean. I have orders."

Marina will promise that Kasparov will meet the press for just two questions. Because everyone is tired. Because for Kasparov, after five days in prison, and for herself, after two marches and three days of picketing, all they really want is to go home to their own beds.

At precisely five o'clock Masha Gaidar will show up in the courtyard carrying a huge bouquet of white flowers. And Marina will tell Masha, "Masha, go inside. Garry's home already. He's waiting for you there in the apartment." Turns out, they use the formal "you."

But Masha won't go inside. Masha is going to wait for Kasparov at the entrance, despite the freezing cold, because she will want to give Kasparov his bouquet in front of the television camera lens. And Marina will think that Masha shouldn't get in front of television cameras just because she's giving him a bouquet. And Marina will again say to Masha, "Masha, go inside!"

But Masha will have no intention of doing that. The doors of the entry will open, and first Kasparov's guard will come out into the courtyard, having also spent five days in jail for resisting arrest and trying to keep them from crippling Kasparov while detaining him. And behind him Kasparov himself will appear. And Masha Gaidar will rush up, embrace him, and offer him the bouquet. And Marina Litvinovich will shout, "Garry! Garry!" so that Kasparov approaches the cameras quickly and quickly drop that damn bouquet, because international reports (Russian television naturally will show nothing about Kasparov), should not be about Masha Gaidar giving Garry Kasparov a bouquet but about Garry Kasparov being released.

And I will think, What has to happen for these dear and decent people whom I deeply admire to stop calculating just for a moment how many seconds of air time they're going to get?

The reporters will line up, the spies will line up behind the reporters, and Kasparov will walk up to them and answer two questions: "How do you feel?" and "How do you assess the prospects for the parliamentary elections?"

A child would answer these questions: "I feel fine. There's nothing good about prison, of course, but if you're an opposition politician in Russia, sooner or later you'll wind up in prison"—and that's how Kasparov will probably answer. And about election prospects he will say, naturally, that there are no elections in Russia, that they are a profanation, not elections, and the Putin regime must be dismantled by peaceful means.

After these two questions the TV cameramen will run to film Kasparov going back to the door, his boots striding through the snow, his guard opening the door wide for him, and the door slamming shut. Because television people don't care whether their reports make any sense. They care about there being "synchrony," that is, what the main character says, and "cut-ins," that is, the slamming door and boots striding through the snow, and the "standup," that is, the words of the reporter himself standing with a microphone in the tiny court-yard of the building on the Arbat byway where Garry Kasparov lives. "Today Garry Kasparov, leader of the United Civil Front, was freed. Kasparov spent five days in confinement. He was arrested. . ." This is what the reporters will say, each into his own camera, but all more or less the same thing, against the backdrop of the closed entry door, and all very energetically, because that's how it's done and because for every reporter the "standup" is the main part of his report. Reporters, too, value the seconds of television air alloted them more than anything else in this world.

"Want to go inside?" Marina will ask me.

I will nod. Of course I want to go inside.

INTERVIEW FOR POSTERITY

I will walk in. Going up in the elevator with me will be an affable man, a guard, evidently. Two more affable men will be standing watch on the landing. In the vestibule I'll have to remove my boots and put on slippers. And from the number of boots under the coat rack, I will conjecture that there are about ten people in the living room.

Garry Kasparov's apartment proves comically predictable. In the 1970s, if smart little Garry from Baku imagined what kind of home he would have in Moscow when he was some-body, then he would have imagined an apartment exactly like this. Furniture with curlicues. Crystal glassware in light wood corner cabinets. Karelian birch, apparently. Mirrors and candlesticks. A whole wall of photographs of Garry: Garry at the chessboard, Garry receiving a cup, Garry at ten, Garry at twenty, Garry at thirty . . . In the middle of the living room there is a huge table, and on the wall above the table is a huge mirror that doubles the number of guests and makes the already huge table look twice as big and the dishes on it twice as many.

We'll have tea. The huge table will be covered with Azerbaijani sweets prepared by hand by Kasparov's mother, Klara Shagenovna. And Klara Shagenovna herself will be sitting on a little chair in the corner. No, not at the table. She doesn't sit at the table. She bakes these exotic sweets, lays them out for the guests, and brews the tea, but does not sit at the table. She is a "selfless mother," if you know what I mean. The kind of mother a person has to have in order to become the world chess champion or a great musician or scholar. A combination of concern and despotism. A mother who believes unconditionally in her son's outstanding talent, who makes sure her boy eats nutritious puréed soups, goes to bed at the right time, goes for his walk at the right time, and breathes fresh air but also puts six hours a day into studying his mysterious art, which, the greater her son's successes, the less his mother understands. She will sit in the corner on her little chair, drink plain water from a plain glass, watch her son, and remember the night before the deciding game for the title of world champion.

That was nearly thirty years ago. His match against Karpov. Karpov was the ideal Soviet champion, a champion with the face of a Young Communist functionary. And Kasparov was a talented young upstart. Even people who didn't understand chess followed this match because it was a battle between the old, boring, and Soviet, and the new, talented, and fresh. Karpov was leading, five to zero. And the match was on its way to six wins. If Karpov won the sixth game, that would spell the death of Kasparov's career. Because you can lose a match for world champion to a current champion, of course, but if you lose it without winning a single game, then the whole world writes you off as a loser. And Karpov was leading, five to zero. Klara Shagenovna was certain that one of her son's trainers was spying for Karpov and telling the champion about the variations the challenger was coming up with during the breaks. She was certain someone was spying, but there was nothing she could do. On the eve of the decisive game, Garry was sleeping in his hotel room and she was standing by the window. First she'd open a pane so her boy could breathe fresh air, then she'd close it so her boy wouldn't catch cold. She stood like that by the window the whole night, opening and closing the pane . . . And the next day she was sitting in the hall, the former hall of the assembly of the nobility, in the Hall of Columns of the House of Unions. She didn't really understand what was happening on the board. She just felt the tension and caught her son's mood. He made a mistake. Nikitin, his trainer, leaned over to Klara Shagenovna and whispered, "This is the end, Klara." On the stage Garry, too, saw that the move was a mistake and that if Karpov saw his mistake he could not avoid defeat—in the game and the match. So Garry stood up, took off his jacket, hung it on the back of his chair, and walked to the edge of the stage, as if stretching his legs. In the hall, Klara Shagenovna felt that this was an element of the game, too, a distracting maneuver, a bluff, as in poker. And that it might work. And it did. Karpov didn't notice the mistake, and after a long and persistent struggle Kasparov became the world champion.

Klara Shagenovna will recall this and watch her son recounting how he spent his five days in prison, and she won't be as afraid as she was the night she spent opening and closing the pane. It will seem to her that Garry has more game chances now than in the House of Union's Hall of Columns when he took off his jacket and walked to the edge of the stage. It will seem to her that now he can still win, and she will believe he is winning, as always.

Kasparov's wife Dasha will also sit at a distance from the table, on the couch, wearing a distraught expression on her face. When she got married she realized, of course, that her husband was not just a great chess player who had earned every possible title and who could now simply rest on his laurels, write books, and take his young wife traveling between the Hôtel Le Bristol in Paris and the Château Saint-Martin hotel on the Côte d'Azur. She realized she was marrying an opposition politician and fully shared his views, but she apparently was not prepared for her husband going to prison. Prison had not occured to her.

Now she will listen to her husband recounting what his five days in prison had been like and will not understand why he is talking about prison so breezily. Kasparov will recount how the warden stopped by to see him in prison and prophesied that Putin would be gone soon and Kasparov would be tsar.

"Do you have a wife?" the warden asked.

"Yes," Kasparov replied.

"Well, she'll be the tsaritsa," the warden summed up. "A young wife?"

"Yes."

"Not your first?"

"Fourth."

"Then"—the warden whistled in an expression of delight and envy—"then you'll be sultan."

His guests will laugh. Dasha will cast her distraught gaze over them, struggling to understand why her husband is having so much fun talking about prison and his guests are having so much fun listening. And it will seem to Dasha that all these people know some secret she doesn't.

Only men will be sitting at the table. And because of this Garry Kasparov's by no means Caucasian home will seem

Caucasian because there will be Caucasian sweets on the table and only men sitting at it, men who have taken their shoes off at that.

Kasparov will be sitting at the head of the table. Opposite Kasparov will be a video camera on a tripod. Everything he is saying will be videotaped. For history, probably. Because for now he can't tell anyone but this close circle of friends. Kasparov will tell them how the policemen who arrested him and the guards in the prison and the investigators all treated him like a future president. Just in case. What if this prisoner becomes president? He will tell them that he'd been allowed extra walks. And been brought packages from Klara Shagenovna. He will say that the whole five days in prison he ate only his mother's cooking and no prison food, for fear they would poison him. When he says "poison," Dasha will shudder, and there will be fear in her eyes. Kasparov will turn to me and ask me not to tell anyone what I've heard here, otherwise the guards, investigators, and policemen will be in trouble for treating a prisoner like a future president. And I will promise not to tell anyone anything. I will be lying, of course.

Sitting on his right will be Aleksandr Osovtsov, the former head of Khodorkovsky's Open Russia, who, when Khodorkovsky was imprisoned but Open Russia was still in existence, organized political discussions, invited Kasparov to them, and in this way drew the chess player into politics.

Sitting on his left will be Boris Nemtsov, one of the leaders of the oppositionist party Union of Right Forces. Nemtsov, who in 2004, when his party failed to win a seat in parliament for the first time, created Committee 2008, an odd organization that attempted to unite the democratic parties. Nemtsov, who invited Kasparov to head up Committee 2008 and agreed to say that the committee's goal was not to unite the democrats but to defend the very institution of elections. Nemtsov, who had been transformed so gradually from a liberal obedient to the authorities into a genuine oppositionist. We won't know at the time that in the forthcoming elections his party will not only lose but lose with a bang. And Nemtsov will be nominated for president, but Nemtsov will withdraw his candidacy in order not to disgrace himself. Six months later the party will be completely disbanded, and in its place the Kremlin will create a new party of marionette liberals, which Nemtsov will refuse to have anything to do with, and with Kasparov he will begin to create the Solidarity movement, of which nothing will ever come.

We will know none of this. Nemtsov will drink tea and seemingly envy Kasparov a little for having spent five days in prison as a hero, whereas he, Nemtsov, was detained by the police only for a few hours.

Sitting opposite Nemtsov will be Vladimir Ryzhkov, a former State Duma deputy. Ryzhkov, who in 2004 in Committee 2008 said that they shouldn't unite the existing democratic parties but create a new party. He believed that this party should be registered because the Kremlin should have a loyal opposition in order to appear legitimate in the eyes of its Western partners. At the time Kasparov told Ryzhkov that the party would not be registered and the Kremlin wouldn't give a damn how it looked in the eyes of its Western partners as long as oil cost a hundred dollars a barrel and Europe depended on Russian natural gas. So the party was not registered. And Ryzhkov will be sitting at the table at Kasparov's as part of the underground, not the loyal opposition.

Sitting next to him will be human-rights activist Lev Ponomarev, who will be completely in his element. Because any semblance of democracy had ended. Because we had returned to the Soviet Union, to a life we knew. When, no matter who you were, you could not have any effect on the regime or rise to power. When the regime was somewhere there, behind the Kremlin walls and OMON cordons, on the television screen, in the cars with the flashing lights. While you are here, in a living room, in a kitchen, with your books, with witnesses' stories about what is actually happening in Chechnya and Ingushetia and what actually happened in Beslan. You are here, meeting your prison mates and preparing for prison . . . and in an odd way, this is a life we know how to live.

Kasparov will be talking and laughing, shuffling the pieces of paper on which he recorded, hour by hour, what was happening to him during those five days in prison. But I will gradually realize that he is recounting all of this to convince himself and his comrades that this new life, in which we are no longer members of parliament, or leaders of parties, or politicians, or journalists, but underground men, this life is not so frightening. It might even be entertaining, and the people depriving us of our freedom might even sympathize with us. And any number of desperate situations might reveal new opportunities to us.

Any situation other than death, I will think, recalling Yury Chervochkin, a National Bolshevik beaten by the police. A young man who will die a few days after the events described.

POSSIBLE PLAYS

In 2005, when Garry Kasparov first formulated the key phrase of the United Civic Front's manifesto, the first thing he did was decide to travel around the country and talk to the people. "We are not left wing or right wing," the manifesto said. "We are in favor of dismantling the regime."

Kasparov chartered a plane (at that time you could still charter a plane if you were Kasparov), and, taking a few journalists along, he headed for Makhachkala, Vladikavkaz, Stavropol, and Rostov. Halls were rented in all of these cities for public meetings. But as soon as Kasparov arrived, something would happen in these halls. Either the sewer line would break, or the plumbing would burst, or there would be a slip-up and it would turn out that a children's drawing contest had been previously scheduled for the same time as Kasparov's public meeting. In Vladikavkaz, when they refused Kasparov the hall he had rented and he announced he would meet with people on the square, the children's drawing contest suddenly turned out to be a children's chalk-drawing contest outdoors, in the square, on the asphalt. The square was ringed by police, and the police herded the children into it and forced the children to draw until Kasparov left.

He didn't even get to fly to Rostov. The Rostov airport refused to receive Kasparov's plane, saying that rocks had shown up out of nowhere and were lying in disarray on the runway. Kasparov and Litvinovich got into a car, drove to Rostov, arrived at the library where the meeting with supporters had been scheduled, and discovered that there had been a flood in the library, naturally; a pipe had burst. They had to hold the meeting on the library steps.

That evening the Rostov airport's administration announced that now it definitely would not allow Kasparov's plane on its runway to take the world champion and the reporters back to Moscow. Kasparov sat in the hotel and looked through the local newspaper, which announced a rally of Communists scheduled for the next day in Rostov.

"Good," Kasparov said. "If they won't let me fly out of Rostov, then tomorrow I'll go to the Communists' rally."

Fifteen minutes later the news that the leader of the United Civic Front was planning to go to the Communist rally appeared on the news feeds. Half an hour later the airport administration gave Kasparov's plane permission to land, on condition that Kasparov board the plane he'd chartered and fly out immediately. Kasparov had a good laugh. He rejoiced at this unexpected move, the way he occasionally rejoiced at an unexpected move on the chessboard.

On the day he gets out of prison, Kasparov will tell me at his apartment that the situation does not seem desperate to him.

"In any case," Kasparov will say, "there are more possible plays. In any case, it's easier now than when it was five-zero in the match with Karpov."

"Yes," I will object, "but that was just a game, chess."

"Oh-ho, just a game!" Harsh notes will appear in Kasparov's voice, indicating that he is insulted. "For me it was my whole life."

"But still just a game," I will insist. "Whereas this is for real. They're beating people on the head with truncheons for real, they're putting people in prison for real, and people could die for real."

"Don't you dare utter that word!" Kasparov's mother, Klara Shagenovna, will stand up from her corner, from her little chair, come up to me, give me a stern look, and say, "Don't you dare utter that word!"

And I will hold my tongue.

Here, at the roadside café, which I have made up, there have as yet been no deaths in the ranks of dissenters. National Bolshevik Yury Chervochkin has been beaten by policemen and is lying in the ICU, but we still don't know that he's going to die. We don't know that at his funeral, when Kasparov and Limonov are standing near the grave and one of the dead man's comrades tries almost in a whisper to utter the National Bolshevik slogan, "Yes! Death!" Yury's fiancée will shout, "Be quiet! Be quiet! Don't you dare utter that word!" The exact same way Garry Kasparov's mother will forbid me to utter that word on the day her son got out of prison and told funny stories about prison.

We still don't know that Garry Kasparov will get out of prison safely. We don't know that subsequent Dissenters' Marches will be routed with particular brutality, and as a result the organizers will stop informing the authorities about the marches, as the law requires. New possible plays: the dissenters will be harassed so brutally that they will pop up here and there, avoiding checks and controls. The marches will arise unexpectedly, at subway stations and on the streets. While the police are assembling, the dissenters will be able to shout out their slogans and run away.

We still don't know that not a single opposition party will get into parliament in the elections. We don't know that Dmitry Medvedev will be the next president, that Putin will become prime minister, and that the presidential term will be extended to six years, evidently so that Putin could return. We don't know there will be a war with Georgia. We don't know that Ilya Yashin will be driven out of Yabloko and Masha Gaidar will leave the Union of Right Forces. That Nikita Belykh will receive an offer from President Medvedev to become governor of Vyatka and that he will accept the offer, and yesterday's supporters will not know whether to consider this a betrayal or rejoice at this appointment as a sign of a thaw.

We don't know there will be an economic crisis and that the bubble of oil smugness will burst for the people who now look at us with contempt for coming out to protest with the price of oil at $120 a barrel. We don't know that the reason for the protests will be not the absence of freedom that oppresses us but the tariffs on the import of foreign cars, cars that people evidently need more than they do freedom.

We don't know a damn thing here in the roadside café between Moscow and Petersburg. Garry Kasparov, who wrote a book, *Chess as a Metaphor for Life,* is missing. The man who calculates the variations and constructs algorithms. We don't calculate the variations or construct algorithms. We say goodbye to Gregor, whom I've made up, or rather, moved here from a different trip and a different highway. Gregor hugs me and says, "Hey! Take it easy!" We get into our cars and drive to Petersburg, which, on the eve of the impending parliamentary elections, has been hung with signs that say "You are part of Putin's plan." Two hours before dawn the city is empty, if you don't count the police posted everywhere and the OMON brigades brought in from Novgorod, Pskov, and Petrozavodsk for our benefit.

Palace Square, where we are supposed to hold our Dissenters' March, has been blocked with street-cleaning trucks. Transformed into a parking lot for street-cleaning trucks.

We have nowhere to assemble, but dawn is coming soon, and we'll be making our way to the square regardless.

ON THE MARCH

The march is starting at the Petersburg headquarters of the Yabloko party, on a tiny street not far from Ligovsky Prospect. You can't move in the few small rooms there. I'm smoking outside when Boris Nemtsov calls me. He's flown in and wants to know where we are and where we're going.

"Borya, I don't know where we are. We're at Yabloko headquarters, but I don't know the name of the street. And I don't know where we're going, probably to Palace Square, but all of Nevsky is blocked by OMON, and we'll probably get about fifty meters."

There are about two hundred of us. We're moving. Many are carrying flowers. I don't know where Marina Litvinovich has gone. Walking next to me is a red-haired young woman wearing a pin that says "Sorry, I live here." In front of us, OMON soldiers have formed a chain blocking the street. There really are about fifty meters between us and them. We have nowhere to go. Nowhere. Thirty meters, twenty, ten, and someone in our ranks shouts, "We need another Russia!"

In response to the shout, the OMON men cut into our flimsy ranks, grab their truncheons, and start swinging them at shoulder height. They aren't expecting us to resist. They aren't expecting that the National Bolsheviks walking with us will take iron bars out from under their coats or that the bars will start whistling in the air. Or that Nikita Belykh will use his huge fists to start scattering the OMON soldiers, take away someone's truncheon, and arm himself with it, snarling, "Fight! Fight!"

The OMON soldiers aren't expecting us to start fighting. And rightly so. No, no, of course not. We're a peaceful demonstration. We don't resist when they twist our arms behind our backs. We don't resist when they beat us over the head with truncheons. When four OMON men drag him away, enormous Nikita Belykh merely explains politely that he is a candidate for State Duma deputy and by law he cannot be detained without the sanction of the general prosecutor. They drag him about twenty meters and then let him go, evidently having understood that he's a parliamentary deputy candidate. They don't let the rest go. They grab, drag, beat, and throw them on buses. A huge OMON man waves his truncheon over my head. With my shoulder, I shield the redhead with the "Sorry, I live here" pin. The blow is glancing, but my shoulder still hurts. After striking me, the OMON soldier moves on, having decided for some reason not to arrest me and the redhead, just as not long ago another OMON man in Moscow decided not to arrest me and Masha Gaidar. For some reason they don't touch couples. We find ourselves behind the OMON chain, and the redhead cries, watching powerlessly as they finish off what is left of our march.

Five minutes later the street is empty. The only ones left are Nikita Belykh, the red-haired young woman, a couple of candidates for deputy from the Petersburg Yabloko party, and me.

"Where'd they take them?" Nikita asks about the people detained.

And right then Nemtsov arrives. Our clothes are torn and dirty, but Nemtsov is wearing clean blue jeans, a clean leather coat, and polished boots. He says we should go rescue our comrades. I say we should go to Palace Square. I've received a text message from Marina Litvinovich: "I'm at Palace, they're picking up people here. Bring one of the leaders, if you can."

I say, "Borya, we don't need to go to the police station. Nothing's going to happen to them. They'll sit there for five hours and leave."

"They're our comrades," Nemtsov objects.

"Nothing is going to happen to our comrades. But there are people on Palace. You summoned people to Palace Square, Borya. People have come, and you're not there."

We keep talking like this while we're hotfooting it to the police station near the Moscow Train Station, which is in the opposite direction from Palace Square.

Nemtsov says, "What do you want from me?"

I say, "I want you to go to the square. Because people are there, your supporters, who you called there, and you're not there."

Nemtsov says, "I have to free our comrades from the police."

I say, "Don't lie, Borya! You just know it's safer at the station than on the square. But you also know you should be on the square. And if you don't go to the square, Borya, then you're a worthless piece of shit."

Nemtsov is as hurt as a little boy. "I am not."

"Then let's go to the square."

We flag down a car. We're riding down Nevsky, which is solidly lined with OMON. Palace Square is blocked by street-cleaning trucks, and in the little square in front of the Hermitage there are more OMON. And very few people. The distracted, distraught people on the sidewalk don't know what they should do. There aren't any banners. You can't tell Dissenters' March participants from the people waiting for the trolleybus at the trolleybus stop. Therefore the OMON men sometimes pick up people who were just waiting for the trolleybus.

We drive up and I see Marina Litvinovich being dragged toward an OMON bus. Nemtsov gets out. Reporters with cameras and OMON soldiers rush up to him simultaneously.

"Boris Yefimovich!" the reporters shout.

"Get in the bus!" the OMON soldiers shout.

They twist Nemtsov's arms behind his back and drag him away. He just manages to shout to me, "This is just what you wanted, provocateur! Look what you did. They arrested me! Is that what you wanted?"

"Yes," I reply. "That's what I wanted."

The bus is full of arrested people. Everyone's cheerful, telling jokes, singing songs. Only one young man is crying. He's crying and saying, "I'm not with them. There's been a mistake. I'm a correspondent for Russian Television. I'm not with them. Let me go. There's been a mistake."

Marina Litvinovich walks up to the correspondent, puts her hand on his shoulder, and says, "You're part of Putin's plan, sonny!"—the words written on the ruling party's campaign posters hanging all over town.

Later, the OMON escort stationed at the bus door is replaced. Marina gets a guide to St. Petersburg out of her purse, walks up to the OMON man and says, "Excuse me, please, what's going on here?" She is an unassuming, skinny blonde with a guide in her hands.

"Where did you come from?" The OMON man is amazed, looking at the skinny blonde.

"I don't know. I was just walking down the street and all of a sudden they grabbed me. I don't understand. Forgive me, I'm so afraid."

"Where were you going?" the OMON man asks again.

"The Hermitage." Marina smiles and, to back up her words, sticks the guide under the OMON man's nose.

The OMON man looks around. None of the officers seems to be looking, so he tells the unassuming blonde, "Get out of here, little girl. What a time to go to the Hermitage. Get out of here!"

"Thank you!"

The unassuming blonde smiles and runs off the bus. Then in the blink of an eye she jumps onto a parapet and shouts in her rally voice, "Join me! People! We're assembling here! We're going to the Bronze Horseman! We need another Russia!"

And she hops off the parapet. The OMON man sees about fifty people who had been scattered over the square form up behind the quiet, unassuming blonde he let go. They unfurl banners, wave flags, shout "Russia without Putin!" and walk about fifty meters in the direction of the Bronze Horseman until another OMON brigade scatters them and shoves them into buses.

They don't arrest me. It's as if I'm invisibile. Or I'm just lucky today. Or I'm behaving in a cowardly way. But I have justification: I'm a journalist, I have to write a report for the newspaper about how the Dissenters' March in Petersburg was routed.

An hour later the square will be empty and I will go to the editorial office and write my report. The editor will throw out the episode about Marina Litvinovich in the OMON bus. The editor will say the story is entertaining, certainly, but inappropriate for the newspaper's sober style.

Later I'll go out onto Nevsky alone and think, "Where can I get a drink?" I'll walk a hundred meters or so and think, "Damn, it doesn't matter where. I need a drink right away, I don't care where." And at that moment I will get a text message from Marina Litvinovich, who hadn't been answering her telephone since she was arrested for the second time on her way to the Bronze Horseman. The text will say, "Where are you? Can you meet me in fifteen minutes where we parted this morning?" That morning Marina and I had parted on Ligovka across from the Oktyabrskaya Hotel. I will realize that Marina has been released. But they eavesdrop on conversations and inspect text messages, so you can't set up a meeting directly, you have to beat around the bush. Fifteen minutes later, on

Ligovka, when I see Marina from a distance walking toward me wearing a jauntily cocked torn cap and a dirty coat, I will feel tenderness toward her.

We will go to the Pushkinskaya 10 café and drink wine. The place will be filled with people. No one except us will be talking about the Dissenters' Marches.

ABOUT THE AUTHOR

Valery Panyushkin was born in Leningrad in 1969. He has worked as a special correspondent for the newspapers *Kommersant* and *Vedomosti*. He wrote a regular column in *Gazeta.ru*, and earned the Golden Pen award for his journalism. He is the author of the books *Mikhail Khodorkovsky: a Prisoner of Silence*, *Gazprom: The New Russian Weapon*, and *Something Unnoticeable*. He lives in Moscow and currently works as a correspondent for *Snob* magazine.

Europa Editions publishes in the USA and in the UK. Not all titles are available in both countries. Availability of individual titles is indicated in the following list.

Carmine Abate
Between Two Seas
"A moving portrayal of generational continuity."
—*Kirkus*
224 pp • $14.95 • 978-1-933372-40-2 • Territories: World

Salwa Al Neimi
The Proof of the Honey
"Al Neimi announces the end of a taboo in the Arab world: that of *sex!*"
—*Reuters*
144 pp • $15.00 • 978-1-933372-68-6 • Territories: World

Alberto Angela
A Day in the Life of Ancient Rome
"Fascinating and accessible."
—*Il Giornale*
392 pp • $16.00 • 978-1-933372-71-6 • Territories: USA & Canada

Muriel Barbery
The Elegance of the Hedgehog
"Gently satirical, exceptionally winning and inevitably bittersweet."
—Michael Dirda, *The Washington Post*
336 pp • $15.00 • 978-1-933372-60-0 • Territories: USA & Canada

Gourmet Rhapsody
"In the pages of this book, Barbery shows off her finest gift: lightness."
—*La Repubblica*
176 pp • $15.00 • 978-1-933372-95-2 • Territories: World (except UK, EU)

Stefano Benni
Margherita Dolce Vita
"A modern fable...hilarious social commentary."—*People*
240 pp • $14.95 • 978-1-933372-20-4 • Territories: World

Timeskipper
"Benni again unveils his Italian brand of magical realism."
—*Library Journal*
400 pp • $16.95 • 978-1-933372-44-0 • Territories: World

Romano Bilenchi
The Chill
120 pp • $15.00 • 978-1-933372-90-7 • Territories: World

Massimo Carlotto
The Goodbye Kiss
"A masterpiece of Italian noir."
—*Globe and Mail*
160 pp • $14.95 • 978-1-933372-05-1 • Territories: World

Death's Dark Abyss
"A remarkable study of corruption and redemption."
—*Kirkus* (starred review)
160 pp • $14.95 • 978-1-933372-18-1 • Territories: World

The Fugitive
"[Carlotto is] the reigning king of Mediterranean noir."
—*The Boston Phoenix*
176 pp • $14.95 • 978-1-933372-25-9 • Territories: World

(with Marco Videtta)
Poisonville
"The business world as described by Carlotto and Videtta
in *Poisonville* is frightening as hell."
—*La Repubblica*
224 pp • $15.00 • 978-1-933372-91-4 • Territories: World

Francisco Coloane
Tierra del Fuego
"Coloane is the Jack London of our times."—Alvaro Mutis
192 pp • $14.95 • 978-1-933372-63-1 • Territories: World

Giancarlo De Cataldo
The Father and the Foreigner
"A slim but touching noir novel from one of Italy's best writers
in the genre."—*Quaderni Noir*
144 pp • $15.00 • 978-1-933372-72-3 • Territories: World

Shashi Deshpande
The Dark Holds No Terrors
"[Deshpande is] an extremely talented storyteller."—*Hindustan Times*
272 pp • $15.00 • 978-1-933372-67-9 • Territories: USA

Helmut Dubiel
Deep in the Brain: Living with Parkinson's Disease
"A book that begs reflection."—*Die Zeit*
144 pp • $15.00 • 978-1-933372-70-9 • Territories: World

Steve Erickson
Zeroville
"A funny, disturbing, daring and demanding novel—Erickson's best."
—*The New York Times Book Review*
352 pp • $14.95 • 978-1-933372-39-6 • Territories: USA & Canada

Elena Ferrante
The Days of Abandonment
"The raging, torrential voice of [this] author is something rare."
—*The New York Times*
192 pp • $14.95 • 978-1-933372-00-6 • Territories: World

Troubling Love
"Ferrante's polished language belies the rawness of her imagery."
—*The New Yorker*
144 pp • $14.95 • 978-1-933372-16-7 • Territories: World

The Lost Daughter
"So refined, almost translucent."—*The Boston Globe*
144 pp • $14.95 • 978-1-933372-42-6 • Territories: World

Jane Gardam
Old Filth
"Old Filth belongs in the Dickensian pantheon of memorable characters."
—*The New York Times Book Review*
304 pp • $14.95 • 978-1-933372-13-6 • Territories: USA

The Queen of the Tambourine
"A truly superb and moving novel."—*The Boston Globe*
272 pp • $14.95 • 978-1-933372-36-5 • Territories: USA

The People on Privilege Hill
"Engrossing stories of hilarity and heartbreak."—*Seattle Times*
208 pp • $15.95 • 978-1-933372-56-3 • Territories: USA

The Man in the Wooden Hat
"Here is a writer who delivers the world we live in...with memorable and moving skill."—*The Boston Globe*
240 pp • $15.00 • 978-1-933372-89-1 • Territories: USA

Alicia Giménez-Bartlett
Dog Day
"Delicado and Garzón prove to be one of the more engaging sleuth teams to debut in a long time."—*The Washington Post*
320 pp • $14.95 • 978-1-933372-14-3 • Territories: USA & Canada

Prime Time Suspect
"A gripping police procedural."—*The Washington Post*
320 pp • $14.95 • 978-1-933372-31-0 • Territories: USA & Canada

Death Rites
"Petra is developing into a good cop, and her earnest efforts to assert her authority...are worth cheering."—*The New York Times*
304 pp • $16.95 • 978-1-933372-54-9 • Territories: USA & Canada

Katharina Hacker
The Have-Nots
"Hacker's prose soars."—*Publishers Weekly*
352 pp • $14.95 • 978-1-933372-41-9 • Territories: USA & Canada

Patrick Hamilton
Hangover Square
"Patrick Hamilton's novels are dark tunnels of misery, loneliness, deceit, and sexual obsession."—*New York Review of Books*
336 pp • $14.95 • 978-1-933372-06-8 • Territories: USA & Canada

James Hamilton-Paterson
Cooking with Fernet Branca
"Irresistible!"—*The Washington Post*
288 pp • $14.95 • 978-1-933372-01-3 • Territories: USA & Canada

Amazing Disgrace
"It's loads of fun, light and dazzling as a peacock feather."
—*New York Magazine*
352 pp • $14.95 • 978-1-933372-19-8 • Territories: USA & Canada

Rancid Pansies
"Campy comic saga about hack writer and self-styled 'culinary genius' Gerald Samper."—*Seattle Times*
288 pp • $15.95 • 978-1-933372-62-4 • Territories: USA & Canada

Seven-Tenths: The Sea and Its Thresholds
"The kind of book that, were he alive now, Shelley might have written."
—*Charles Spawson*
416 pp • $16.00 • 978-1-933372-69-3 • Territories: USA & Canada

Alfred Hayes
The Girl on the Via Flaminia
"Immensely readable."—*The New York Times*
164 pp • $14.95 • 978-1-933372-24-2 • Territories: World